KU-348-787

NEON GENESIS EVANGELION

Special Collector's Edition

Volume 6

Neon Genesis EVANGELION
Special Collector's Editon
Vol. 6

CONTENTS

Stage 1	THE FOURTH CHILD	7
Stage 2	LIGHT, THEN SHADOW	43
Stage 3	CONFESSION	67
Stage 4	THE GIFT	91
Stage 5	AMBUSH	115
Stage 6	THE DUMMY SYSTEM	139
Stage 7	STAINING THE TWILIGHT BLACK	159

This volume contains NEON GENESIS EVANGELION Special Collector's Edition
Book 6 #1 through #4 in their entirety.

Story & Art by Yoshiyuki Sadamoto
Created by GAINAX

English Adaptation by Fred Burke

Translation/Lillian Olsen
Touch-Up Art & Lettering/Bill Schuch
Cover Design/Hidemi Sahara
Layout & Interior Design/Carolina Ugalde
Editor/Carl Gustav Horn
-
Managing Editor/Annette Roman
V.P. of Sales and Marketing/Rick Bauer
V.P. of Editorial/Hyoe Narita
Publisher/Seiji Horibuchi

© GAINAX 2000
Originally published in Japan in 2000 by KADOKAWA SHOTEN PUBLISHING CO., LTD. Tokyo. English translation
rights arranged with KADOKAWA SHOTEN PUBLISHING CO., LTD., Tokyo.

New and adapted artwork and text © 2002 Viz Communications, Inc.
All rights reserved. No unauthorized reproduction allowed. The stories, characters, and
incidents mentioned in this publication are entirely fictional.

Printed in Canada

Published by Viz Communications, Inc.
P.O. Box 77010
San Francisco, CA 94107

10 9 8 7 6 5 4 3 2
First printing, May 2002
Second printing, October 2002

Vizit us at our World Wide Web site at www.viz.com and our Internet magazine, j-pop.com, at www.j-pop.com!

NEON GENESIS EVANGELION SPECIAL COLLECTORS EDITION GRAPHIC NOVELS TO DATE

NEON GENESIS EVANGELION SPECIAL COLLECTORS EDITION VOL. 1
NEON GENESIS EVANGELION SPECIAL COLLECTORS EDITION VOL. 2
NEON GENESIS EVANGELION SPECIAL COLLECTORS EDITION VOL. 3
NEON GENESIS EVANGELION SPECIAL COLLECTORS EDITION VOL. 4
NEON GENESIS EVANGELION SPECIAL COLLECTORS EDITION VOL. 5
NEON GENESIS EVANGELION SPECIAL COLLECTORS EDITION VOL. 6

NEON GENESIS EVANGELION

SPECIAL COLLECTOR'S EDITION

NE
RV

GOD'S IN HIS HEAVEN. ALL'S RIGHT WITH THE WORLD.

Volume 6

Story & Art by
Yoshiyuki Sadamoto
Created by
GAINAX

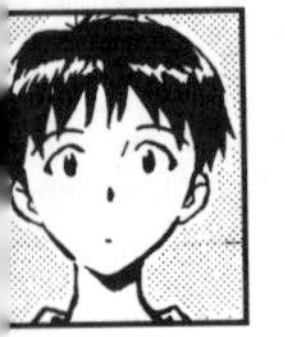

Name: SHINJI IKARI
Identity: EVA UNIT-01 PILOT, NERV/ MIDDLE SCHOOL STUDENT
Age: 14
Notes: Shinji was the "Third Child" chosen to pilot the monstrous Evangelion series: biomechanical weapons developed by the clandestine UN paramilitary agency known as NERV to fight entities code-named "Angels." Despite having no previous knowledge of NERV or combat, and despite his estrangement from NERV's commander, Shinji has successfully fought five Angels.

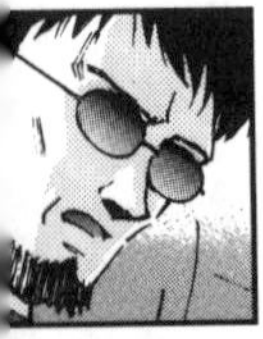

Name: GENDO IKARI
Identity: SUPREME COMMANDER, NERV
Age: 48
Notes: Shinji's father; this ruthless and enigmatic man is the guiding force behind both the development of NERV's Evangelion system, designed to defeat the prophesied return of the Angels, and the even more secret Instrumentality Project. Gendo reports on occasion to the Instrumentality of Man Committee, a.k.a., SEELE ("ZAY-leh," German for "soul"), a shadowy group seeking to control the mysteries of the Dead Sea Scrolls.

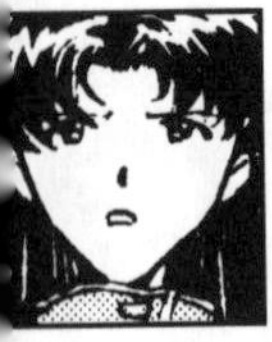

Name: MAJOR MISATO KATSURAGI
Identity: OPERATIONS CHIEF, NERV
Age: 29
Notes: Even though Maj. Katsuragi is the number-three ranking line command officer at NERV, after Gendo and Sub-Commander Fuyutsuki, and oversees the Eva pilots in combat in her role as tactical planner, there are many things about the organization that have been kept from her. A drunk and a slob in her off-hours, Misato has become surrogate family for Shinji and Asuka, with whom she shares an apartment.

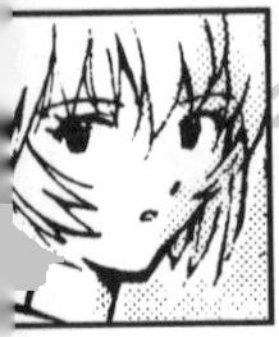

Name: REI AYANAMI
Identity: EVA UNIT-00 PILOT, NERV/ MIDDLE SCHOOL STUDENT
Age: 14
Notes: The "First Child" chosen to pilot an Evangelion, and first to use it in combat, sustaining severe injuries in Unit-01 while fighting the Third Angel. Although Rei barely expresses emotion, she at first regarded Shinji as an interloper. Since she and Shinji fought the Fifth Angel together, they have grown closer, yet Shinji is still mystified at how Rei relates to Gendo in a way he himself cannot.

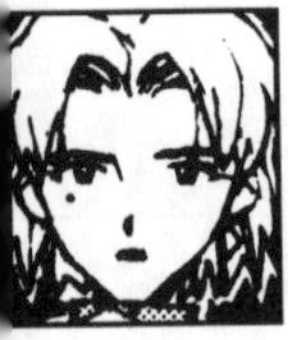

Name: DR. RITSUKO AKAGI
Identity: CHIEF SCIENTIST, NERV
Age: 30
Notes: Technical supervisor for NERV's "Project E (Evangelion)," Dr. Akagi is a polymath genius who rode the wave of scientific revolution that followed the cracking of the human genetic code at the end of the 20th century. Her disciplines include physics, biotechnology and computer science. Dr. Akagi was a friend of Misato's in college.

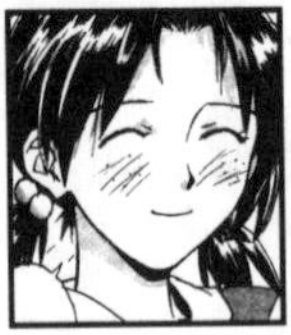

Name: HIKARI HORAKI
Identity: MIDDLE SCHOOL STUDENT
Age: 14
Notes: Believed to be the permanent class representative of Shinji's homeroom, 2-A; responsible for encouraging good order and decorum among her fellow students, including supervising clean-up chores...

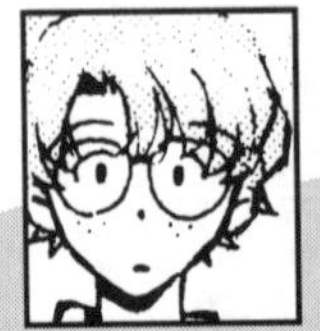

Name: KENSUKE AIDA
Identity: MIDDLE SCHOOL STUDENT
Age: 14
Notes: A devoted fan of military affairs, Aida plays war games in Army costume out in the country, habitually carries a Sony camcorder to capture shots of hardware or combat, and engages in computer hacking to acquire information for his "mania." He has expressed the wish that someone like Misato and/or Asuka would "order him around."

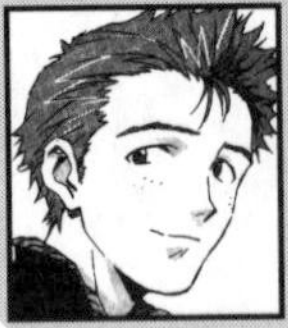

Name: TOJI SUZUHARA
Identity: MIDDLE SCHOOL STUDENT
Age: 14
Notes: Best friend of Aida; speaks with a pronounced accent from his home town, Osaka. His father and grandfather are both part of NERV's research labs. At first he blamed Shinji for injuries his sister suffered during his the attack of the Third Angel and even punched him out; now both Aida and he are friends with Unit-01's pilot.

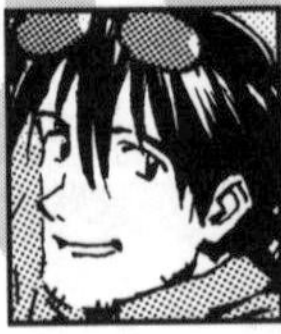

Name: RYOJI KAJI
Identity: DOUBLE AGENT: NERV/JAPANESE MINISTRY OF THE INTERIOR
Age: 30
Notes: Escorted Asuka to Tokyo-3 from Germany bearing the embryonic "Adam." Senior NERV personnel are aware he is also spying for the Japanese government. Yet both he and Gendo consider the arrangement satisfactory—for now, although Kaji suspects his own personal loyalty to the truth may yet cost him his life. Wishes to renew his old college love affair with Major Katsuragi.

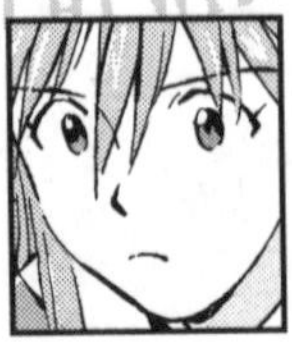

Name: ASUKA LANGLEY SORYU
Identity: EVA PILOT
Age: 14
Notes: Asuka is an United States citizen of mixed Japanese and German ancestry. A boastfully "superior" product of eugenics, Shinji knows that she tries to hide both her bratty nature and pain over the loss of her mother. Asuka is the "Second Child" to be identified as qualified to pilot an Evangelion by the obscure Marduk Agency, and was assigned to Eva Unit-02. Attracted to Ryoji Kaji.

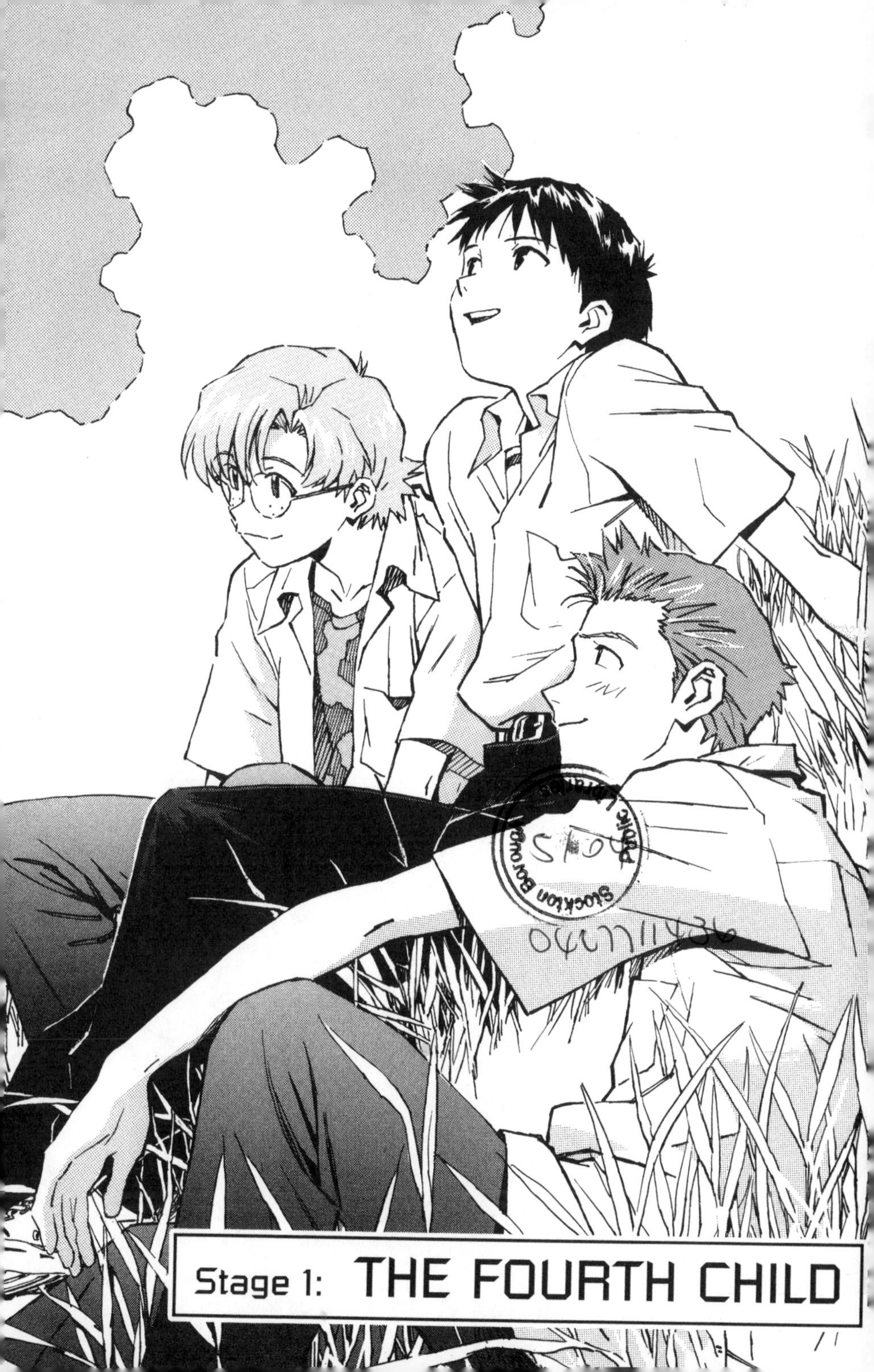

Stage 1: THE FOURTH CHILD

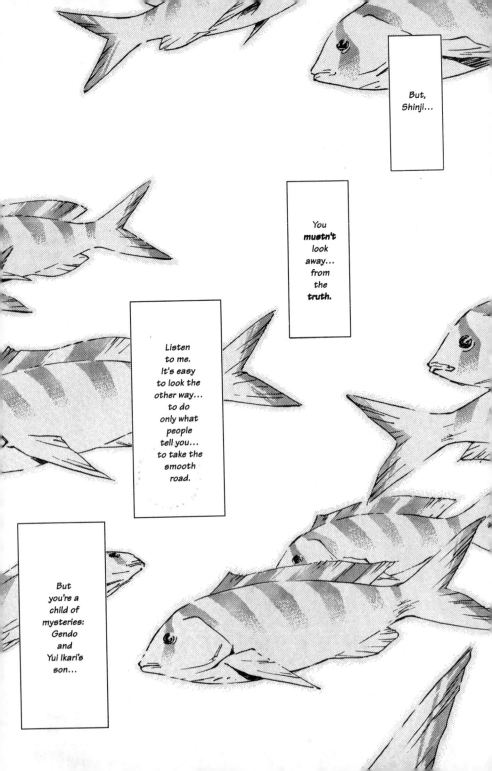

But,
Shinji...

You
mustn't
look
away...
from
the
truth.

Listen
to me.
It's easy
to look the
other way...
to do
only what
people
tell you...
to take the
smooth
road.

But
you're a
child of
mysteries:
Gendo
and
Yui Ikari's
son...

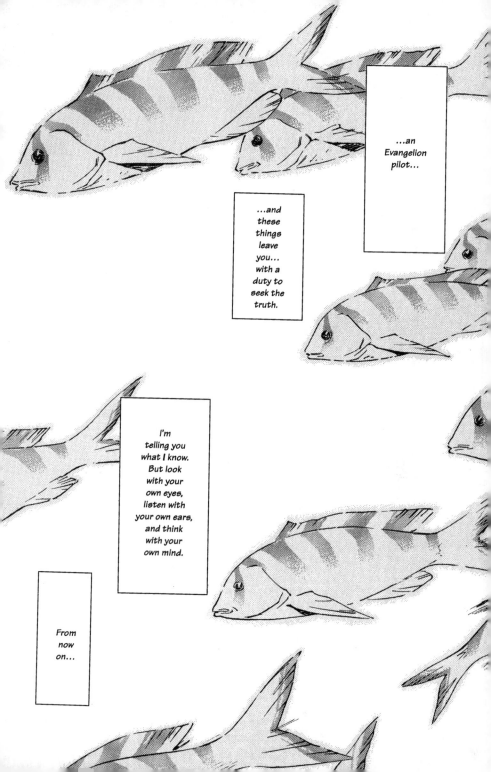

...an Evangelion pilot...

...and these things leave you... with a duty to seek the truth.

I'm telling you what I know. But look with your own eyes, listen with your own ears, and think with your own mind.

From now on...

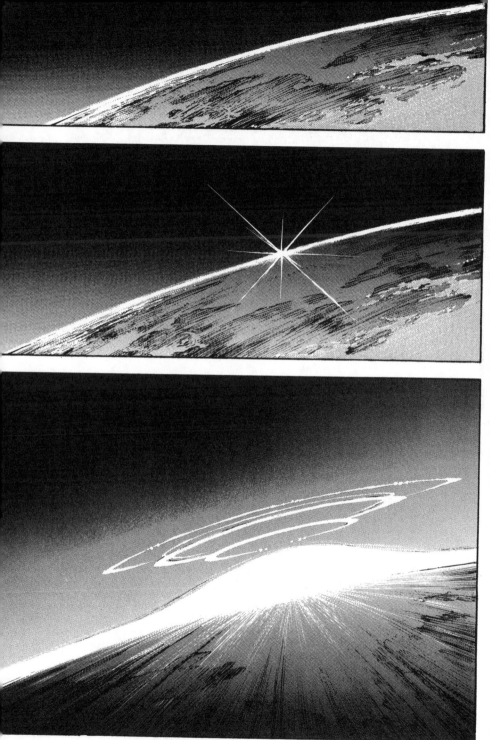

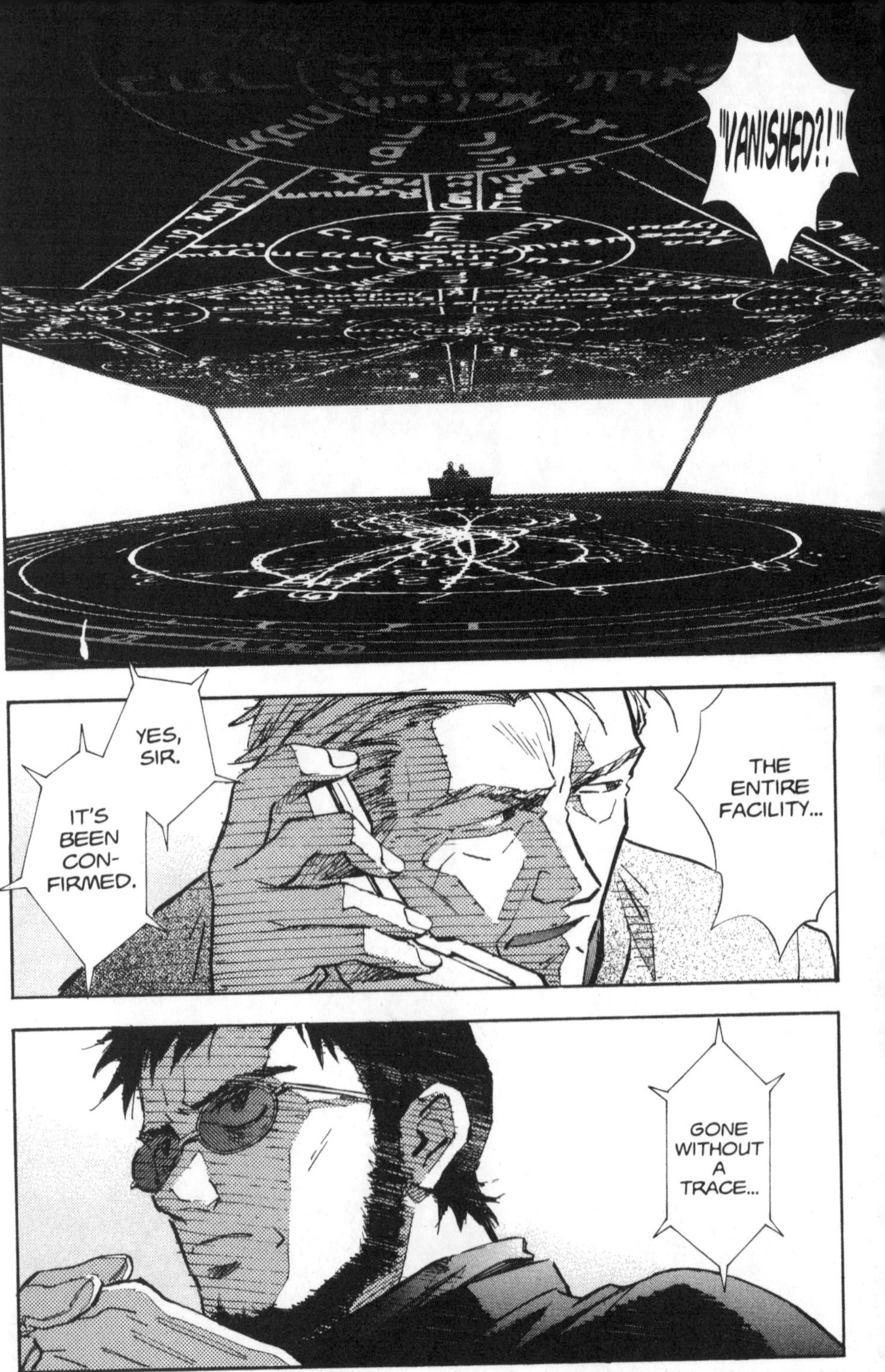
"VANISHED?!"
THE ENTIRE FACILITY...
YES, SIR.
IT'S BEEN CON-FIRMED.
GONE WITHOUT A TRACE...

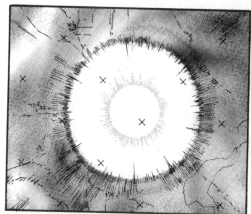
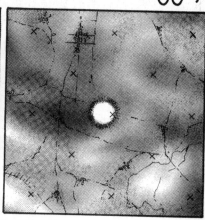
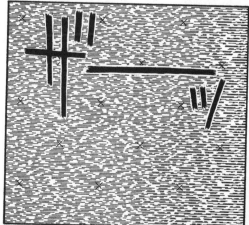
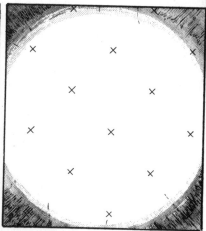

THE ONLY DIRECT EVIDENCE ARE THESE VISUALS FROM OB-SAT 8. IT SIMPLY CEASED TO EXIST.

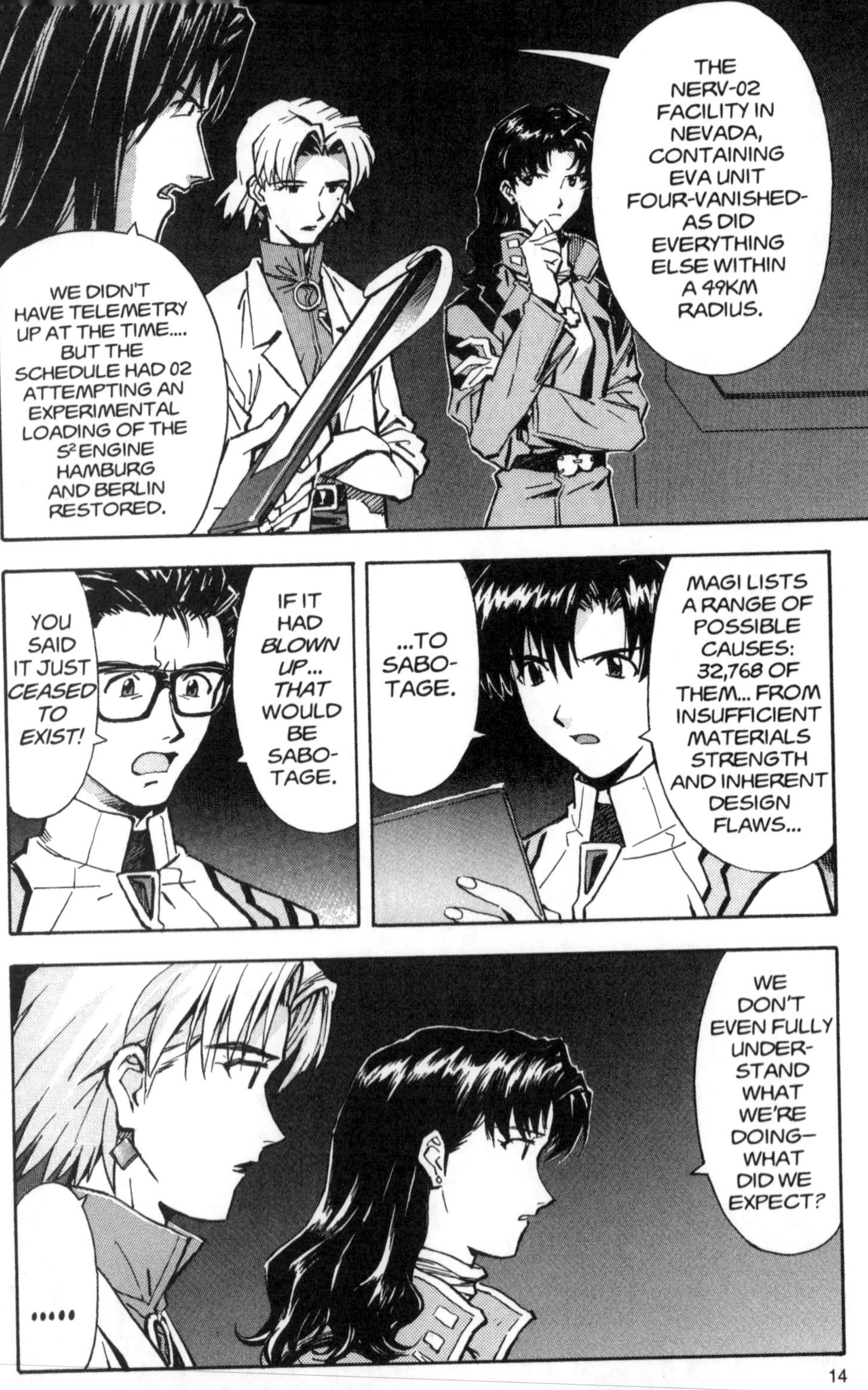
THE NERV-02 FACILITY IN NEVADA, CONTAINING EVA UNIT FOUR-VANISHED-AS DID EVERYTHING ELSE WITHIN A 49KM RADIUS.
WE DIDN'T HAVE TELEMETRY UP AT THE TIME.... BUT THE SCHEDULE HAD 02 ATTEMPTING AN EXPERIMENTAL LOADING OF THE S^2 ENGINE HAMBURG AND BERLIN RESTORED.
MAGI LISTS A RANGE OF POSSIBLE CAUSES: 32,768 OF THEM... FROM INSUFFICIENT MATERIALS STRENGTH AND INHERENT DESIGN FLAWS...
...TO SABO-TAGE.
IF IT HAD *BLOWN UP*... THAT WOULD BE SABO-TAGE.
YOU SAID IT JUST *CEASED TO EXIST!*
WE DON'T EVEN FULLY UNDER-STAND WHAT WE'RE DOING—WHAT DID WE EXPECT?
.....

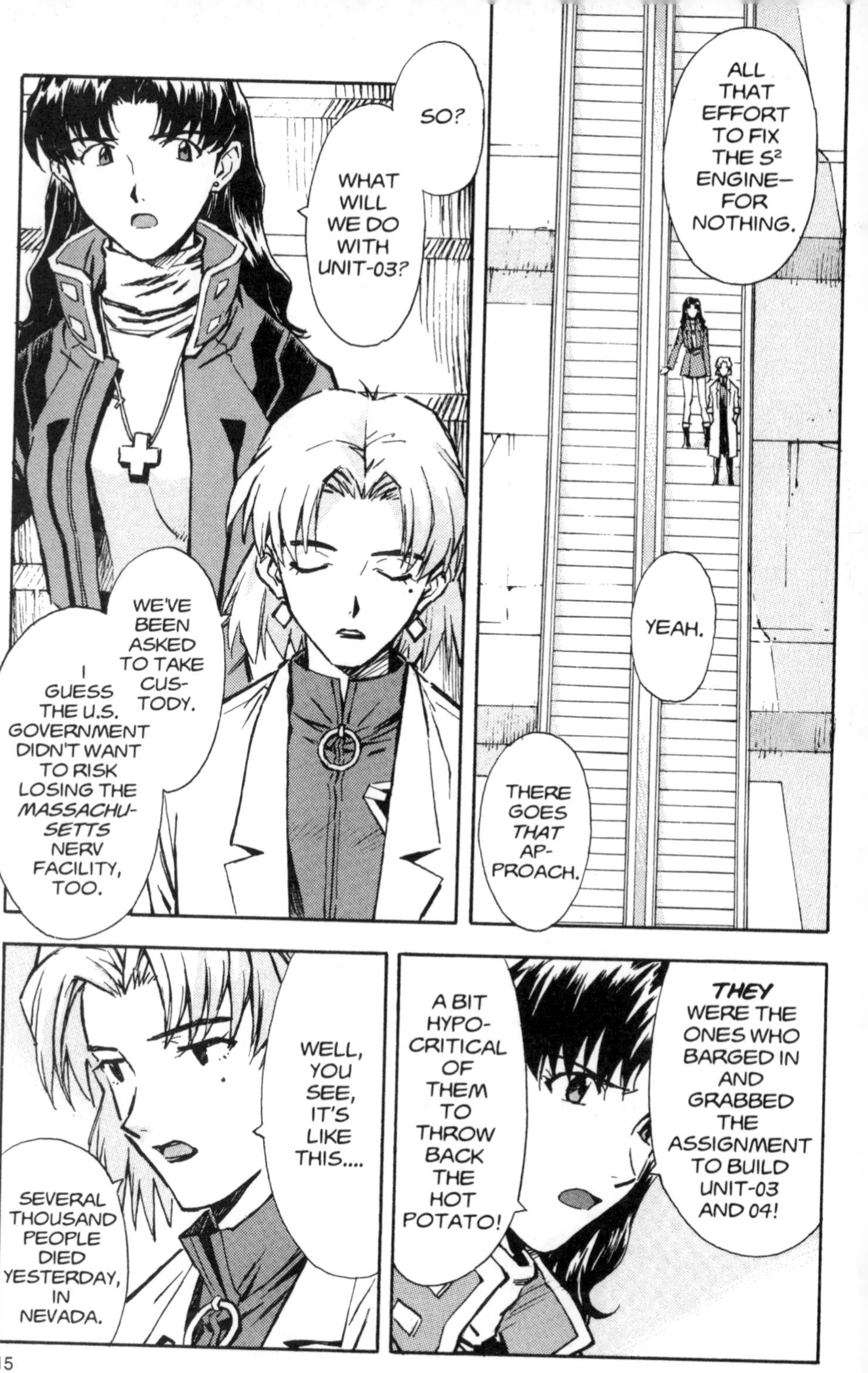
ALL THAT EFFORT TO FIX THE S^2 ENGINE— FOR NOTHING.
YEAH.
THERE GOES *THAT* AP-PROACH.
SO?
WHAT WILL WE DO WITH UNIT-03?
WE'VE BEEN ASKED TO TAKE CUS-TODY.
I GUESS THE U.S. GOVERNMENT DIDN'T WANT TO RISK LOSING THE *MASSACHU-SETTS* NERV FACILITY, TOO.
THEY WERE THE ONES WHO BARGED IN AND GRABBED THE ASSIGNMENT TO BUILD UNIT-03 AND 04!
A BIT HYPO-CRITICAL OF THEM TO THROW BACK THE HOT POTATO!
WELL, YOU SEE, IT'S LIKE THIS....
SEVERAL THOUSAND PEOPLE DIED YESTERDAY, IN NEVADA.

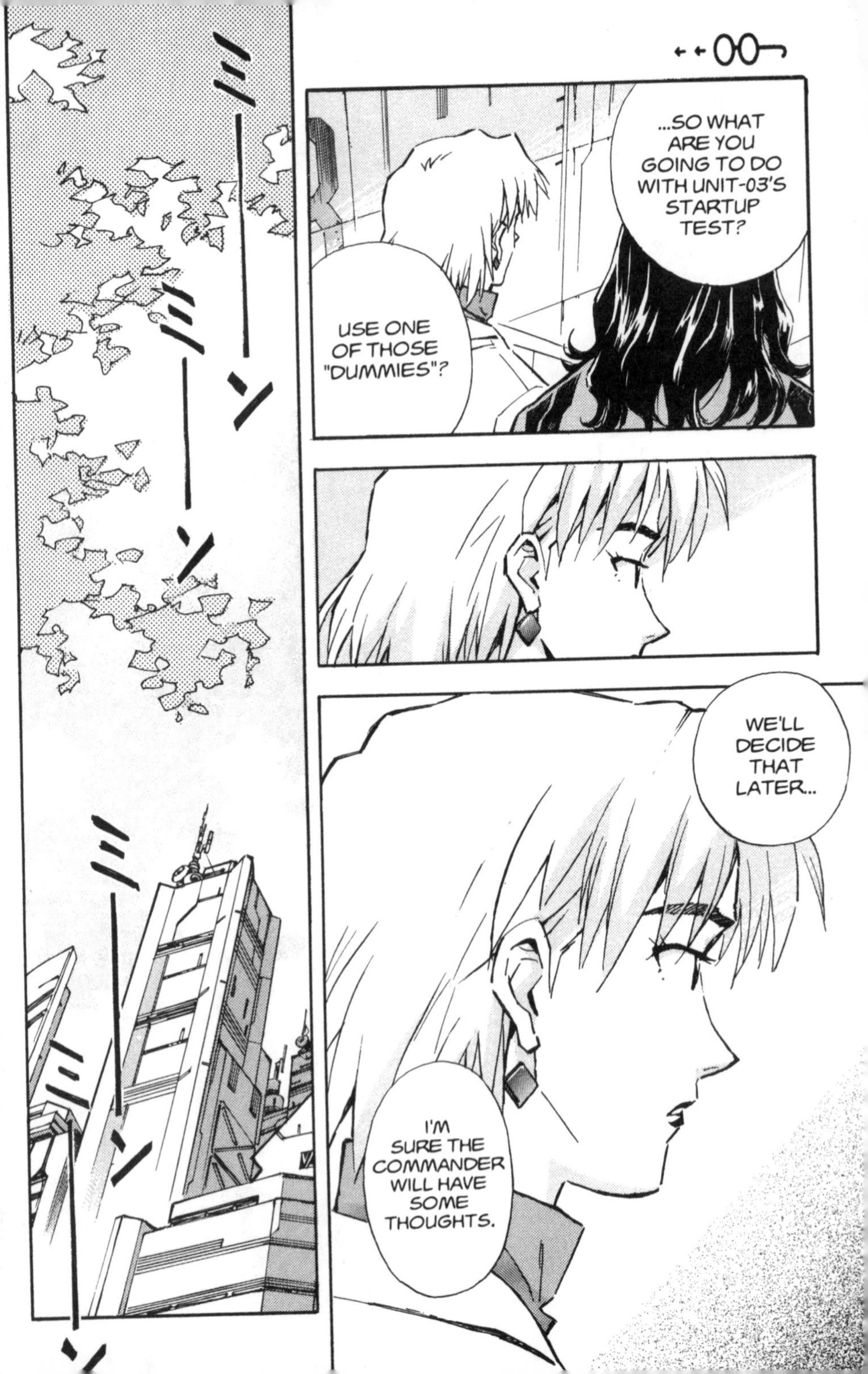
...SO WHAT ARE YOU GOING TO DO WITH UNIT-03'S STARTUP TEST?
USE ONE OF THOSE "DUMMIES"?
WE'LL DECIDE THAT LATER...
I'M SURE THE COMMANDER WILL HAVE SOME THOUGHTS.
ミーン
ミーーン
ミーン
ミーン

WE MIGHT GET IT FOR CHEAP THERE!

WANT TO GO TO NEW YUMOTO?

IT'S SOOO FRIGGIN' HOT TODAY!

ARRGH!

THERE WERE SOME CDS I WANTED, ANYWAY.

THAT'S FINE WITH ME.

I FORGOT— THE NEW MODEL OF "ARMORED GEAR" GOES ON SALE TODAY!

I'LL TAKE A PASS, YOUSE GUYS.

AY.

SEE YA!

BUT, AY! LEMME SEE IT IF YOU BUY IT, YO?

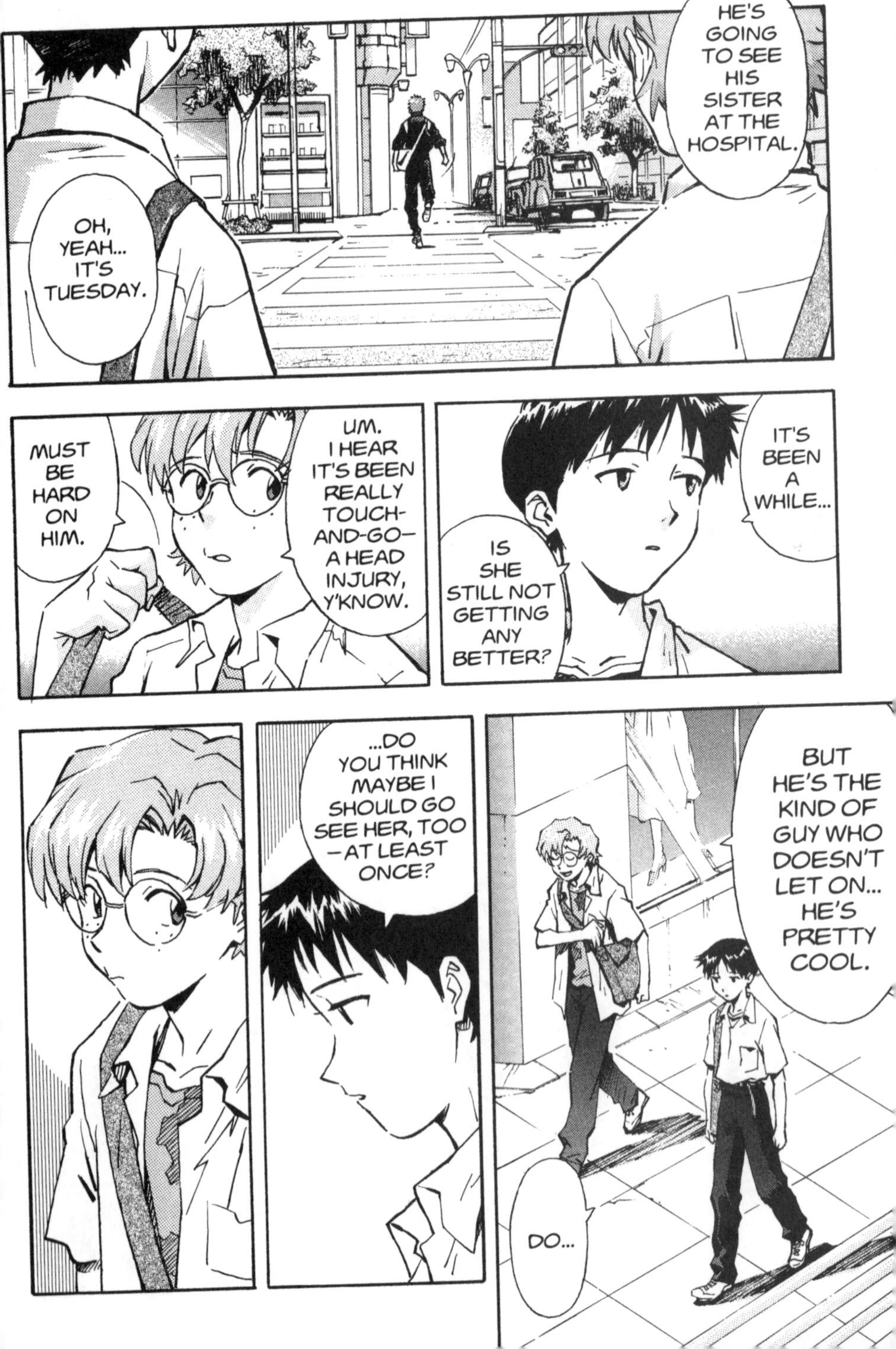
HE'S GOING TO SEE HIS SISTER AT THE HOSPITAL.
OH, YEAH... IT'S TUESDAY.
IT'S BEEN A WHILE...
IS SHE STILL NOT GETTING ANY BETTER?
UM. I HEAR IT'S BEEN REALLY TOUCH-AND-GO—A HEAD INJURY, Y'KNOW.
MUST BE HARD ON HIM.
BUT HE'S THE KIND OF GUY WHO DOESN'T LET ON... HE'S PRETTY COOL.
DO...
...DO YOU THINK MAYBE I SHOULD GO SEE HER, TOO —AT LEAST ONCE?

TOJI'S TOTALLY FORGIVEN YOU NOW.

IF HE WANTED YOU TO COME, HE'D SAY SO.

CUT IT OUT.

WELL, TOJI WAS MAD AT ME....

...THAT IT WAS MY FAULT...

HEY, ARE YOU FEELING RESPONSIBLE OR SOMETHING?

IF THERE'S ONE THING TOJI DOESN'T WANT, IT'S PITY.

HE HATES IT WHEN PEOPLE PUT SYMPATHY ON HIM.

WELL, WE'VE BEEN PALS A LONG TIME.

YOU REALLY UNDERSTAND HIM WELL, YOU KNOW THAT?

WHAT?

.....

19

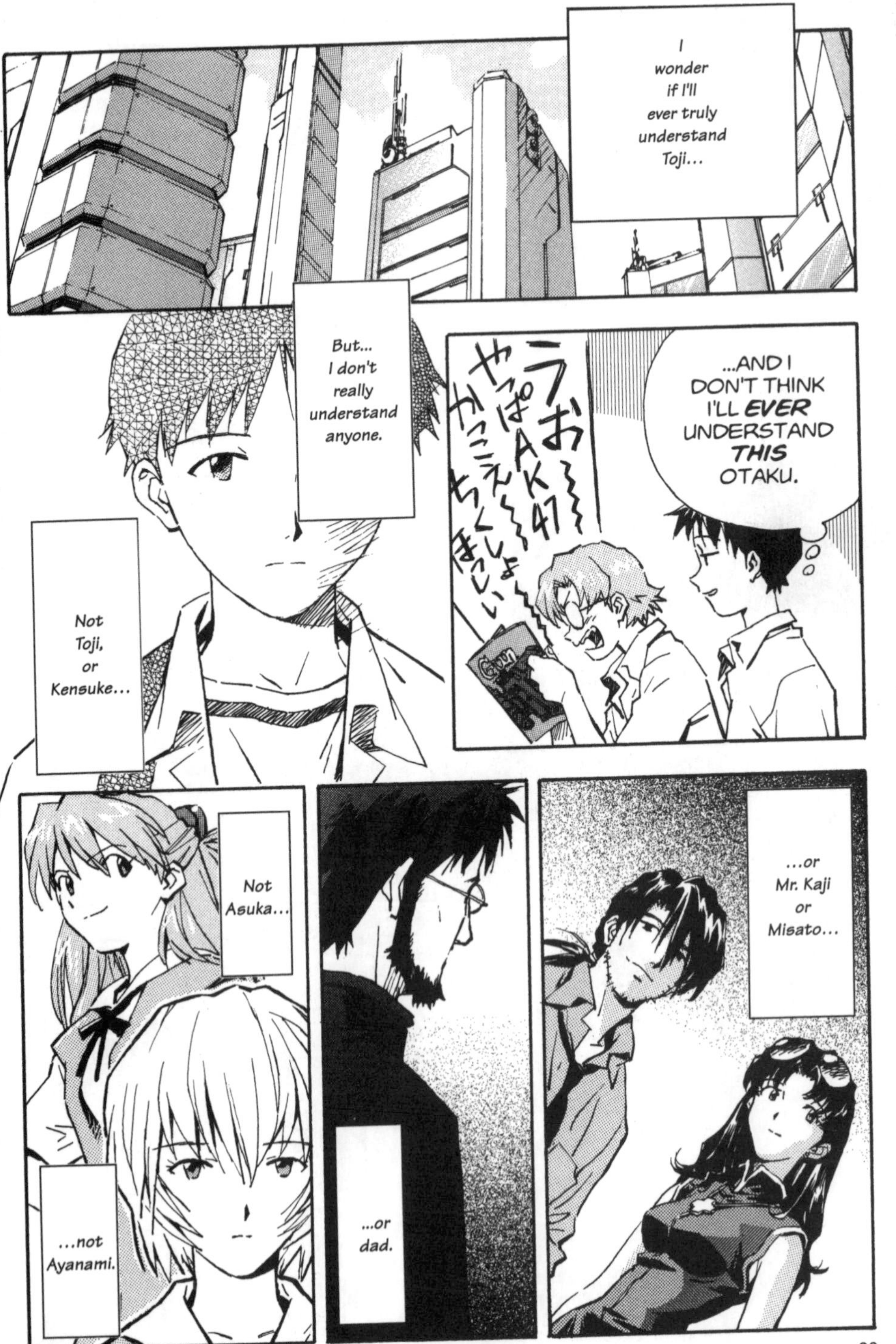
I wonder if I'll ever truly understand Toji…
うお～～～
やっぱAK47
かっこえ～～～
ちくしょ～
ほしい
...AND I DON'T THINK I'LL ***EVER*** UNDERSTAND ***THIS*** OTAKU.
But... I don't really understand anyone.
Not Toji, or Kensuke…
…or Mr. Kaji or Misato…
...or dad.
Not Asuka…
…not Ayanami.

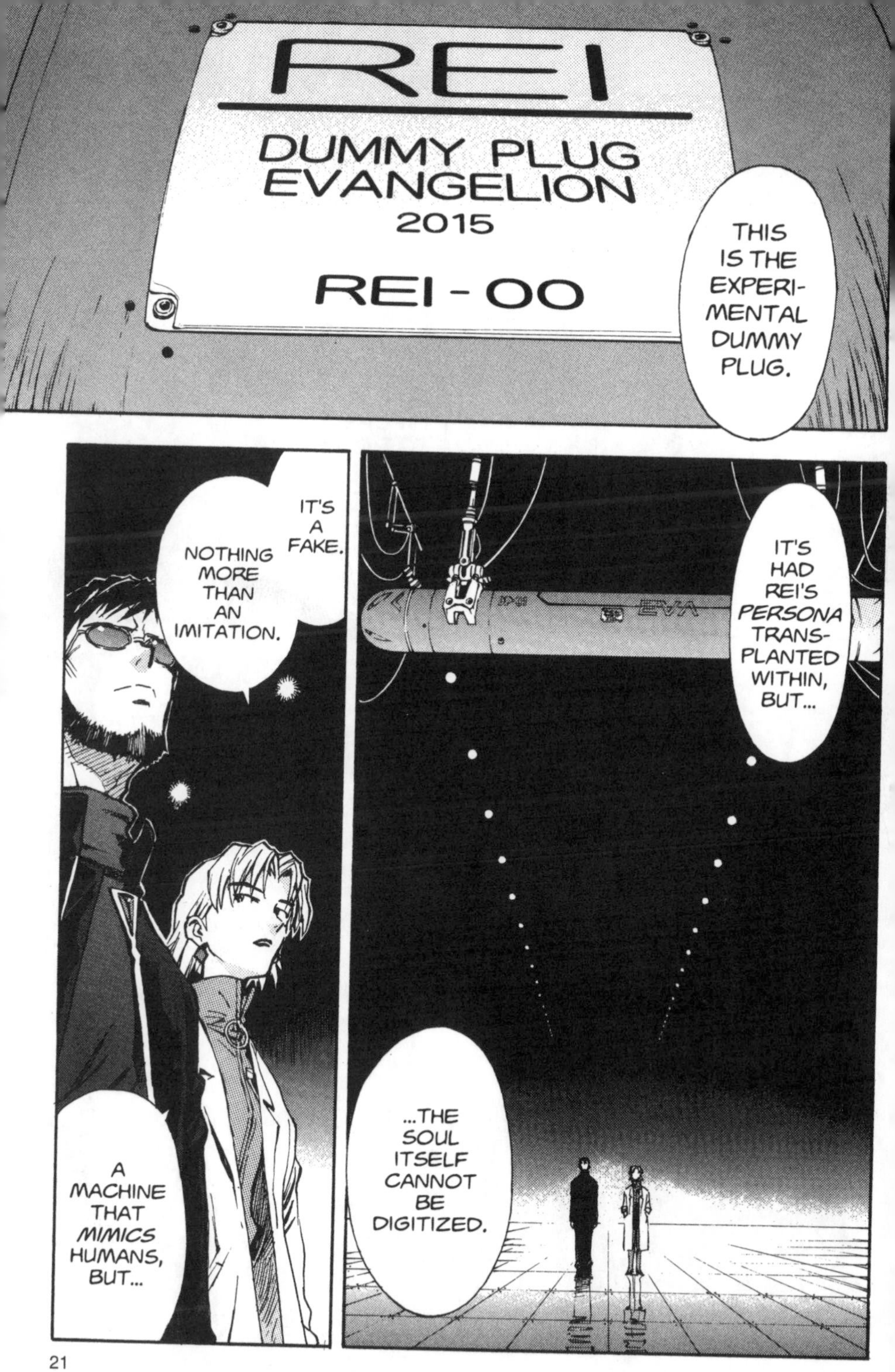
REI
DUMMY PLUG EVANGELION 2015
REI - 00
THIS IS THE EXPERIMENTAL DUMMY PLUG.
EVA
IT'S HAD REI'S *PERSONA* TRANSPLANTED WITHIN, BUT...
...THE SOUL ITSELF CANNOT BE DIGITIZED.
IT'S A FAKE.
NOTHING MORE THAN AN IMITATION.
A MACHINE THAT *MIMICS* HUMANS, BUT...

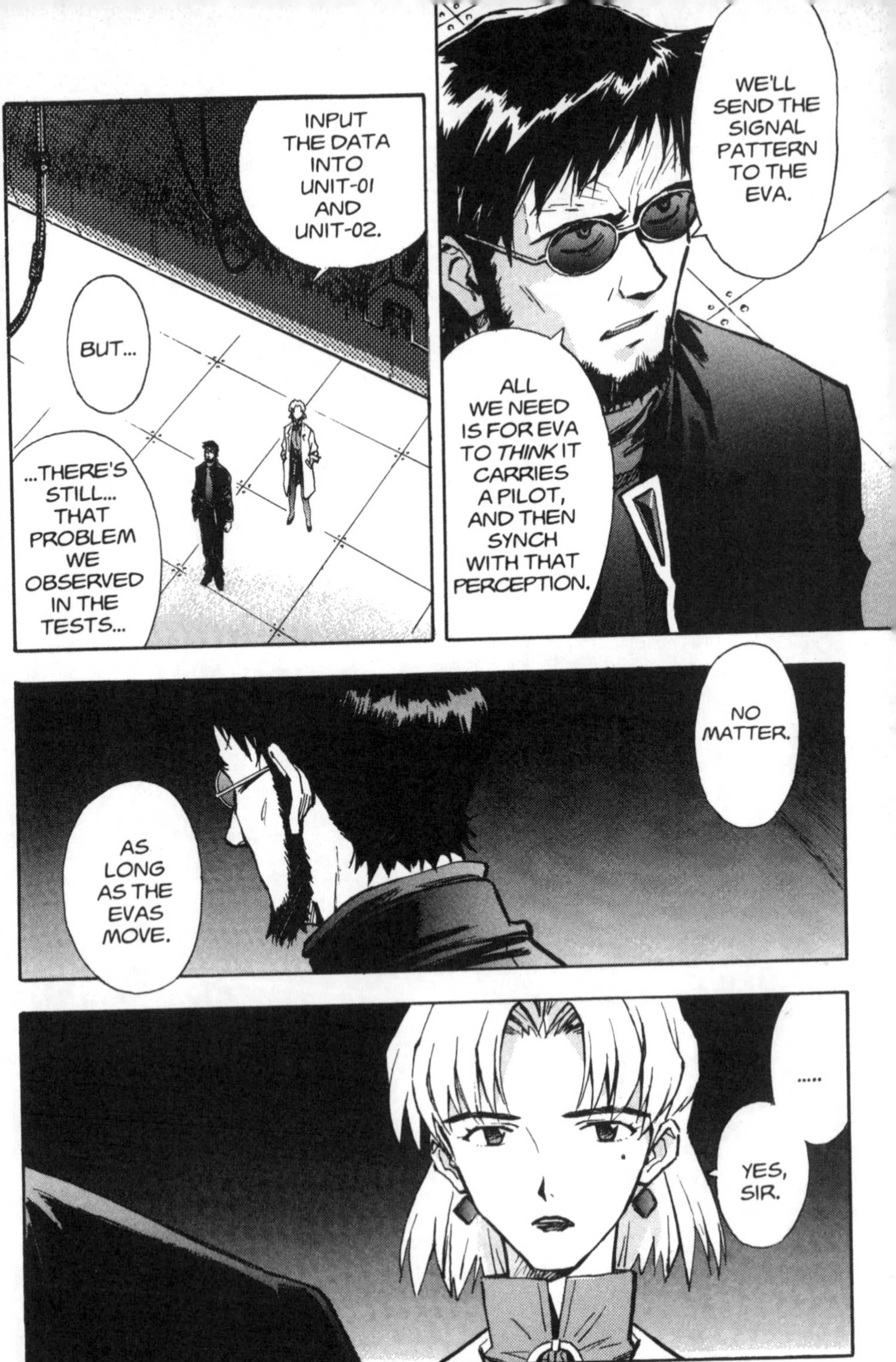
WE'LL SEND THE SIGNAL PATTERN TO THE EVA.
ALL WE NEED IS FOR EVA TO *THINK* IT CARRIES A PILOT, AND THEN SYNCH WITH THAT PERCEPTION.
INPUT THE DATA INTO UNIT-01 AND UNIT-02.
BUT...
...THERE'S STILL... THAT PROBLEM WE OBSERVED IN THE TESTS...
NO MATTER.
AS LONG AS THE EVAS MOVE.
.....
YES, SIR.

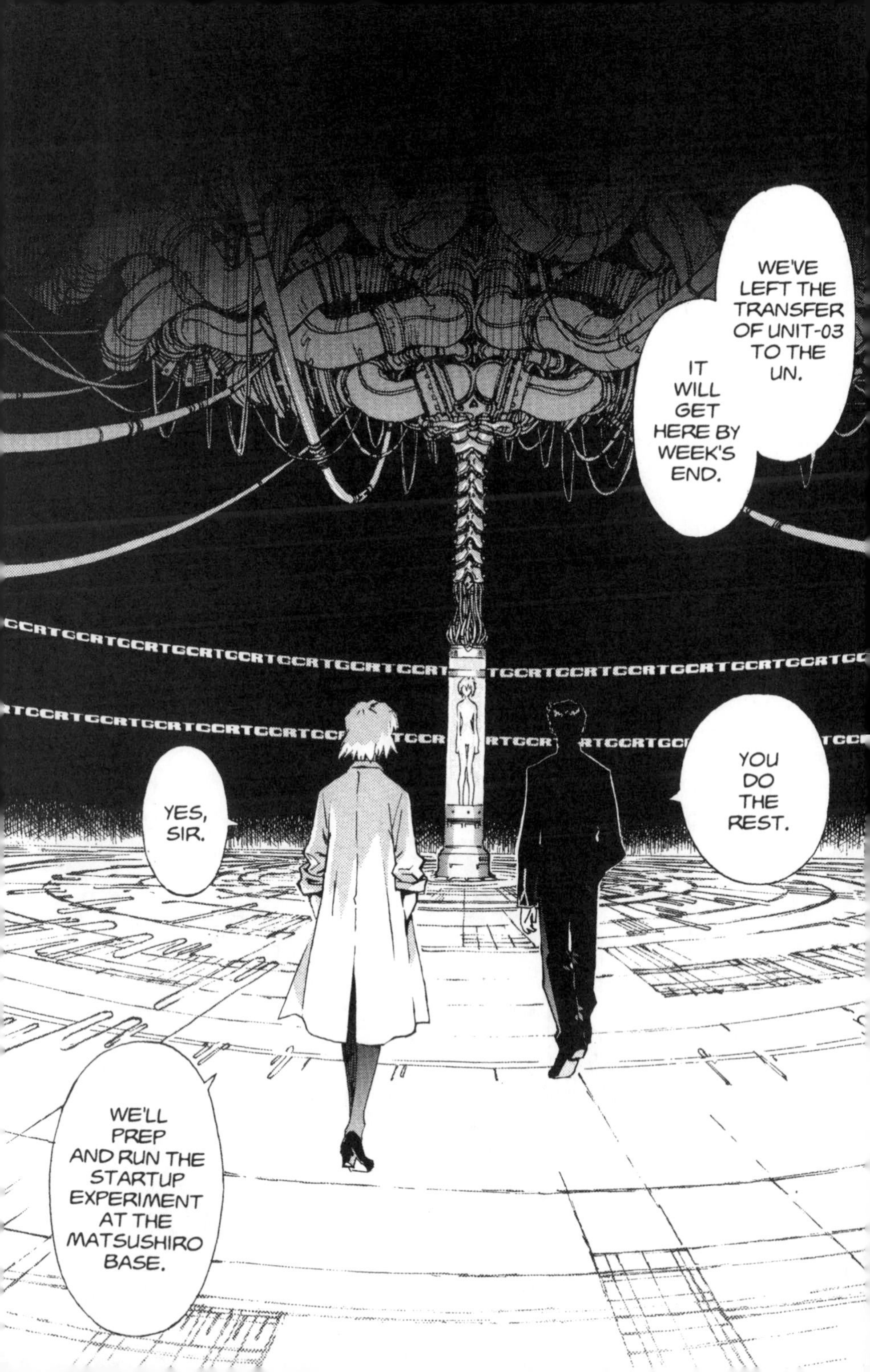
WE'VE LEFT THE TRANSFER OF UNIT-03 TO THE UN.
IT WILL GET HERE BY WEEK'S END.
YOU DO THE REST.
YES, SIR.
WE'LL PREP AND RUN THE STARTUP EXPERIMENT AT THE MATSUSHIRO BASE.

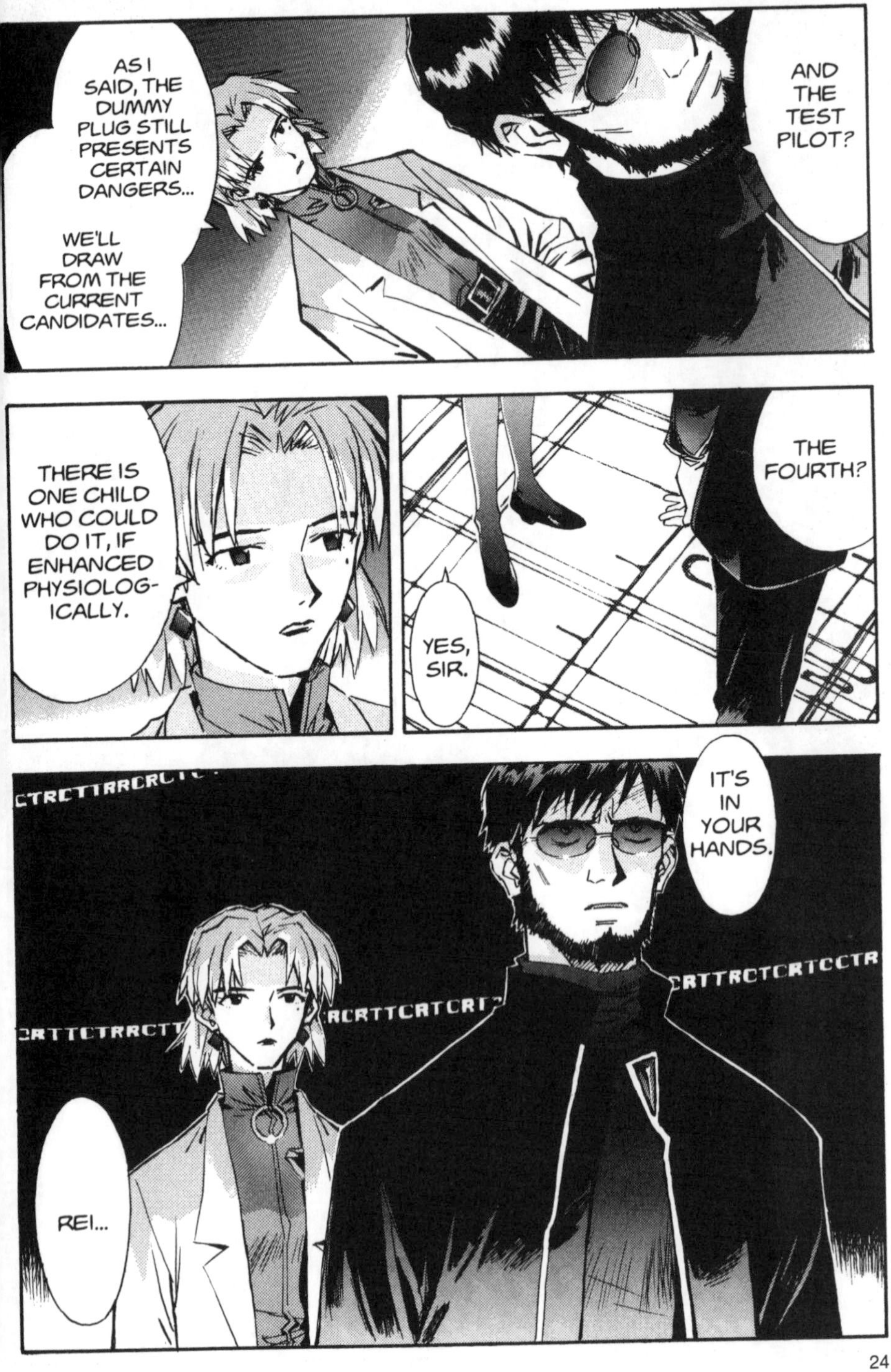
AND THE TEST PILOT?
AS I SAID, THE DUMMY PLUG STILL PRESENTS CERTAIN DANGERS...
WE'LL DRAW FROM THE CURRENT CANDIDATES...
THE FOURTH?
YES, SIR.
THERE IS ONE CHILD WHO COULD DO IT, IF ENHANCED PHYSIOLOG-ICALLY.
IT'S IN YOUR HANDS.
REI...

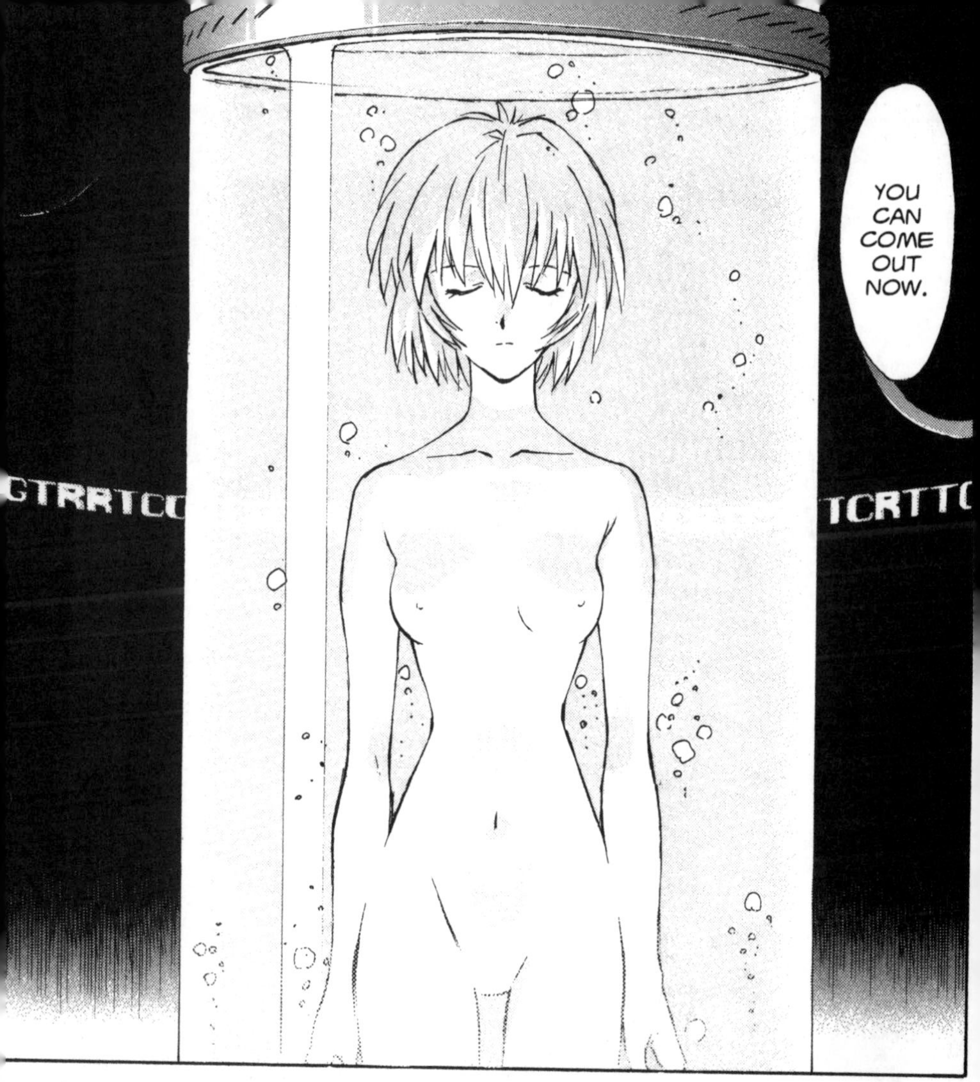
YOU CAN COME OUT NOW.
TCRTTC
GTRRTCC

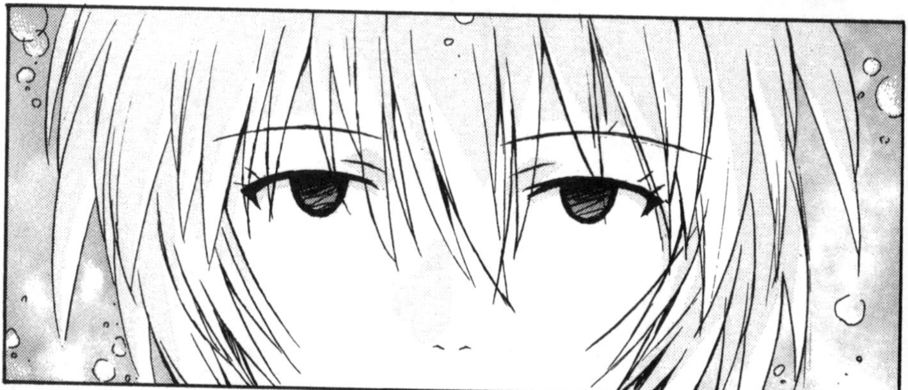

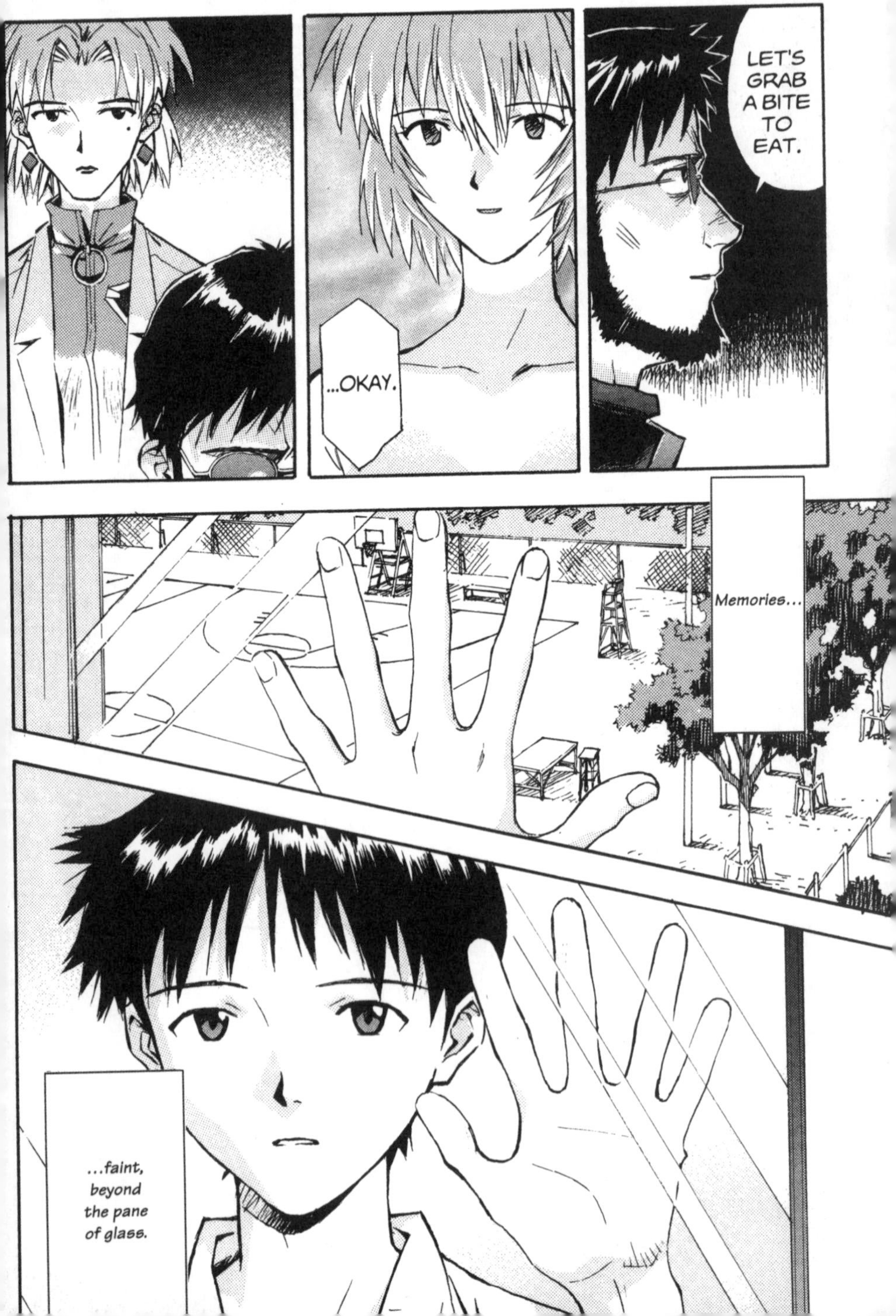
LET'S GRAB A BITE TO EAT.
...OKAY.
Memories...
...faint, beyond the pane of glass.

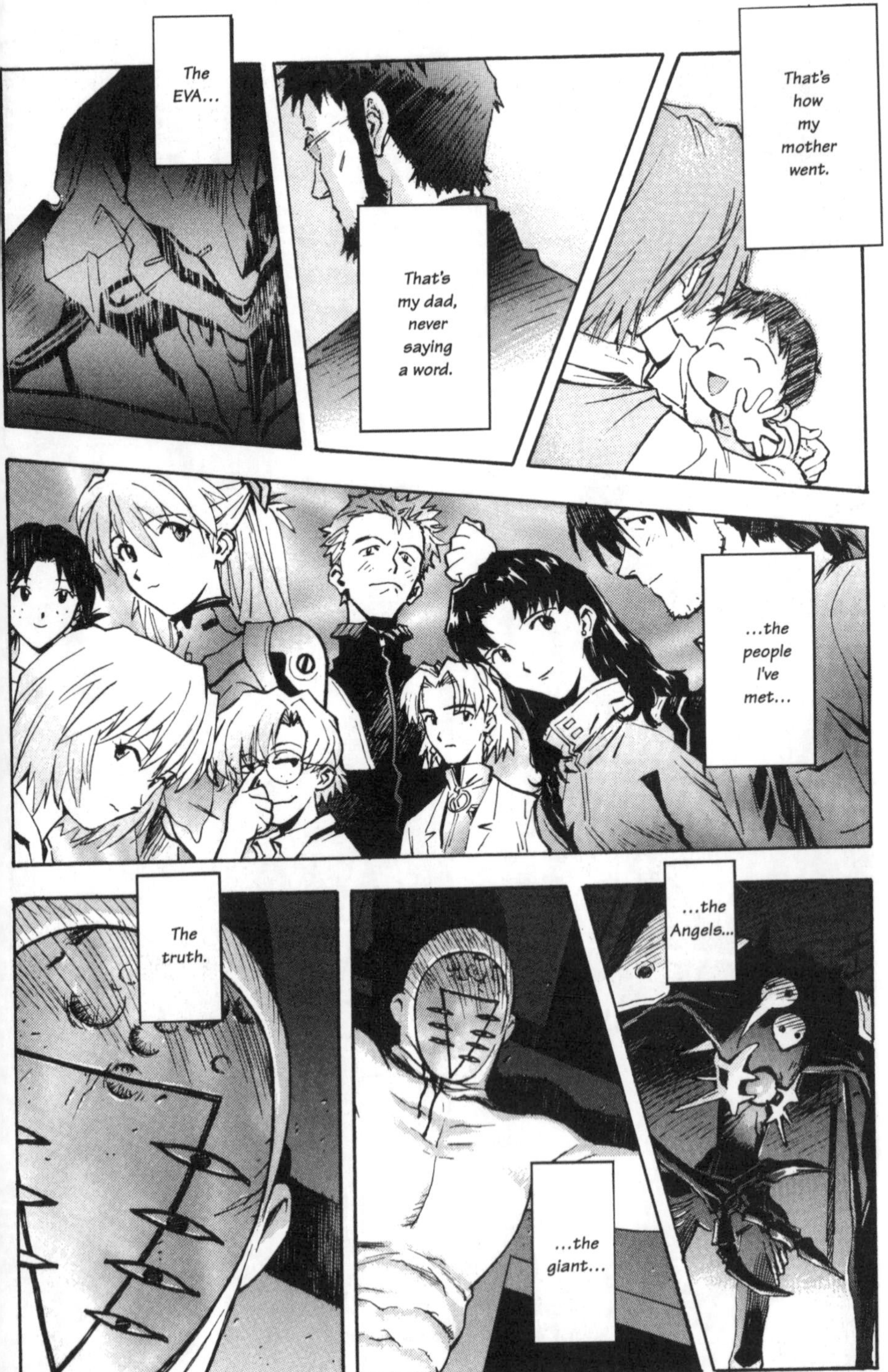
That's how my mother went.
That's my dad, never saying a word.
The EVA...
...the people I've met...
...the Angels...
...the giant...
The truth.

THAT HURT! DON'T HIT ME LIKE THAT, MAN!

IT'S PART A' DA PLAN! IF YOU'RE GONNA PEEP SUCCESSFUL, YA GOTTA PLAY IT RIGHT!

CLEAN UP DIS REVOLTIN' MESS!

OFF YER ASS, SHINJI!

OW...!

SHH! NOT SO LOUD, STUPID.

I'M NOT LIKE YOU!

WHAT DO YOU MEAN?

PRETEND TO WIPE DA FLOOR— LIKE SO....

CAAAAMON! PEEP! AS IN UNDER DA SKOY'TS! I KNOW YOU WAS THINKIN' ABOUT IT!

HUH...? PEEP?

YA GOT TO BE SUBTLE-LIKE... LOOK LIKE YOU'RE WORKIN' HARD...

TILT DA HEAD...

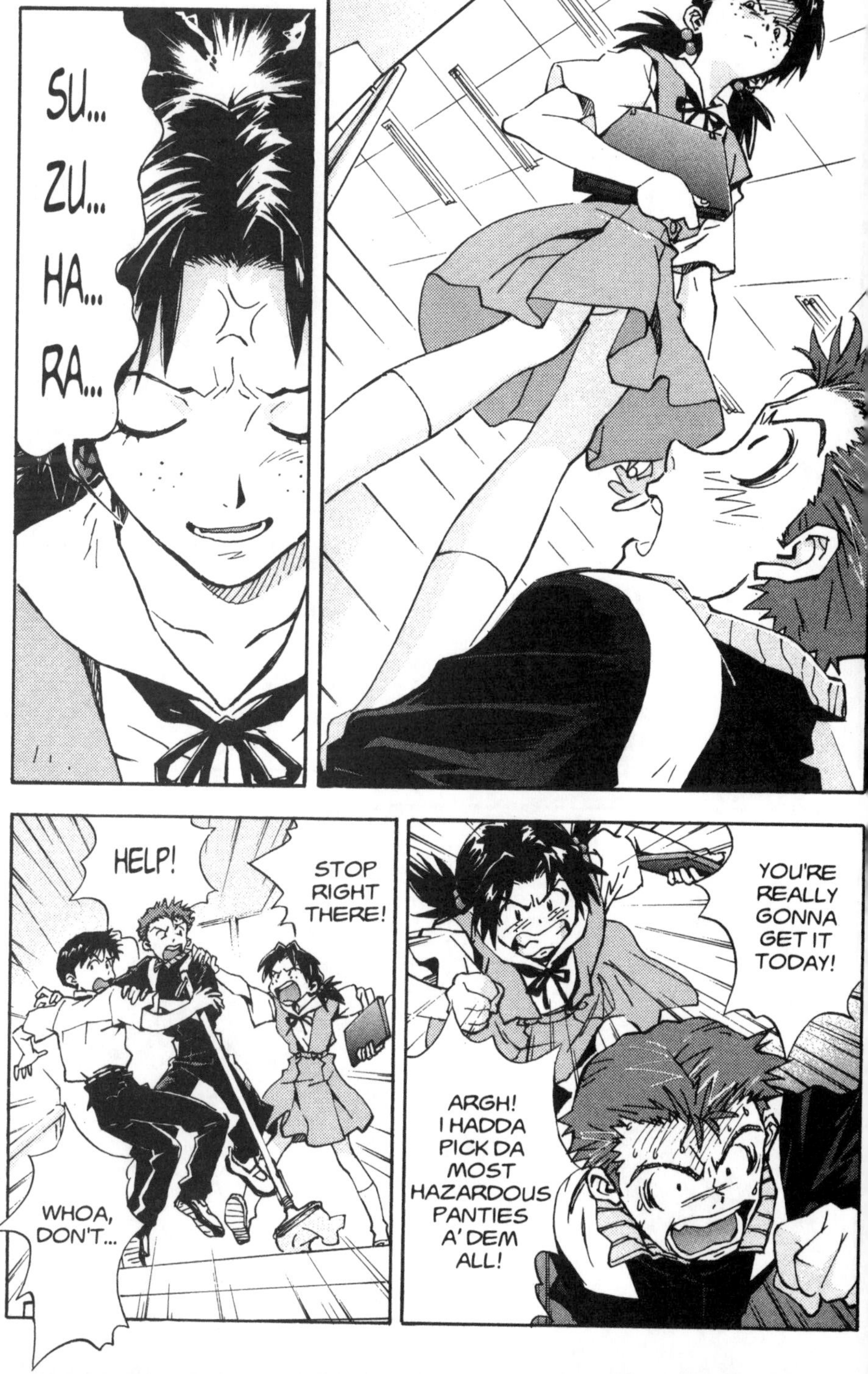
SU... ZU... HA... RA...
YOU'RE REALLY GONNA GET IT TODAY!
ARGH! I HADDA PICK DA MOST HAZARDOUS PANTIES A' DEM ALL!
STOP RIGHT THERE!
HELP!
WHOA, DON'T...

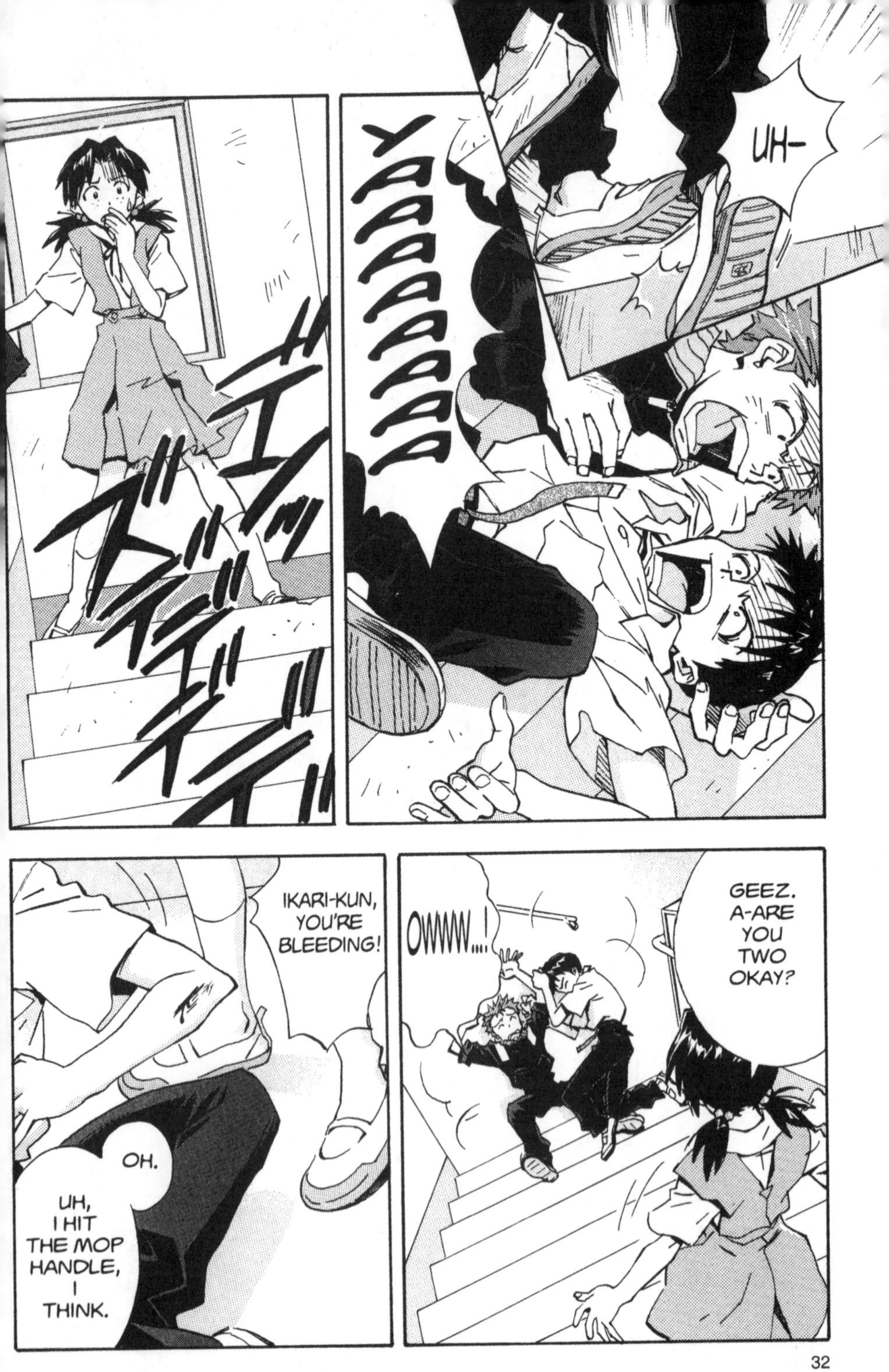
UH-
YAAAAAAAAAA
GEEZ. A-ARE YOU TWO OKAY?
OWWW...!
IKARI-KUN, YOU'RE BLEEDING!
OH.
UH, I HIT THE MOP HANDLE, I THINK.

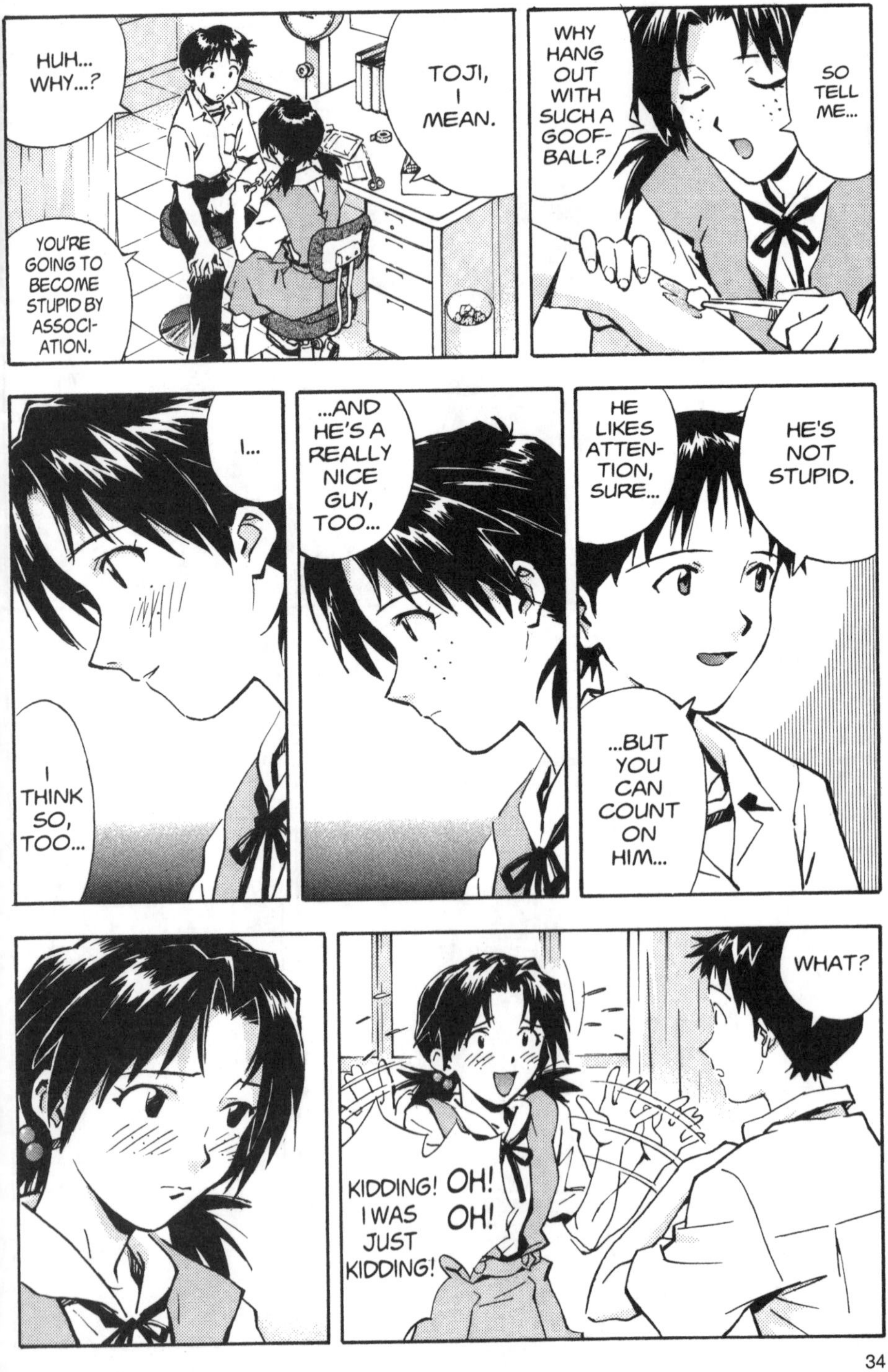
SO TELL ME...
WHY HANG OUT WITH SUCH A GOOF-BALL?
TOJI, I MEAN.
HUH... WHY...?
YOU'RE GOING TO BECOME STUPID BY ASSOCI-ATION.
HE'S NOT STUPID.
HE LIKES ATTEN-TION, SURE...
...BUT YOU CAN COUNT ON HIM...
...AND HE'S A REALLY NICE GUY, TOO...
I...
I THINK SO, TOO...
WHAT?
OH! OH!
KIDDING! I WAS JUST KIDDING!

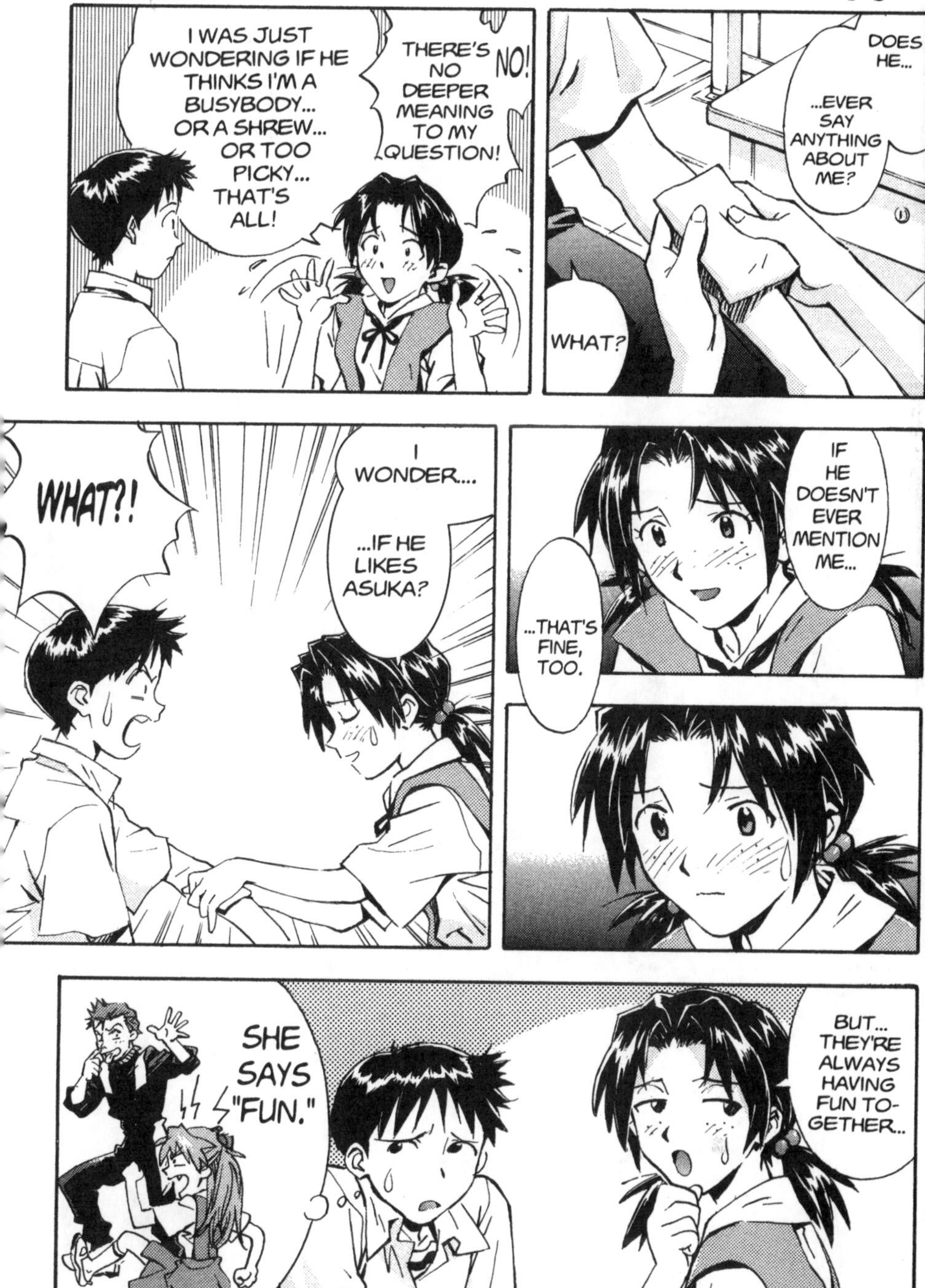
DOES HE...
...EVER SAY ANYTHING ABOUT ME?
WHAT?
NO!
THERE'S NO DEEPER MEANING TO MY QUESTION!
I WAS JUST WONDERING IF HE THINKS I'M A BUSYBODY... OR A SHREW... OR TOO PICKY... THAT'S ALL!
IF HE DOESN'T EVER MENTION ME...
...THAT'S FINE, TOO.
I WONDER....
...IF HE LIKES ASUKA?
WHAT?!
BUT... THEY'RE ALWAYS HAVING FUN TO-GETHER...
SHE SAYS "FUN."

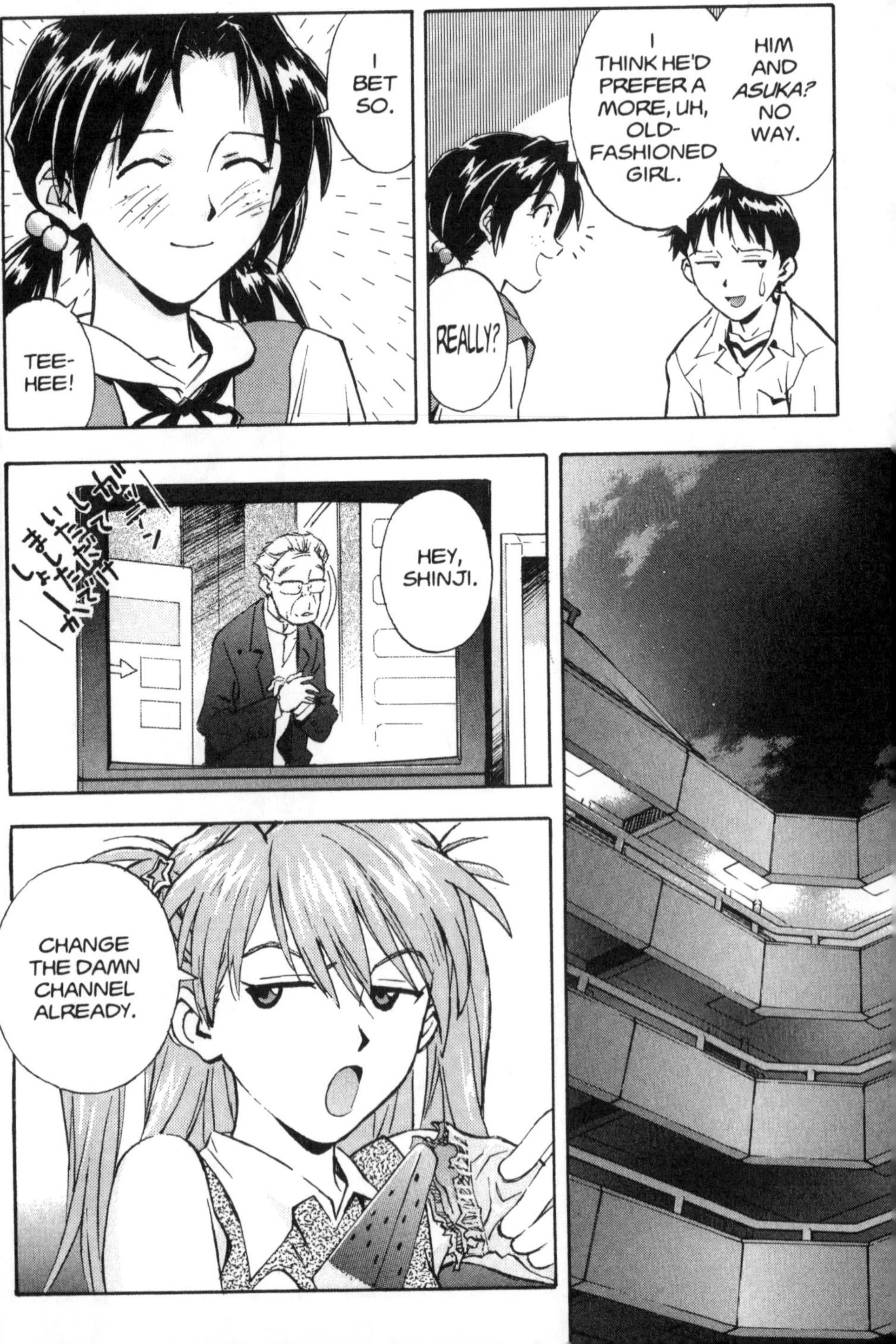
HIM AND ASUKA? NO WAY.
I THINK HE'D PREFER A MORE, UH, OLD-FASHIONED GIRL.
REALLY?
I BET SO.
TEE-HEE!
HEY, SHINJI.
CHANGE THE DAMN CHANNEL ALREADY.

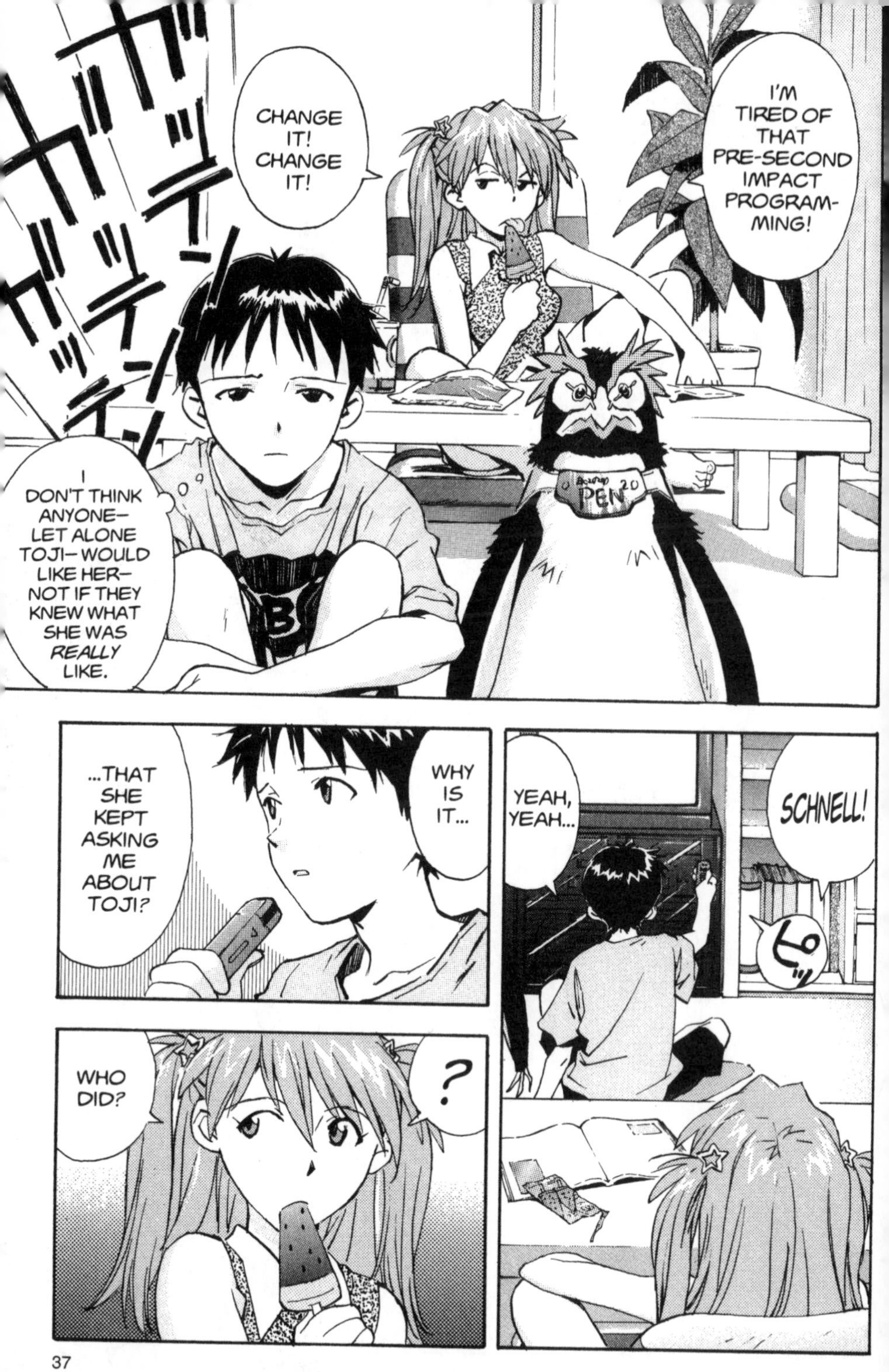
I'M TIRED OF THAT PRE-SECOND IMPACT PROGRAMMING!
CHANGE IT! CHANGE IT!
I DON'T THINK ANYONE—LET ALONE TOJI—WOULD LIKE HER—NOT IF THEY KNEW WHAT SHE WAS *REALLY* LIKE.
SCHNELL!
YEAH, YEAH...
ピッ
WHY IS IT...
...THAT SHE KEPT ASKING ME ABOUT TOJI?
WHO DID?
?

FOR UNIT-03'S STARTUP TEST AT MATSUSHIRO...

...WE'LL BE USING THE FOURTH.

NERV

GOD'S IN HIS HEAVEN, ALL'S RIGHT WITH THE WORLD.

YOU FOUND THE FOURTH CHILD?

WE DID.

FOURTH?

WE'LL HAVE DOCUMENTATION IN TWELVE HOURS.

BUT THERE'S NO REPORT FROM THE MARDUK INSTITUTE...

40

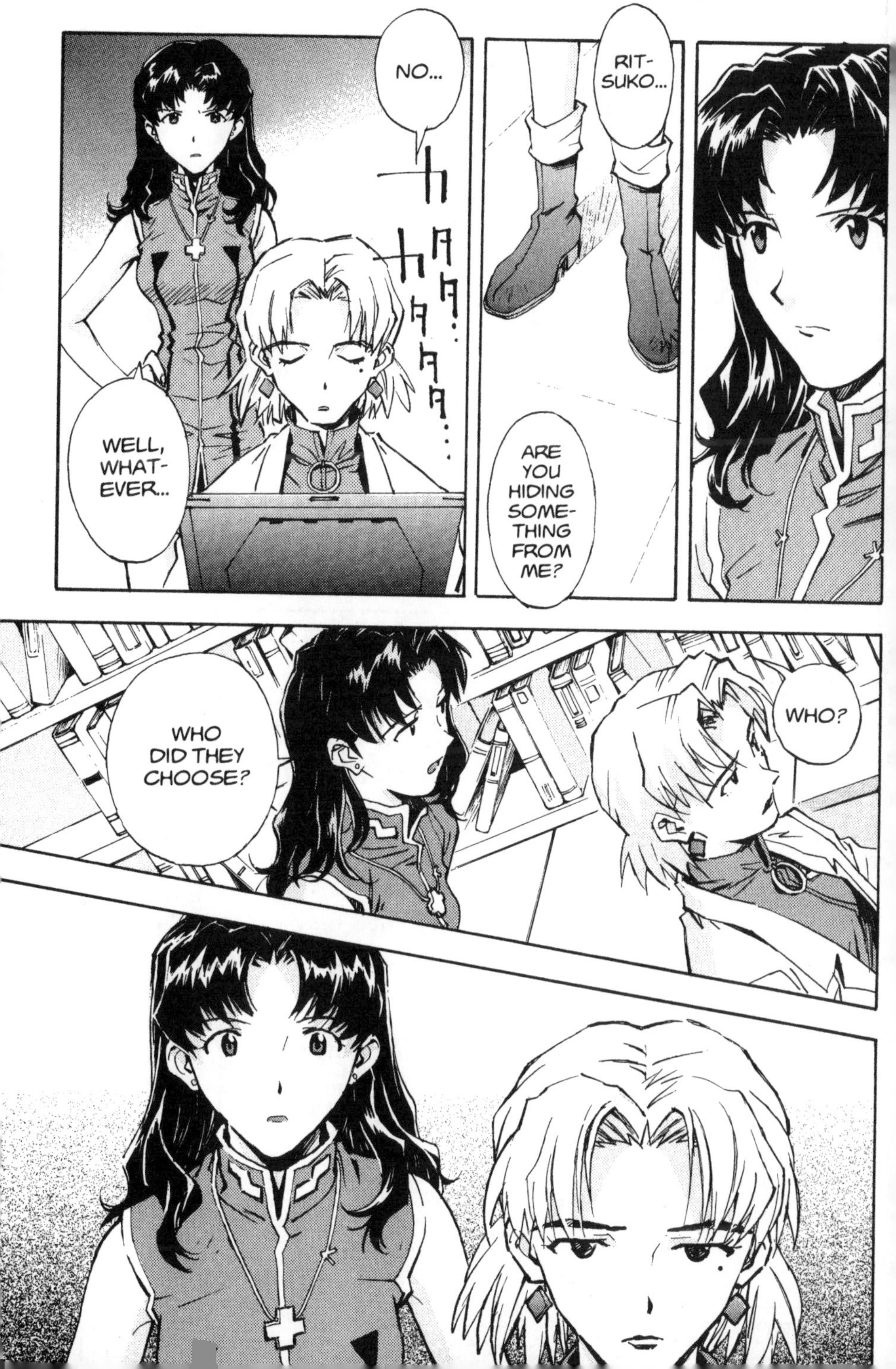
RIT-
SUKO...
ARE YOU HIDING SOME-THING FROM ME?
NO...
WELL, WHAT-EVER...
WHO?
WHO DID THEY CHOOSE?

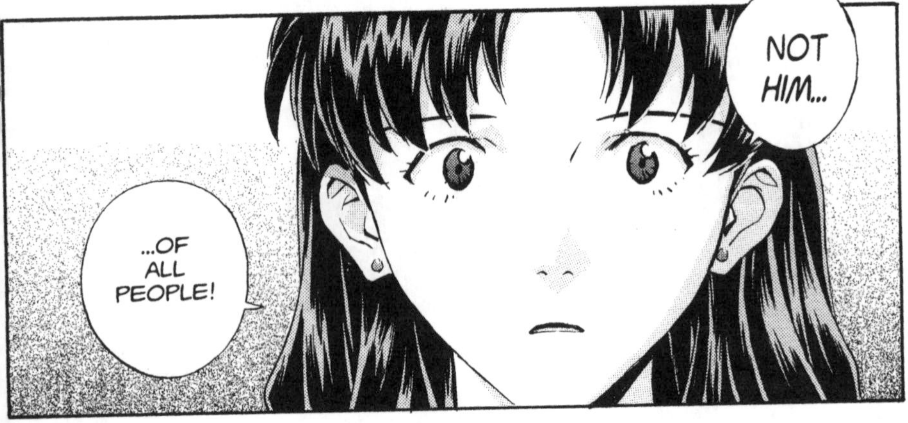
NOT HIM...
...OF ALL PEOPLE!

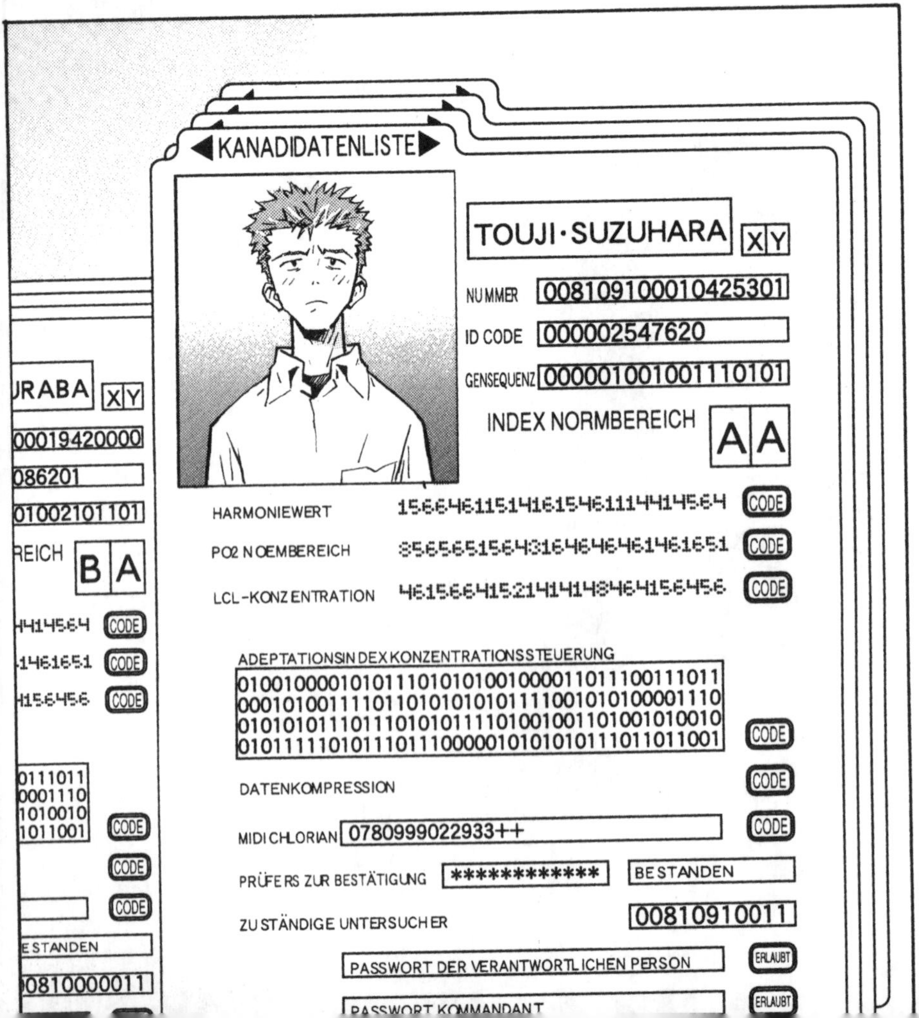
KANADIDATENLISTE
TOUJI·SUZUHARA
XY
NUMMER 00810910001042530 1
ID CODE 000002547620
GENSEQUENZ 00000100100111010 1
INDEX NORMBEREICH
AA
HARMONIEWERT 156646115141615461114414564
CODE
PO2 NOEMBEREICH 856565156431646464614616 51
CODE
LCL-KONZENTRATION 461566415214141484641564 56
CODE
ADEPTATIONSINDEXKONZENTRATIONSSTEUERUNG
01001000010101110101010010000110111001110 11
00010100111101101010101011110010101000011 10
01010101110111010101111010010011010010100 10
01011111010111011100000101010101110110110 01
CODE
DATENKOMPRESSION
CODE
MIDICHLORIAN 0780999022933++
CODE
PRÜFERS ZUR BESTÄTIGUNG ************
BESTANDEN
ZUSTÄNDIGE UNTERSUCHER 00810910011
PASSWORT DER VERANTWORTLICHEN PERSON
ERLAUBT
PASSWORT KOMMANDANT
ERLAUBT
URABA
XY
00019420000
086201
01002101101
REICH
BA
CODE
CODE
CODE
0111011
0001110
1010010
1011001
CODE
CODE
CODE
ESTANDEN
0810000011

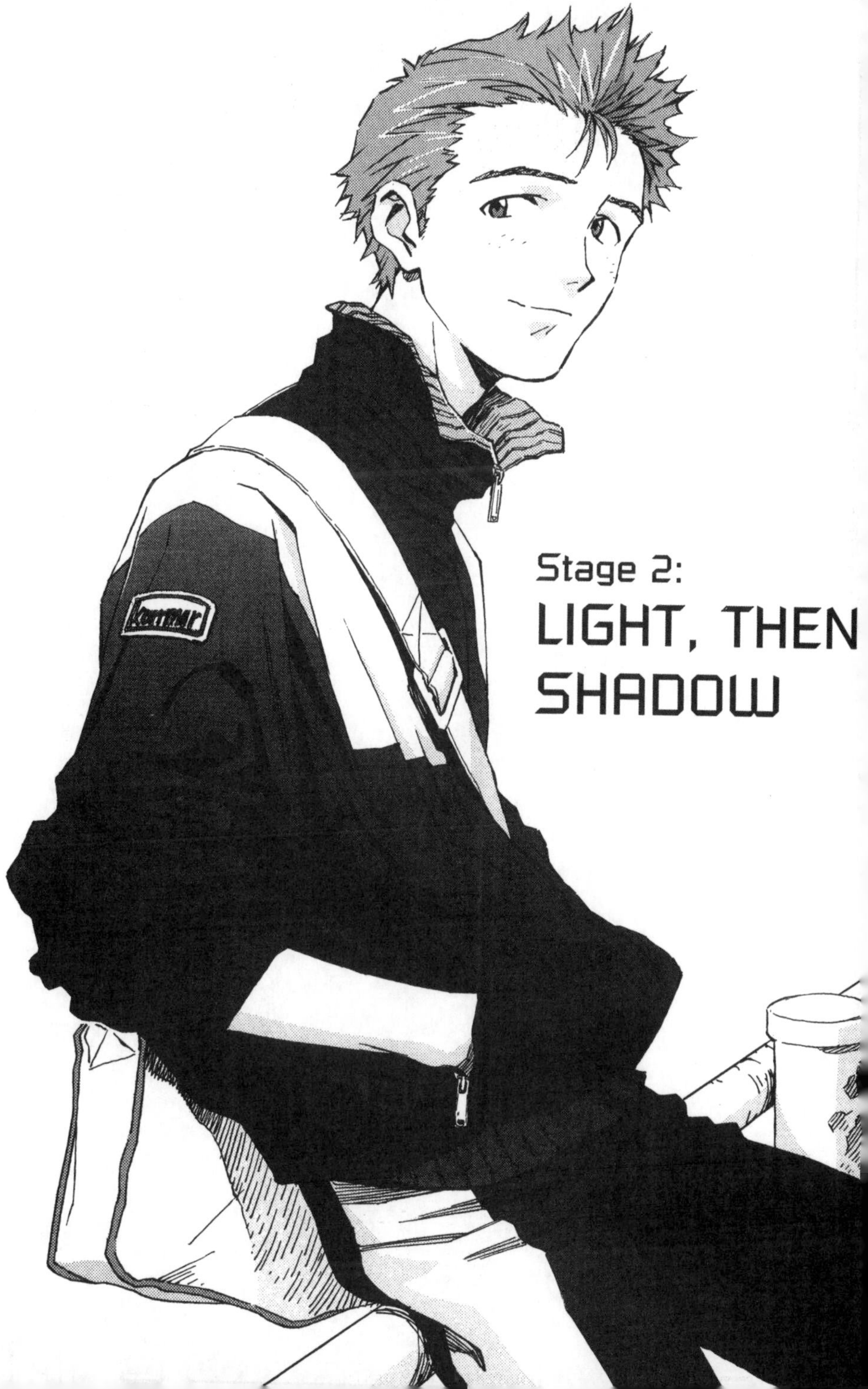

Stage 2: LIGHT, THEN SHADOW

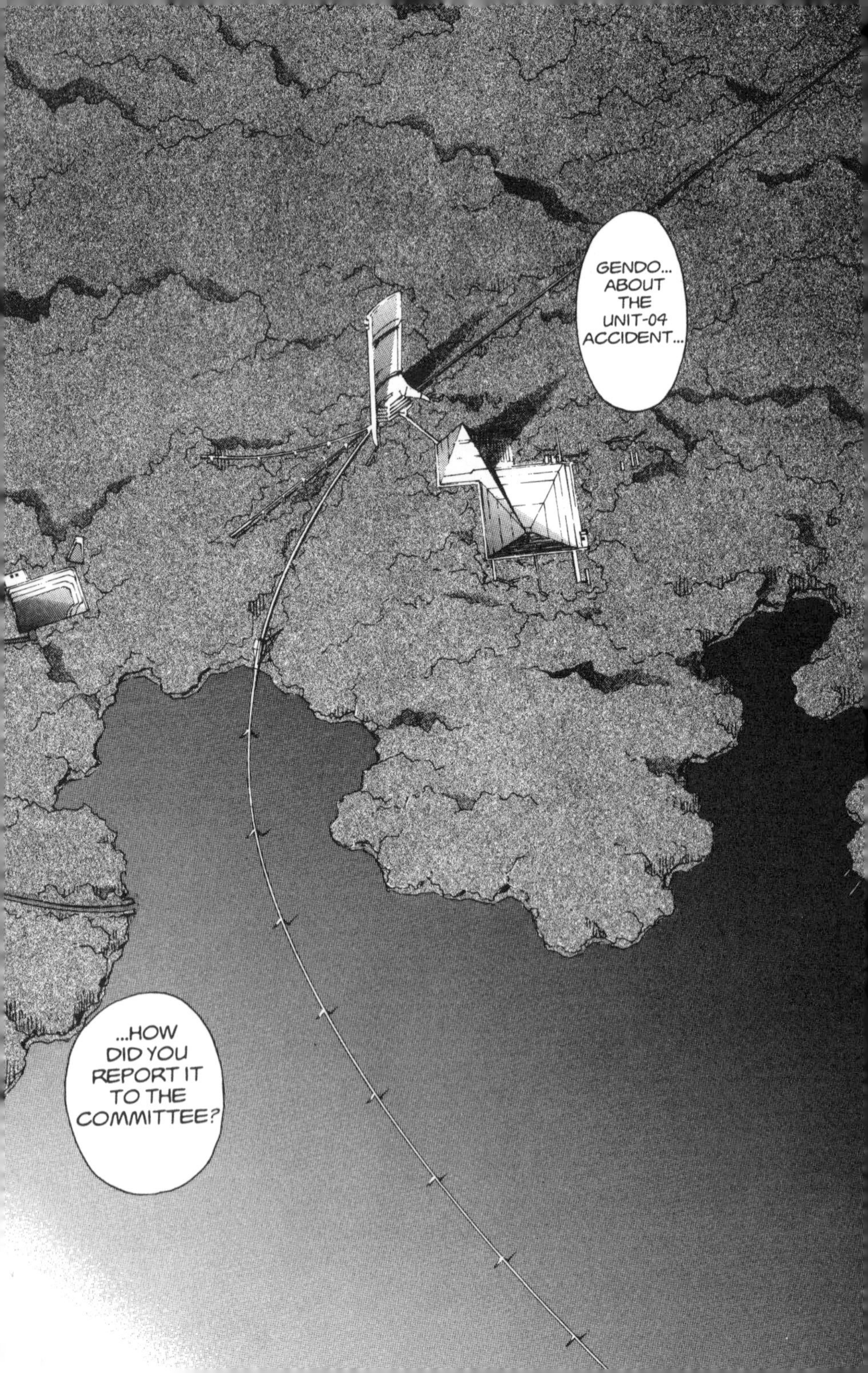
GENDO... ABOUT THE UNIT-04 ACCIDENT...
...HOW DID YOU REPORT IT TO THE COMMITTEE?

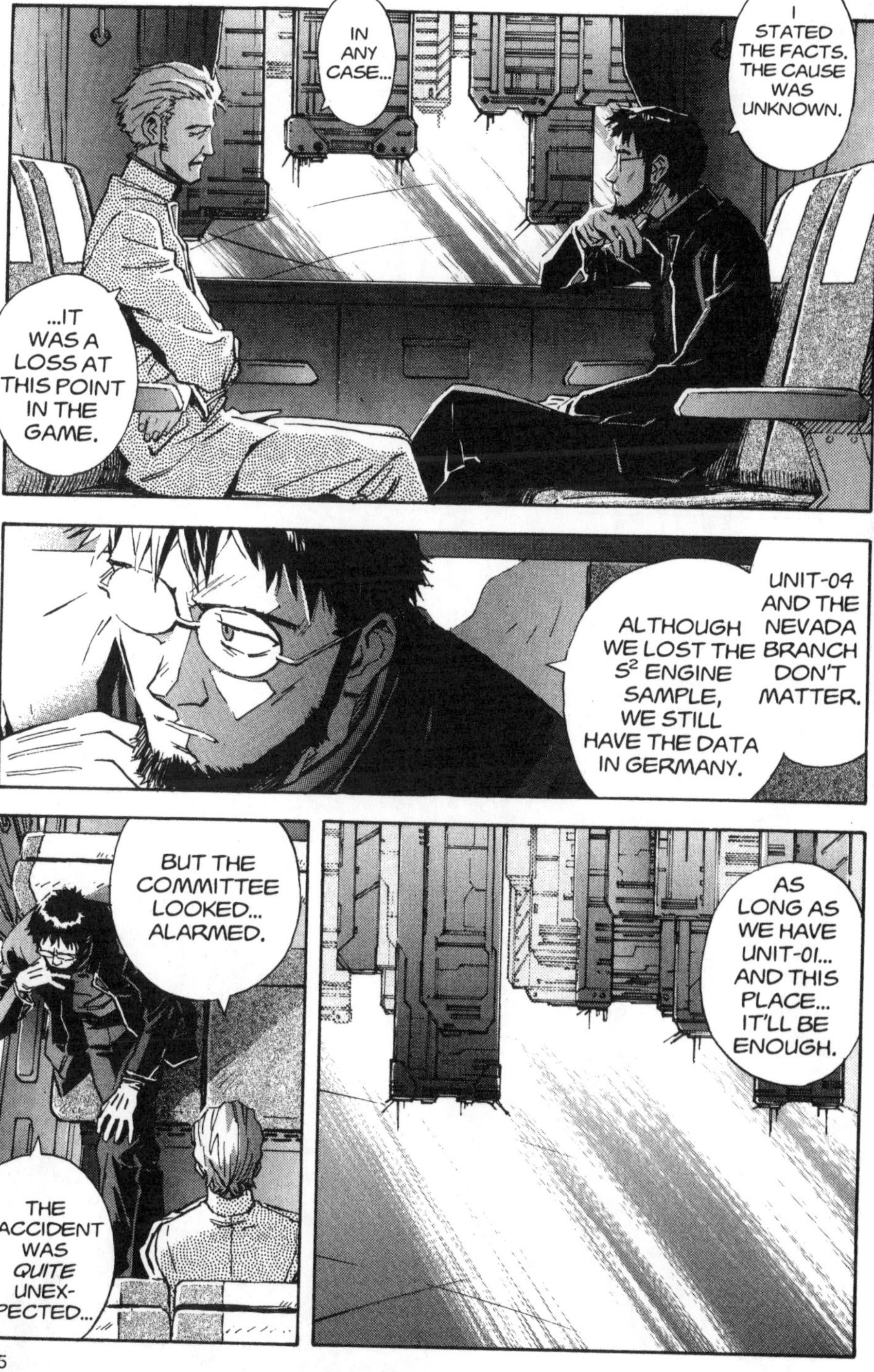
I STATED THE FACTS. THE CAUSE WAS UNKNOWN.
IN ANY CASE...
...IT WAS A LOSS AT THIS POINT IN THE GAME.
UNIT-04 AND THE NEVADA BRANCH DON'T MATTER.
ALTHOUGH WE LOST THE S^2 ENGINE SAMPLE, WE STILL HAVE THE DATA IN GERMANY.
AS LONG AS WE HAVE UNIT-01... AND THIS PLACE... IT'LL BE ENOUGH.
BUT THE COMMITTEE LOOKED... ALARMED.
THE ACCIDENT WAS QUITE UNEXPECTED...

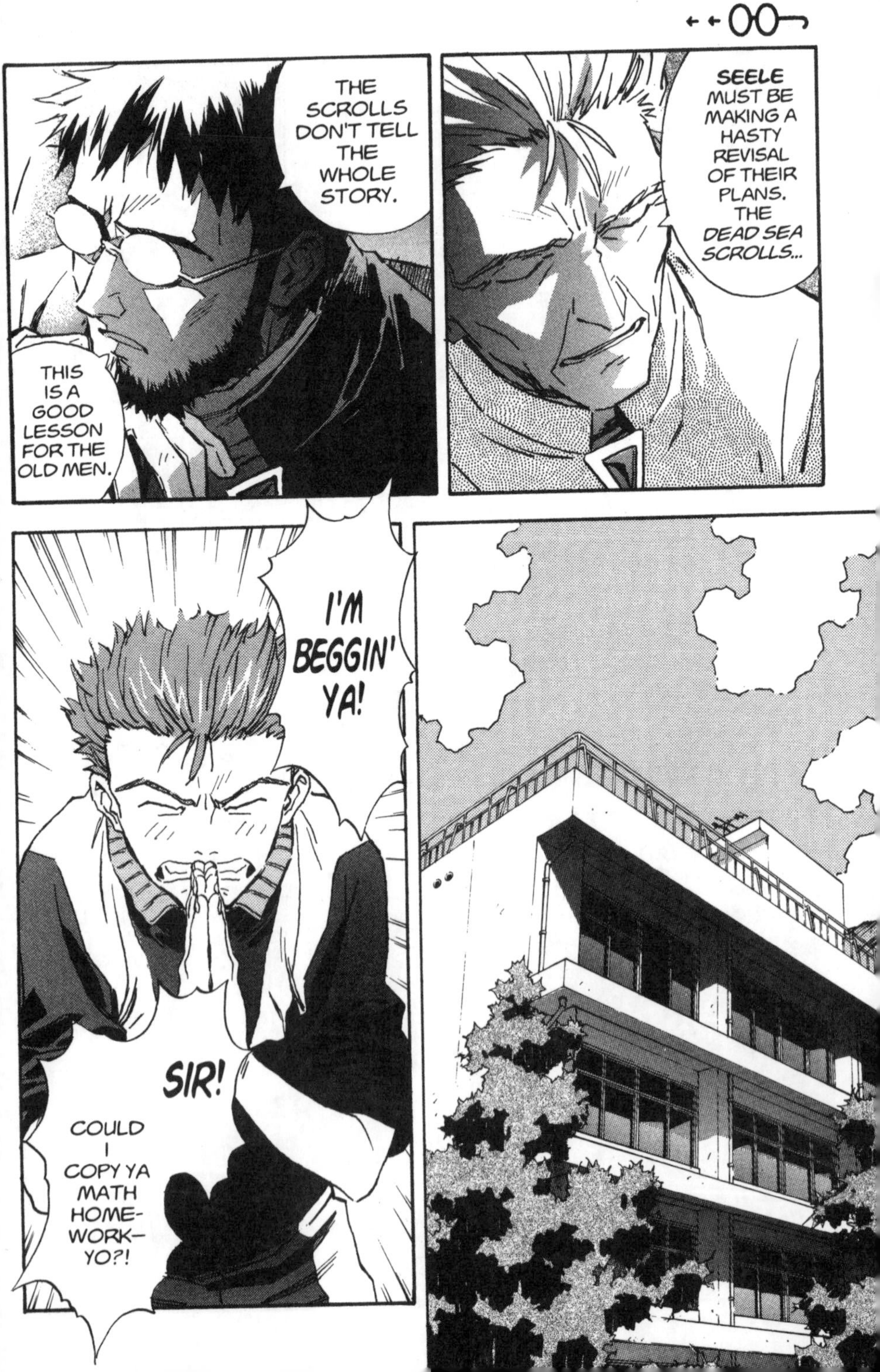
SEELE MUST BE MAKING A HASTY REVISAL OF THEIR PLANS. THE DEAD SEA SCROLLS...
THE SCROLLS DON'T TELL THE WHOLE STORY.
THIS IS A GOOD LESSON FOR THE OLD MEN.
I'M BEGGIN' YA!
SIR!
COULD I COPY YA MATH HOME-WORK-YO?!

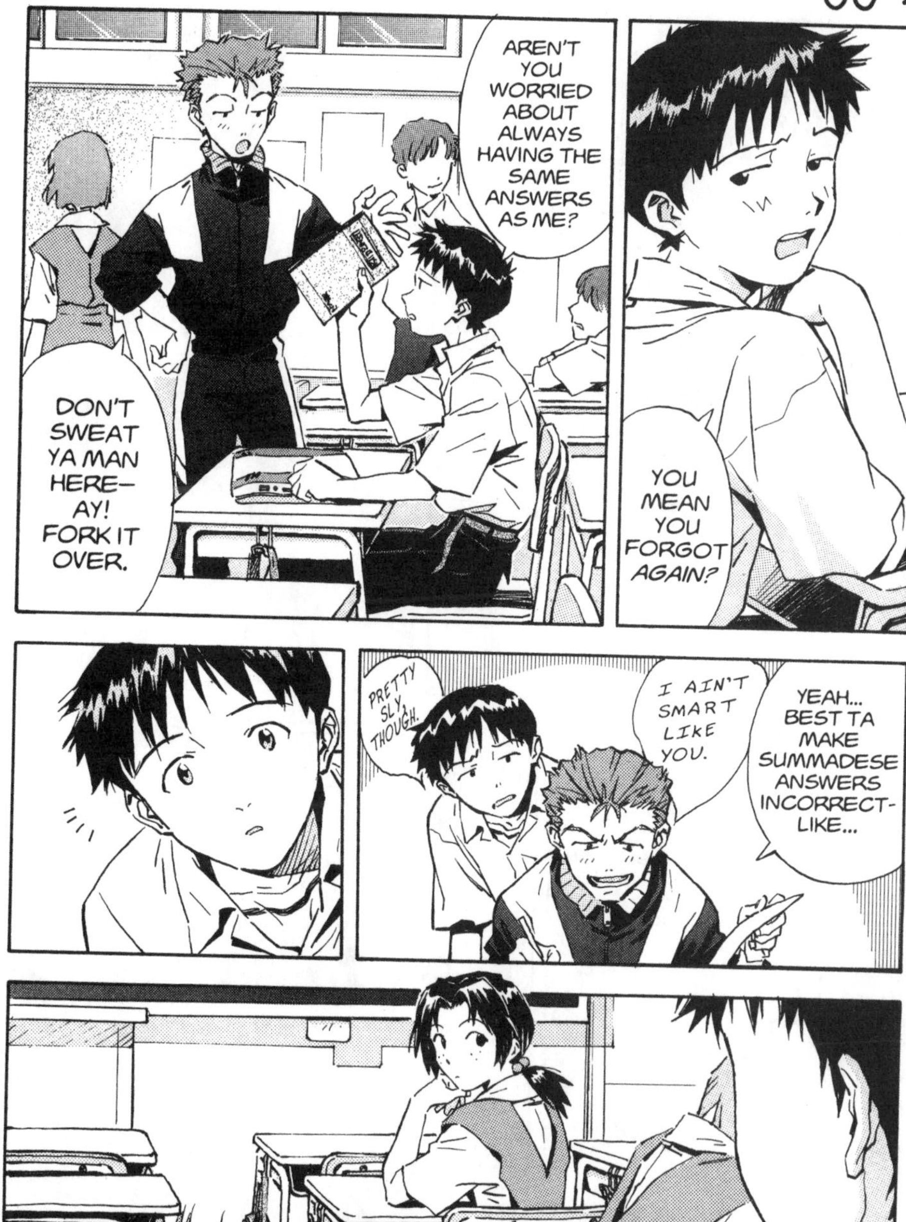
YOU MEAN YOU FORGOT AGAIN?
AREN'T YOU WORRIED ABOUT ALWAYS HAVING THE SAME ANSWERS AS ME?
DON'T SWEAT YA MAN HERE-AY! FORK IT OVER.
YEAH... BEST TA MAKE SUMMADESE ANSWERS INCORRECT-LIKE...
I AIN'T SMART LIKE YOU.
PRETTY SLY, THOUGH.

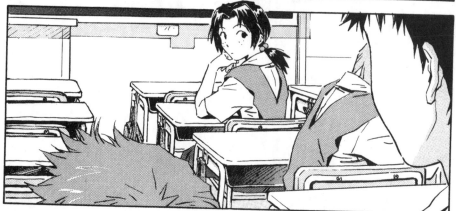

Now I wonder if she's always been glancing over at Toji like that.

I'd never have noticed before she...

WHO'S A... STINGY SQUARE?!

DA STINGY SQUARE A' HOMEROOM 2-A? SHE'D NEVER CONDESCEND T' DAT SIMPLE ACT A' CHARITY!

HMM?

SAY!

LIKE... FROM THE CLASS REP.

FOR THE SAKE OF, UM, STRATEGY, WHY NOT COPY FROM SOMEONE ELSE SOMETIMES?

WHAAAT? HER?

48

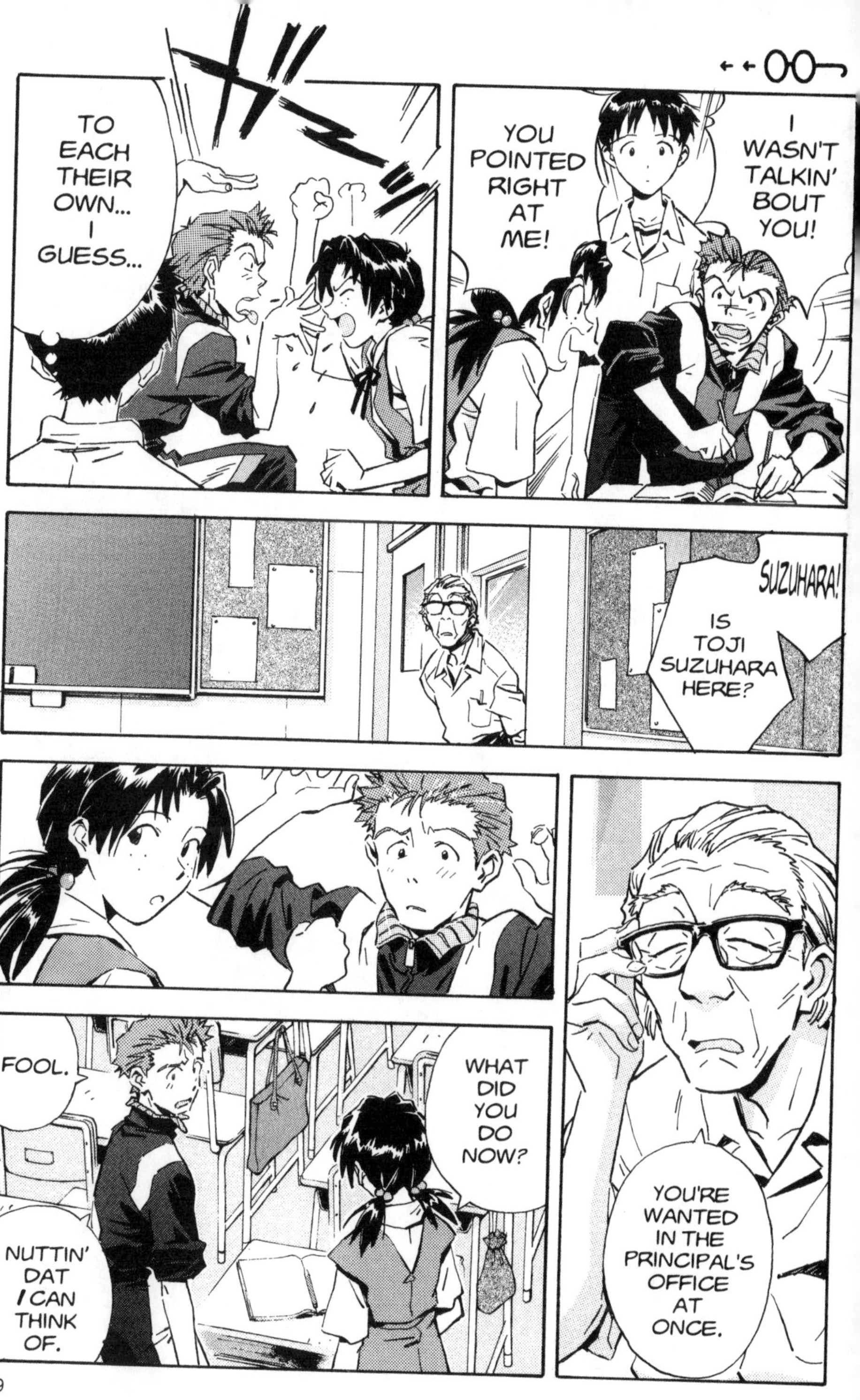
I WASN'T TALKIN' BOUT YOU!
YOU POINTED RIGHT AT ME!
TO EACH THEIR OWN... I GUESS...
SUZUHARA!
IS TOJI SUZUHARA HERE?
YOU'RE WANTED IN THE PRINCIPAL'S OFFICE AT ONCE.
WHAT DID YOU DO NOW?
FOOL.
NUTTIN' DAT *I* CAN THINK OF.

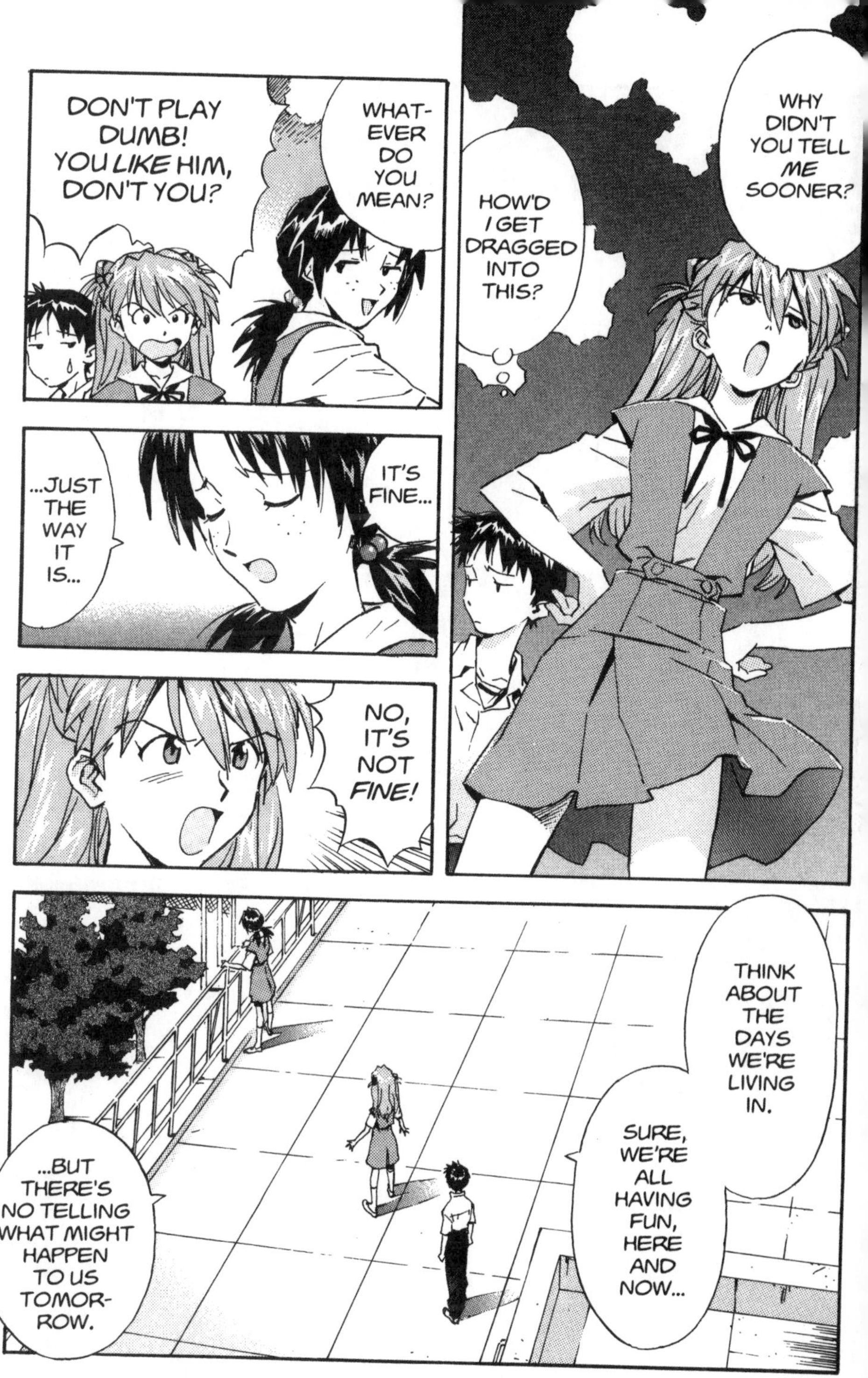
WHY DIDN'T YOU TELL *ME* SOONER?
HOW'D I GET DRAGGED INTO THIS?
WHAT-EVER DO YOU MEAN?
DON'T PLAY DUMB! YOU *LIKE* HIM, DON'T YOU?
IT'S FINE...
...JUST THE WAY IT IS...
NO, IT'S NOT *FINE!*
THINK ABOUT THE DAYS WE'RE LIVING IN.
SURE, WE'RE ALL HAVING FUN, HERE AND NOW...
...BUT THERE'S NO TELLING WHAT MIGHT HAPPEN TO US TOMOR-ROW.

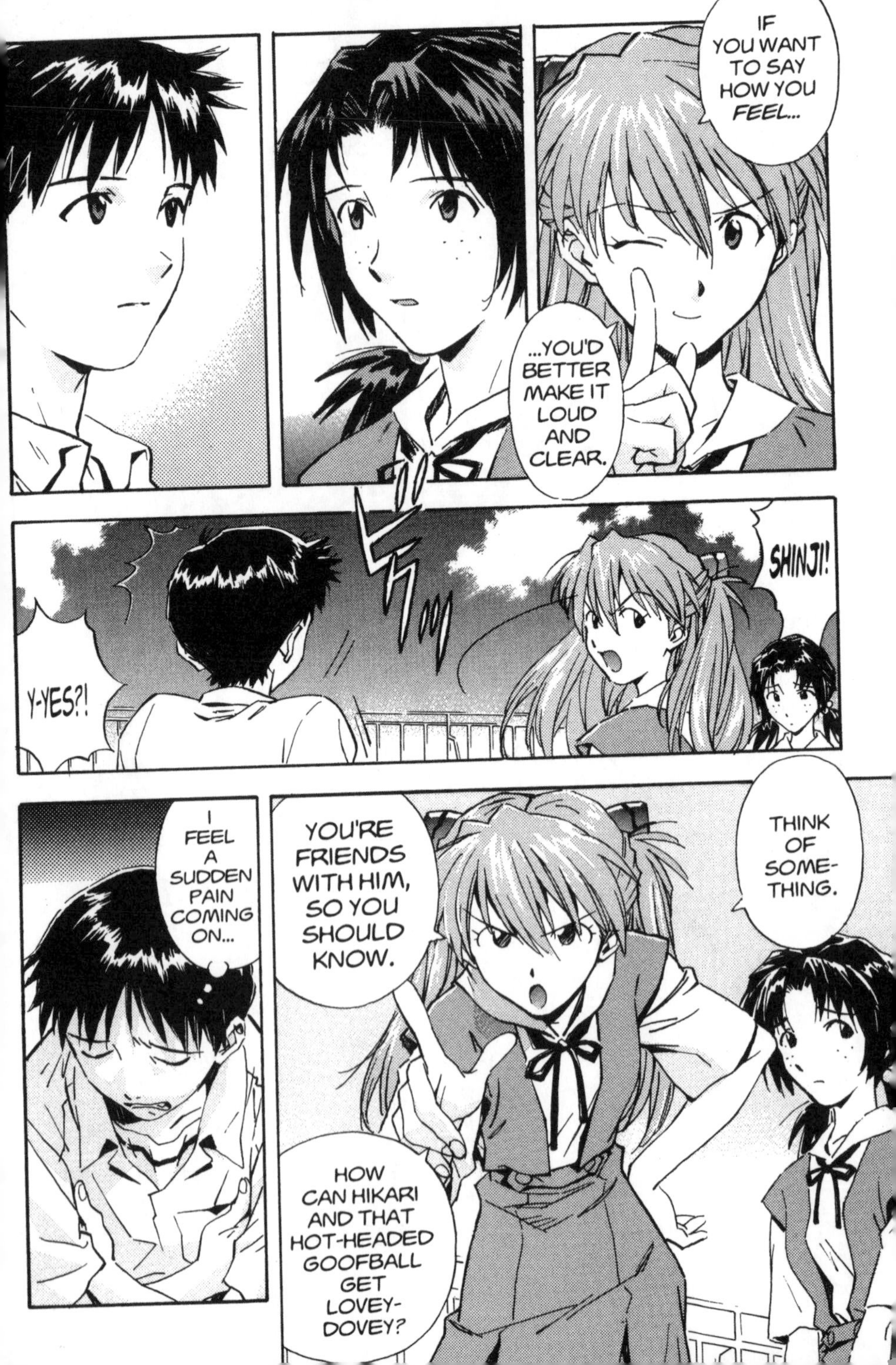
IF YOU WANT TO SAY HOW YOU FEEL...
...YOU'D BETTER MAKE IT LOUD AND CLEAR.
SHINJI!
Y-YES?!
THINK OF SOME-THING.
YOU'RE FRIENDS WITH HIM, SO YOU SHOULD KNOW.
HOW CAN HIKARI AND THAT HOT-HEADED GOOFBALL GET LOVEY-DOVEY?
I FEEL A SUDDEN PAIN COMING ON...

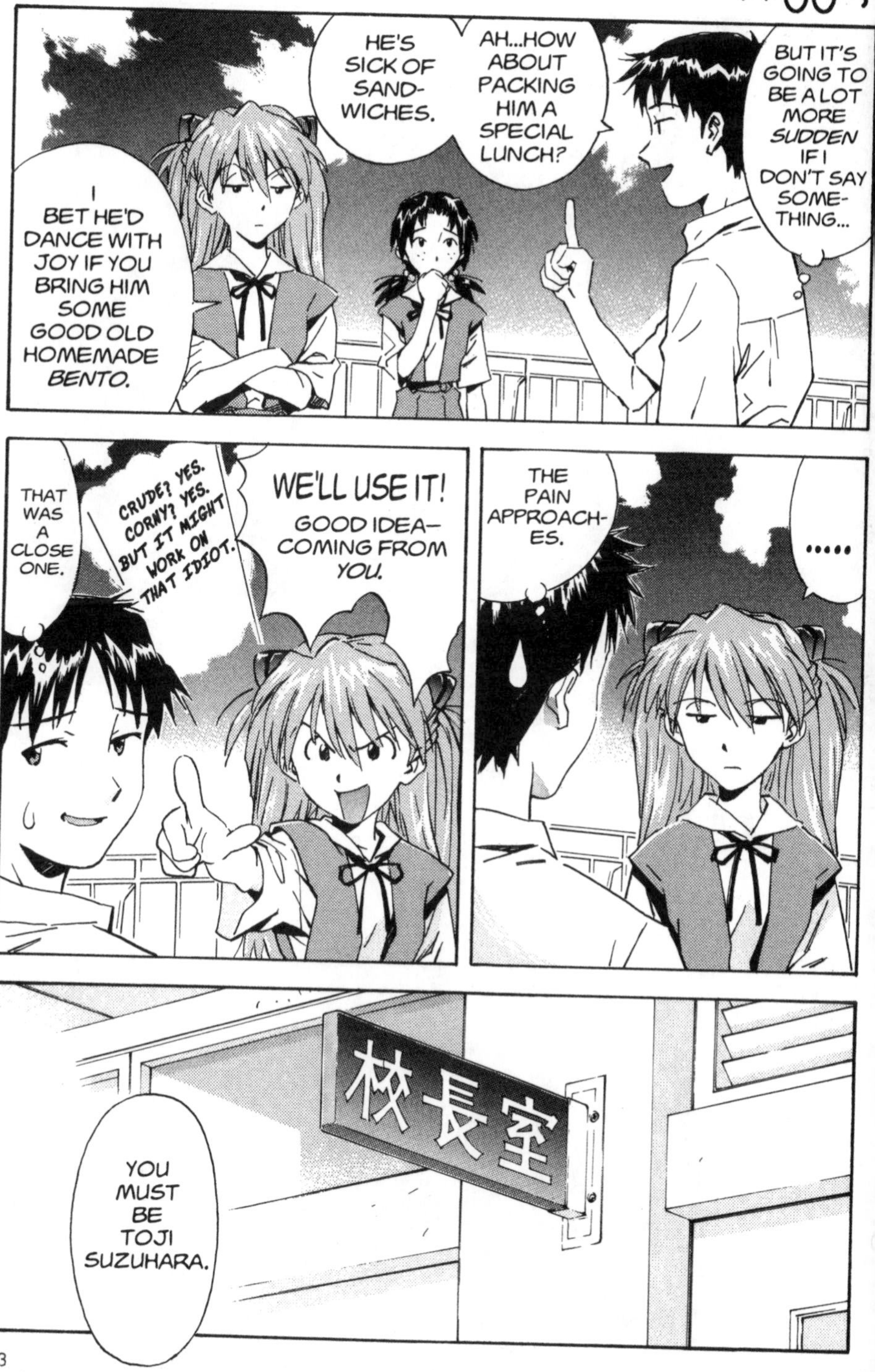
BUT IT'S GOING TO BE A LOT MORE SUDDEN IF I DON'T SAY SOMETHING...
AH...HOW ABOUT PACKING HIM A SPECIAL LUNCH?
HE'S SICK OF SAND-WICHES.
I BET HE'D DANCE WITH JOY IF YOU BRING HIM SOME GOOD OLD HOMEMADE BENTO.
.....
THE PAIN APPROACH-ES.
WE'LL USE IT!
GOOD IDEA—COMING FROM YOU.
CRUDE? YES. CORNY? YES. BUT IT MIGHT WORK ON THAT IDIOT.
THAT WAS A CLOSE ONE.
校長室
YOU MUST BE TOJI SUZUHARA.

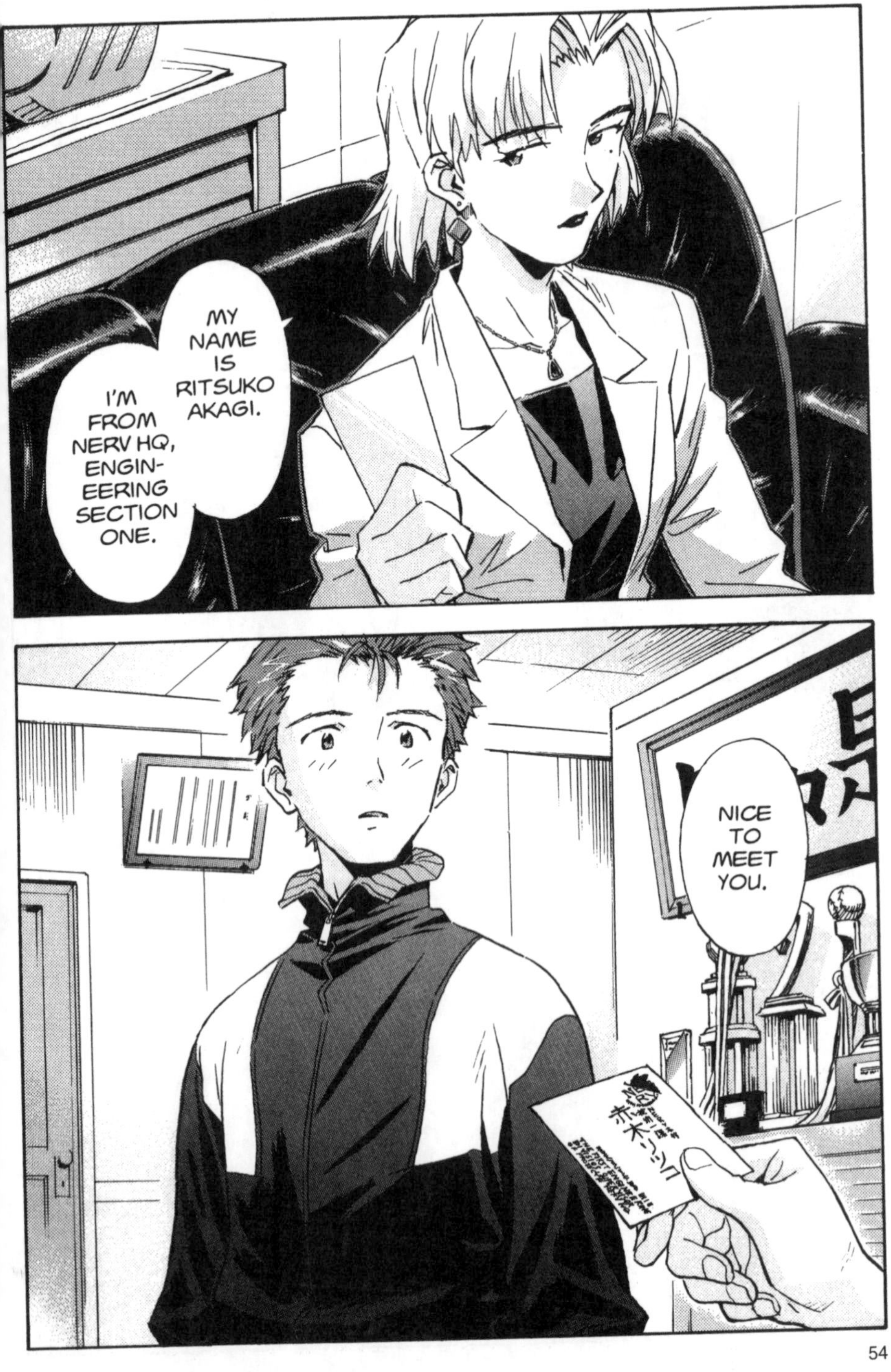
MY NAME IS RITSUKO AKAGI.
I'M FROM NERV HQ, ENGINEERING SECTION ONE.
NICE TO MEET YOU.

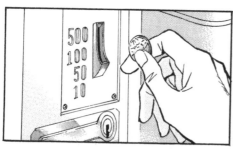

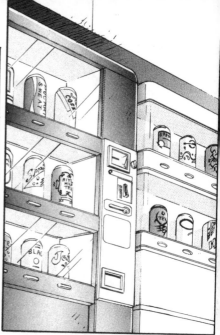

HUH? WHY ASK ME?

...KATSU-RAGI?

COFFEE? MY TREAT.

UH, SO... YOU THINK IT'LL RAIN TOMOR-ROW?

...ANGELS?

THE DISAPPEAR-ANCE OF THE SECOND BRANCH...

55

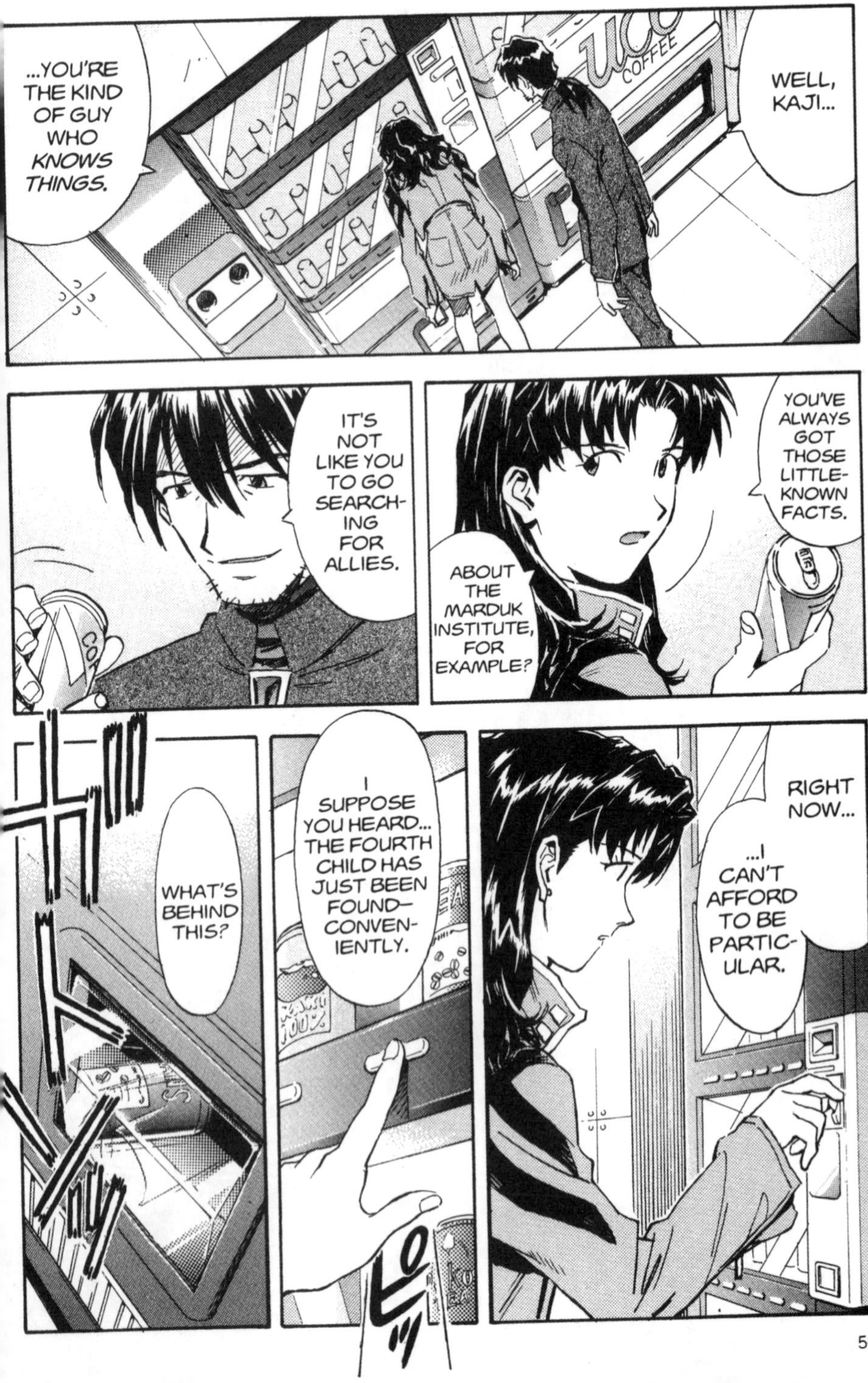
WELL, KAJI...
...YOU'RE THE KIND OF GUY WHO KNOWS THINGS.
YOU'VE ALWAYS GOT THOSE LITTLE-KNOWN FACTS.
ABOUT THE MARDUK INSTITUTE, FOR EXAMPLE?
IT'S NOT LIKE YOU TO GO SEARCHING FOR ALLIES.
RIGHT NOW...
...I CAN'T AFFORD TO BE PARTICULAR.
I SUPPOSE YOU HEARD... THE FOURTH CHILD HAS JUST BEEN FOUND—CONVENIENTLY.
WHAT'S BEHIND THIS?

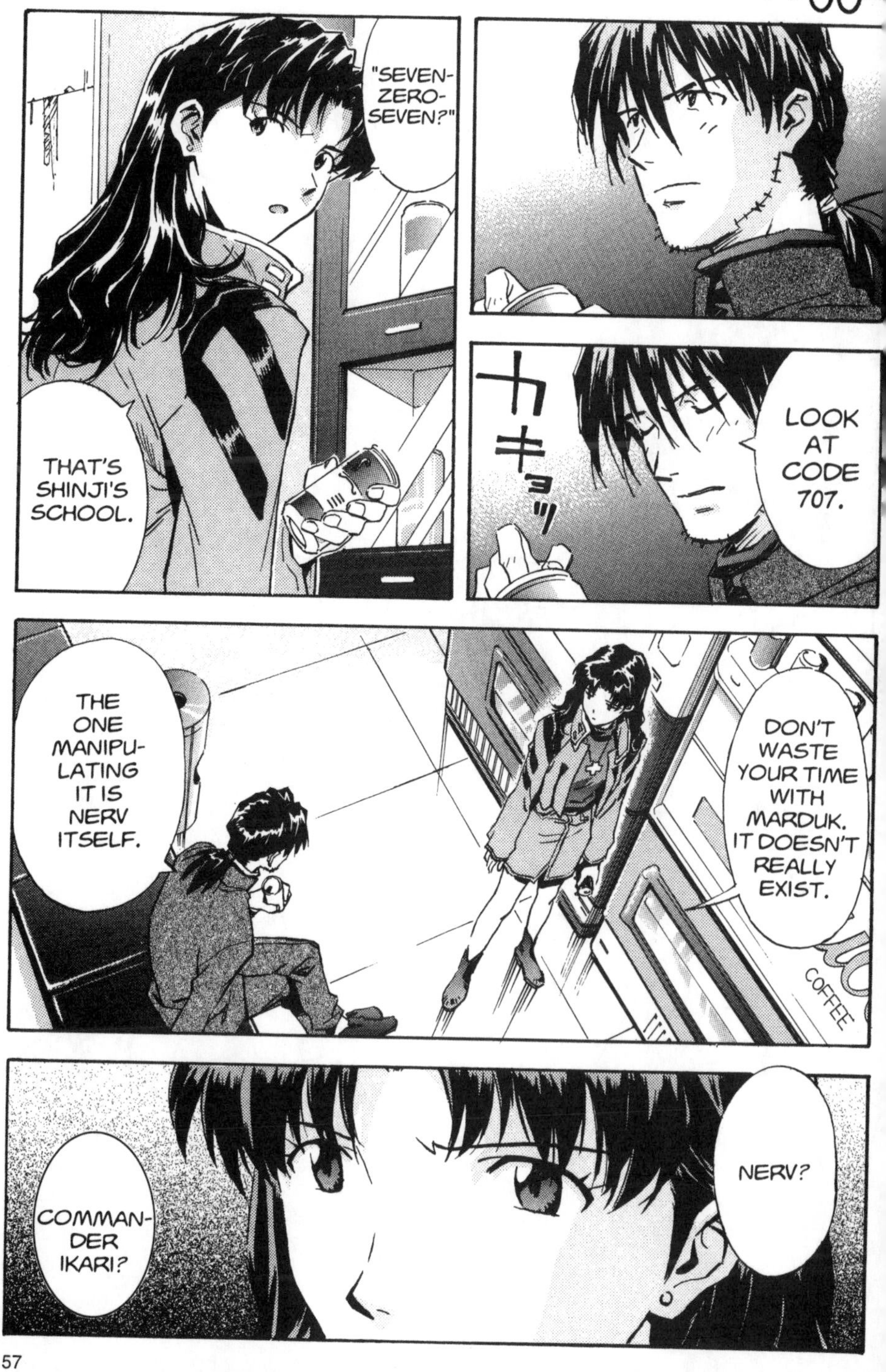
LOOK AT CODE 707.
カキョッ
"SEVEN-ZERO-SEVEN?"
THAT'S SHINJI'S SCHOOL.
DON'T WASTE YOUR TIME WITH MARDUK. IT DOESN'T REALLY EXIST.
COFFEE
THE ONE MANIPULATING IT IS NERV ITSELF.
NERV?
COMMANDER IKARI?

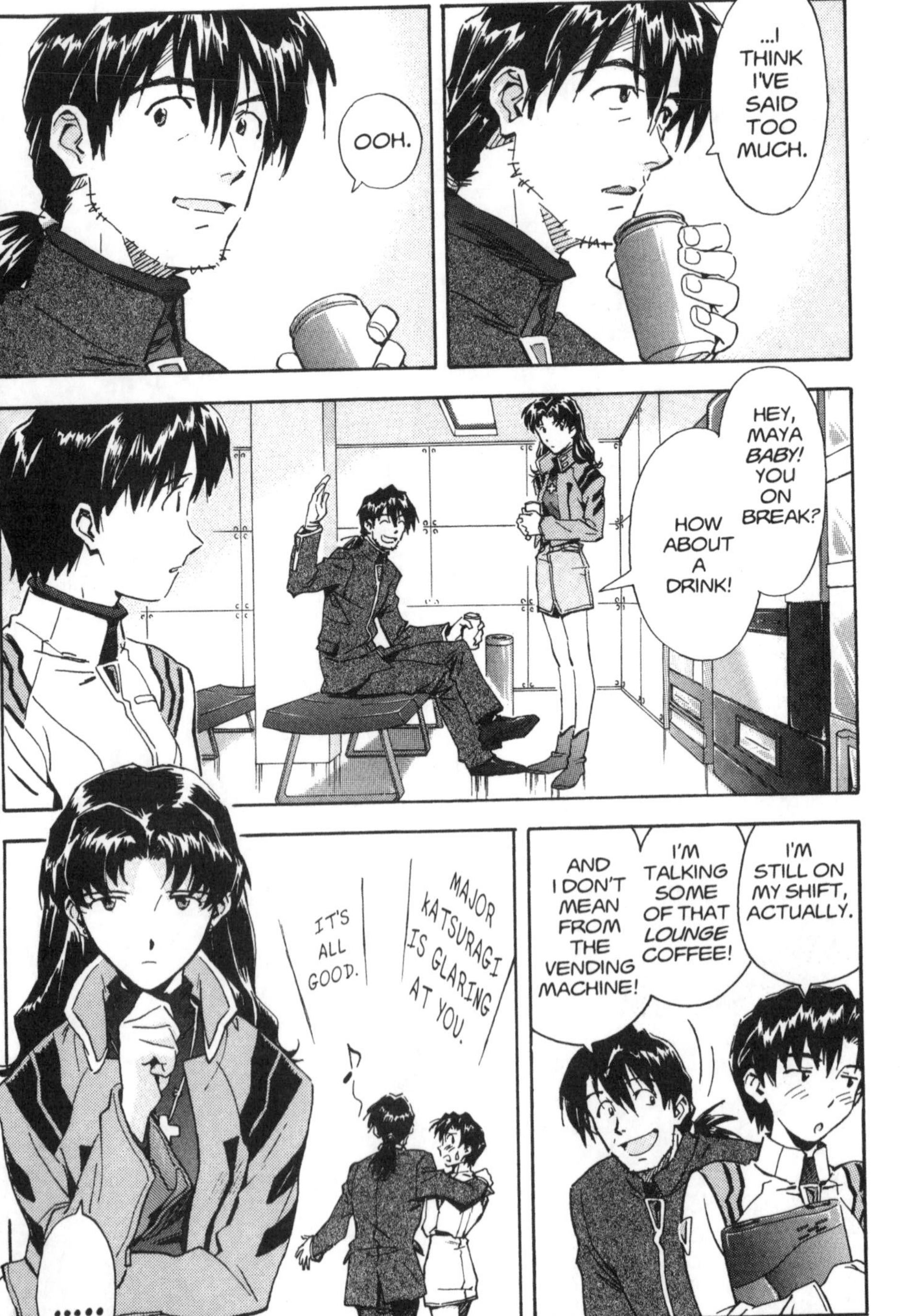
...I THINK I'VE SAID TOO MUCH.
OOH.
HEY, MAYA *BABY!* YOU ON BREAK?
HOW ABOUT A DRINK!
I'M STILL ON MY SHIFT, ACTUALLY.
I'M TALKING SOME OF THAT *LOUNGE* COFFEE!
AND I DON'T MEAN FROM THE VENDING MACHINE!
MAJOR KATSURAGI IS GLARING AT YOU.
IT'S ALL GOOD.
.....

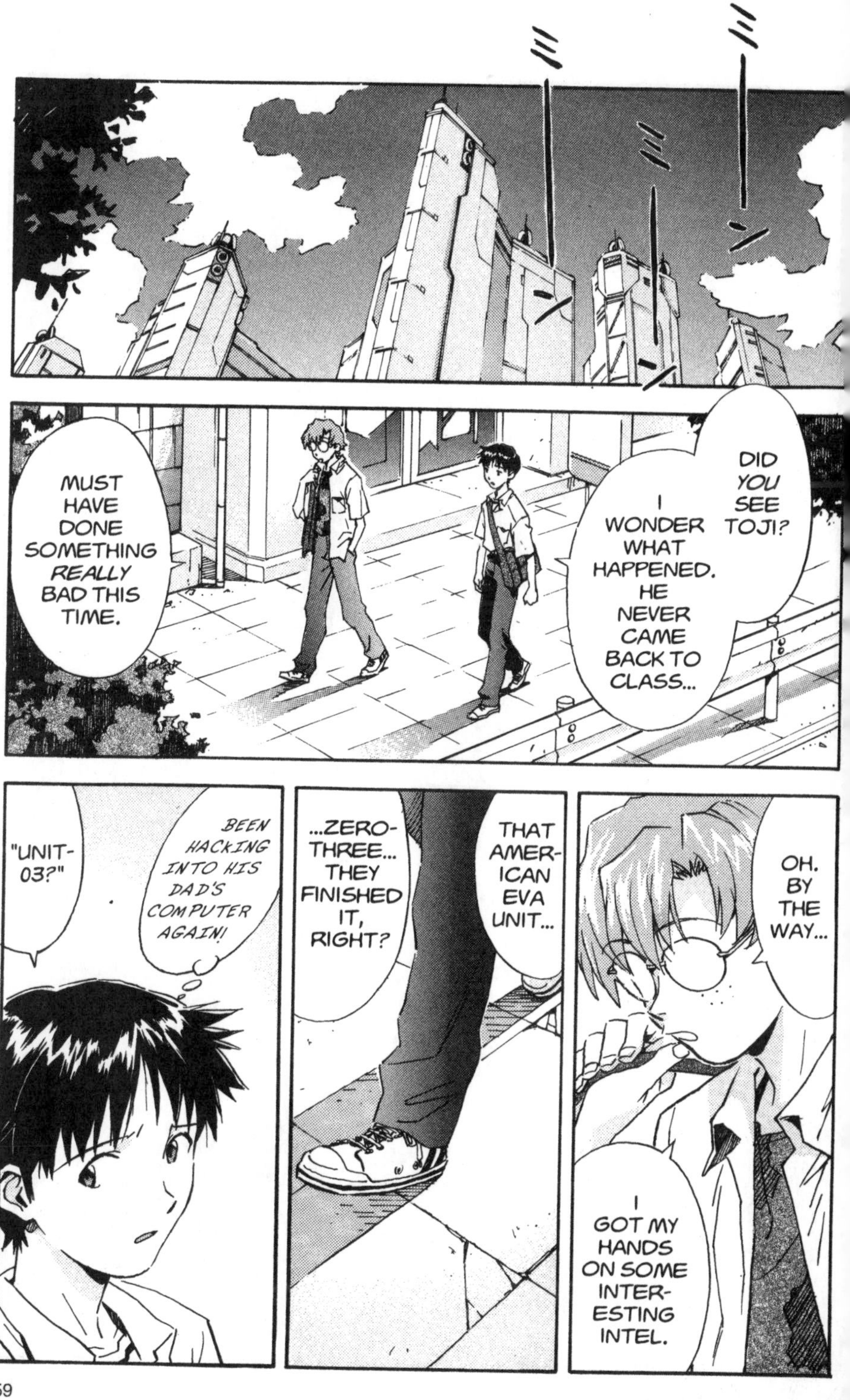
DID YOU SEE TOJI?
I WONDER WHAT HAPPENED. HE NEVER CAME BACK TO CLASS...
MUST HAVE DONE SOMETHING REALLY BAD THIS TIME.
OH. BY THE WAY...
I GOT MY HANDS ON SOME INTERESTING INTEL.
THAT AMERICAN EVA UNIT...
...ZERO-THREE... THEY FINISHED IT, RIGHT?
BEEN HACKING INTO HIS DAD'S COMPUTER AGAIN!
"UNIT-03?"

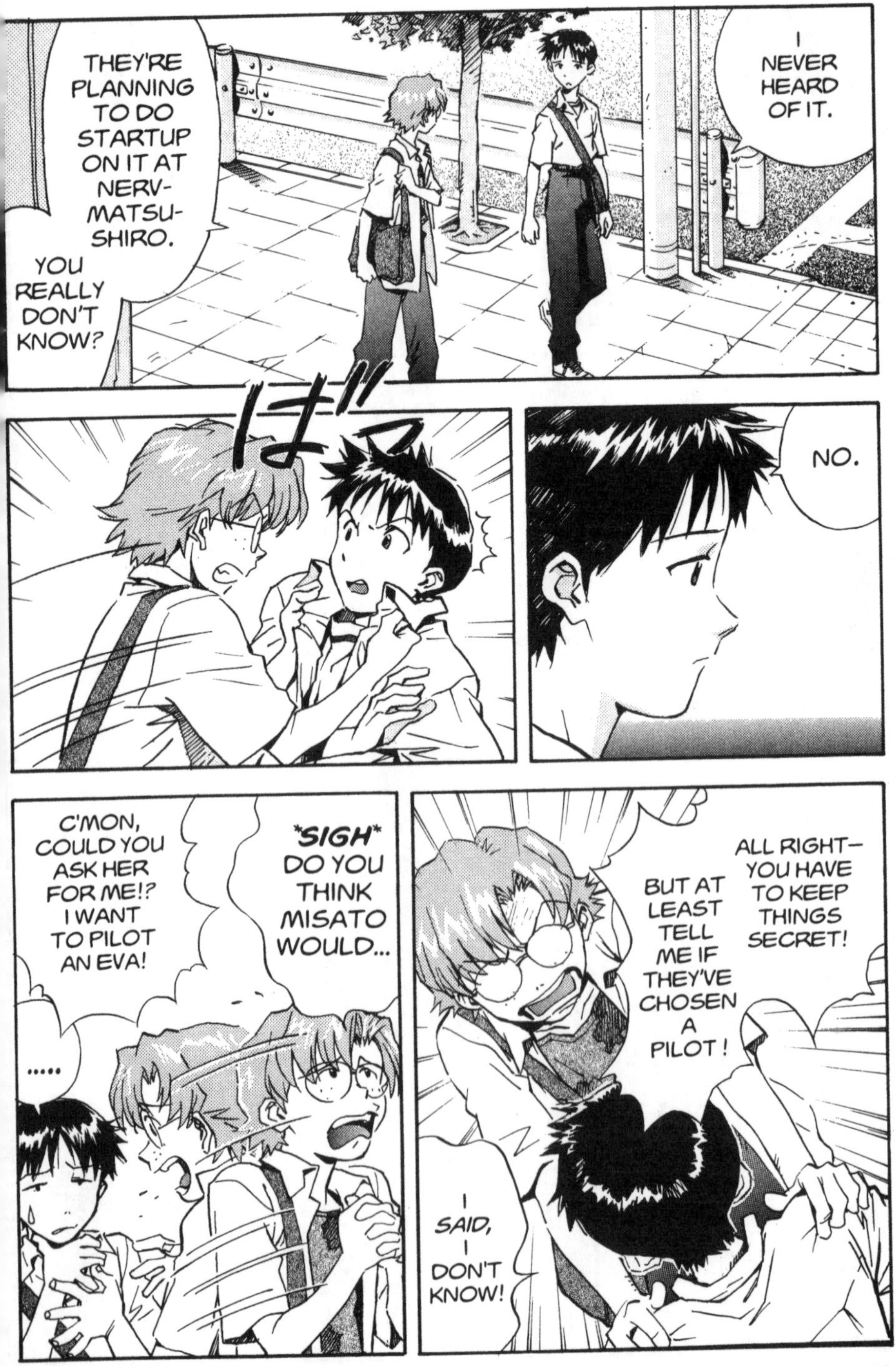
I NEVER HEARD OF IT.
THEY'RE PLANNING TO DO STARTUP ON IT AT NERV-MATSUSHIRO.
YOU REALLY DON'T KNOW?
NO.
ばっ
ALL RIGHT—YOU HAVE TO KEEP THINGS SECRET!
BUT AT LEAST TELL ME IF THEY'VE CHOSEN A PILOT!
I SAID, I DON'T KNOW!
SIGH DO YOU THINK MISATO WOULD...
C'MON, COULD YOU ASK HER FOR ME!? I WANT TO PILOT AN EVA!
......

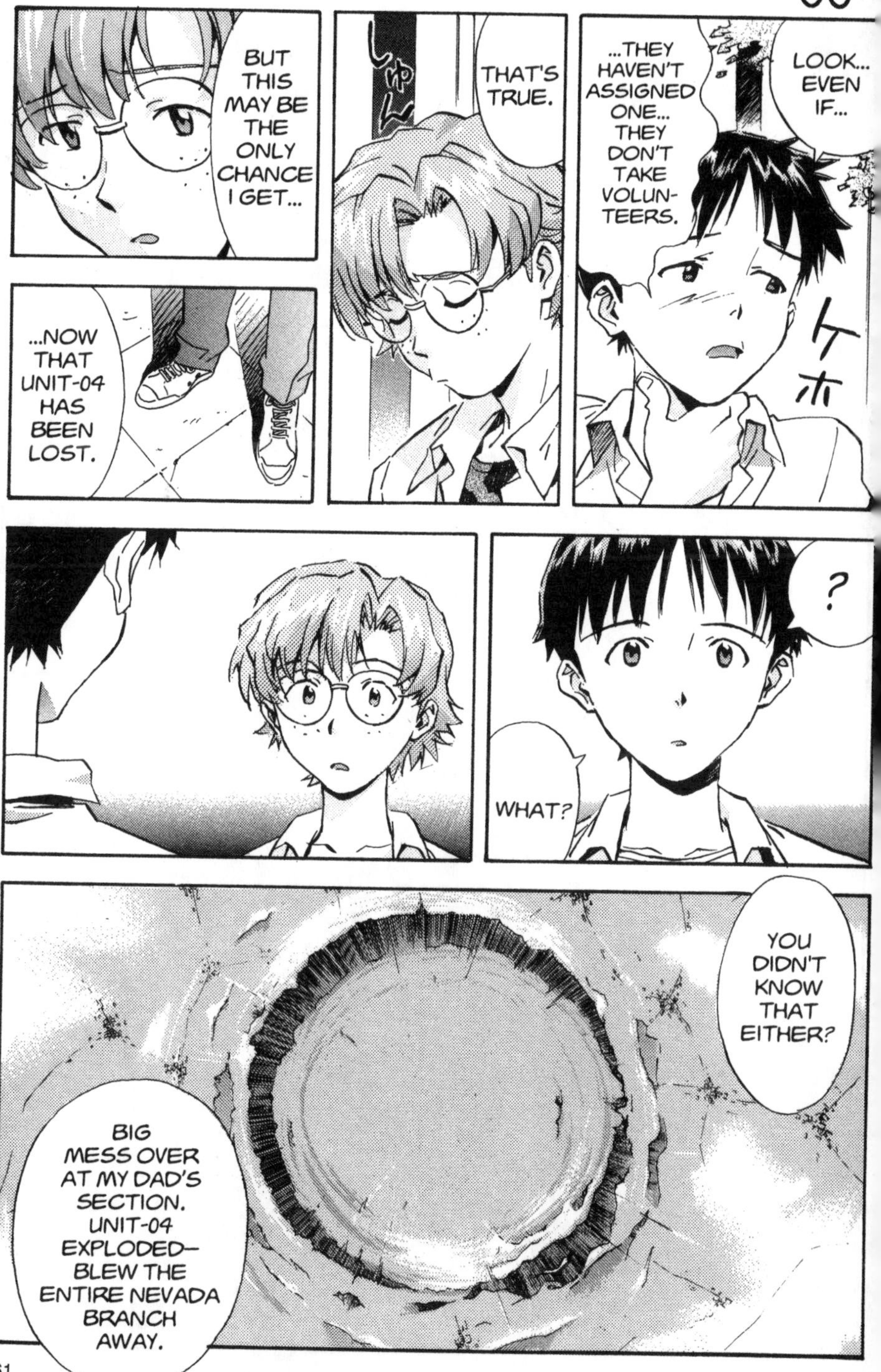
LOOK... EVEN IF...
...THEY HAVEN'T ASSIGNED ONE... THEY DON'T TAKE VOLUNTEERS.
ケホ
しゅん
THAT'S TRUE.
BUT THIS MAY BE THE ONLY CHANCE I GET...
...NOW THAT UNIT-04 HAS BEEN LOST.
?
WHAT?
YOU DIDN'T KNOW THAT EITHER?
BIG MESS OVER AT MY DAD'S SECTION. UNIT-04 EXPLODED— BLEW THE ENTIRE NEVADA BRANCH AWAY.

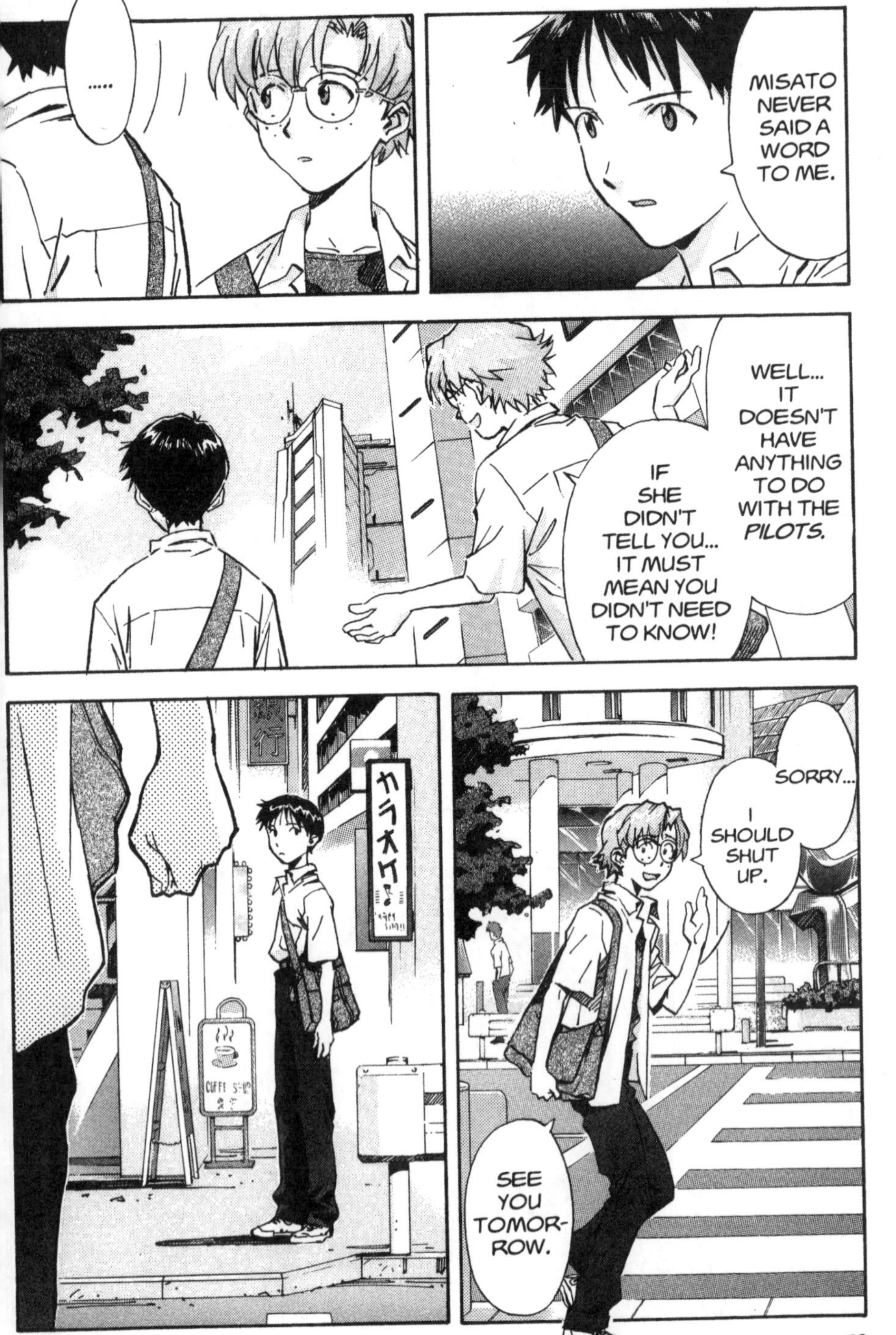
MISATO NEVER SAID A WORD TO ME.
.....
WELL... IT DOESN'T HAVE ANYTHING TO DO WITH THE *PILOTS.*
IF SHE DIDN'T TELL YOU... IT MUST MEAN YOU DIDN'T NEED TO KNOW!
SORRY...
I SHOULD SHUT UP.
SEE YOU TOMOR-ROW.
カラオケ

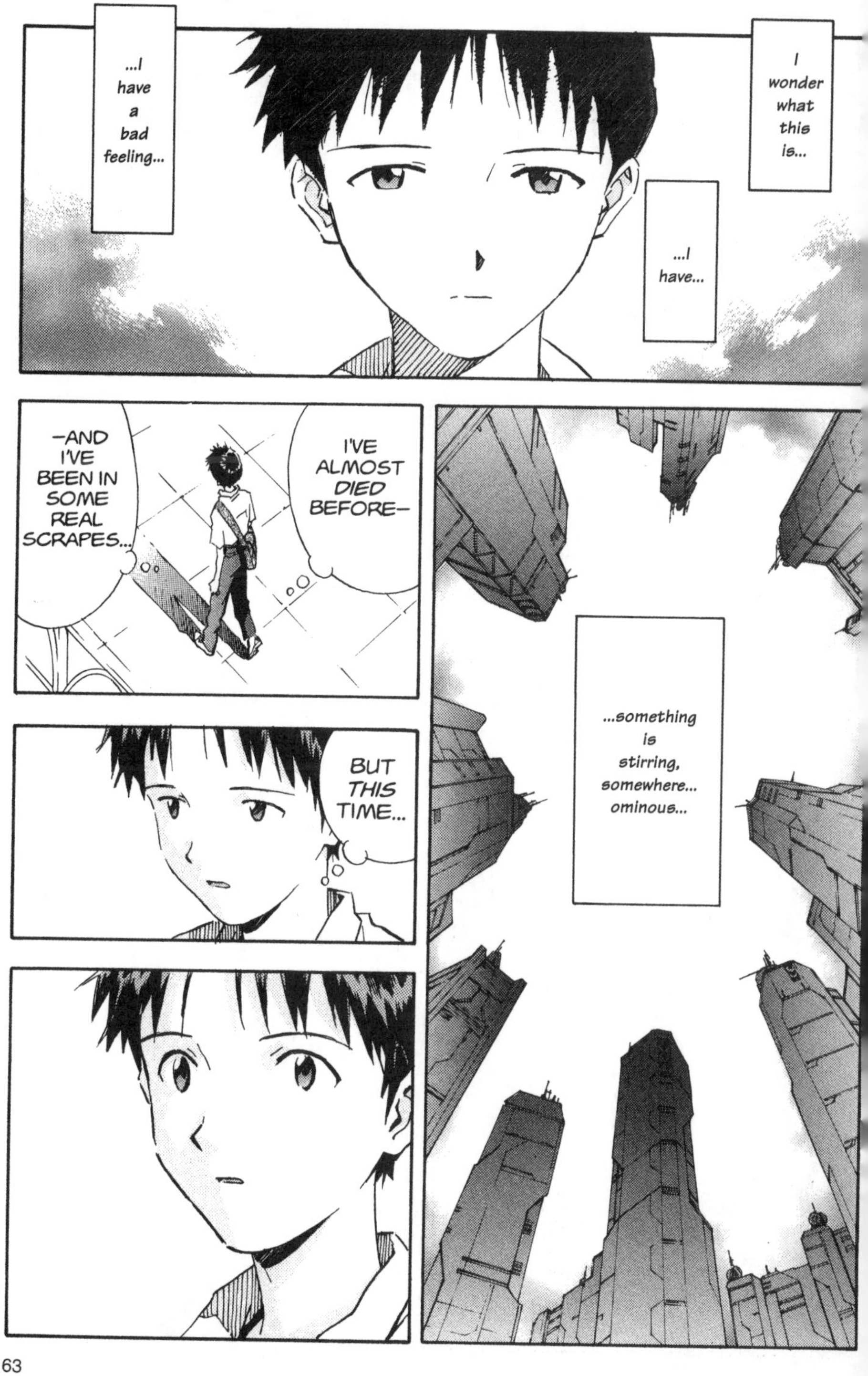
I wonder what this is...
...I have...
...I have a bad feeling...
...something is stirring, somewhere... ominous...
I'VE ALMOST DIED BEFORE—
—AND I'VE BEEN IN SOME REAL SCRAPES...
BUT THIS TIME...

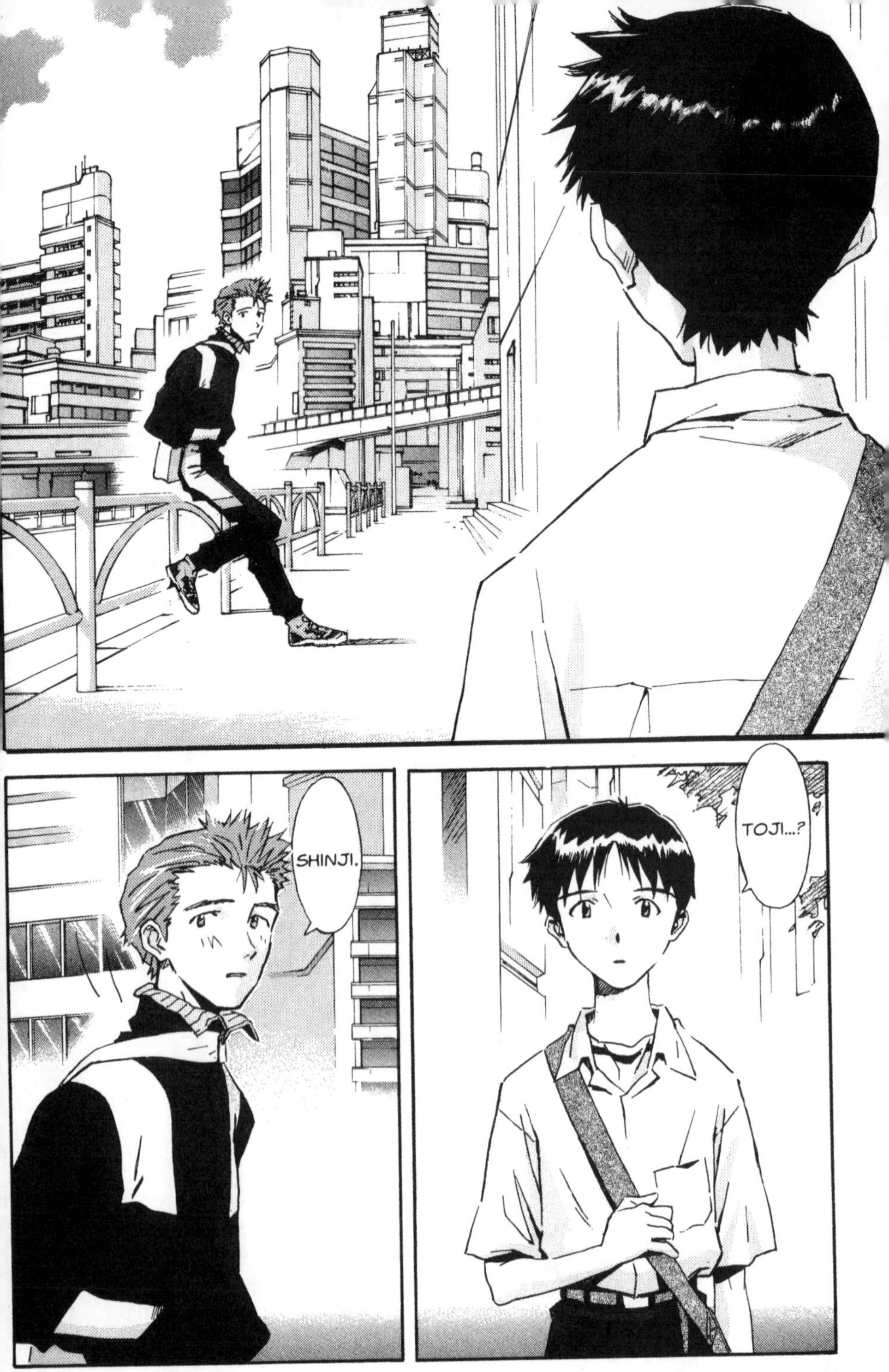
TOJI...?
SHINJI.

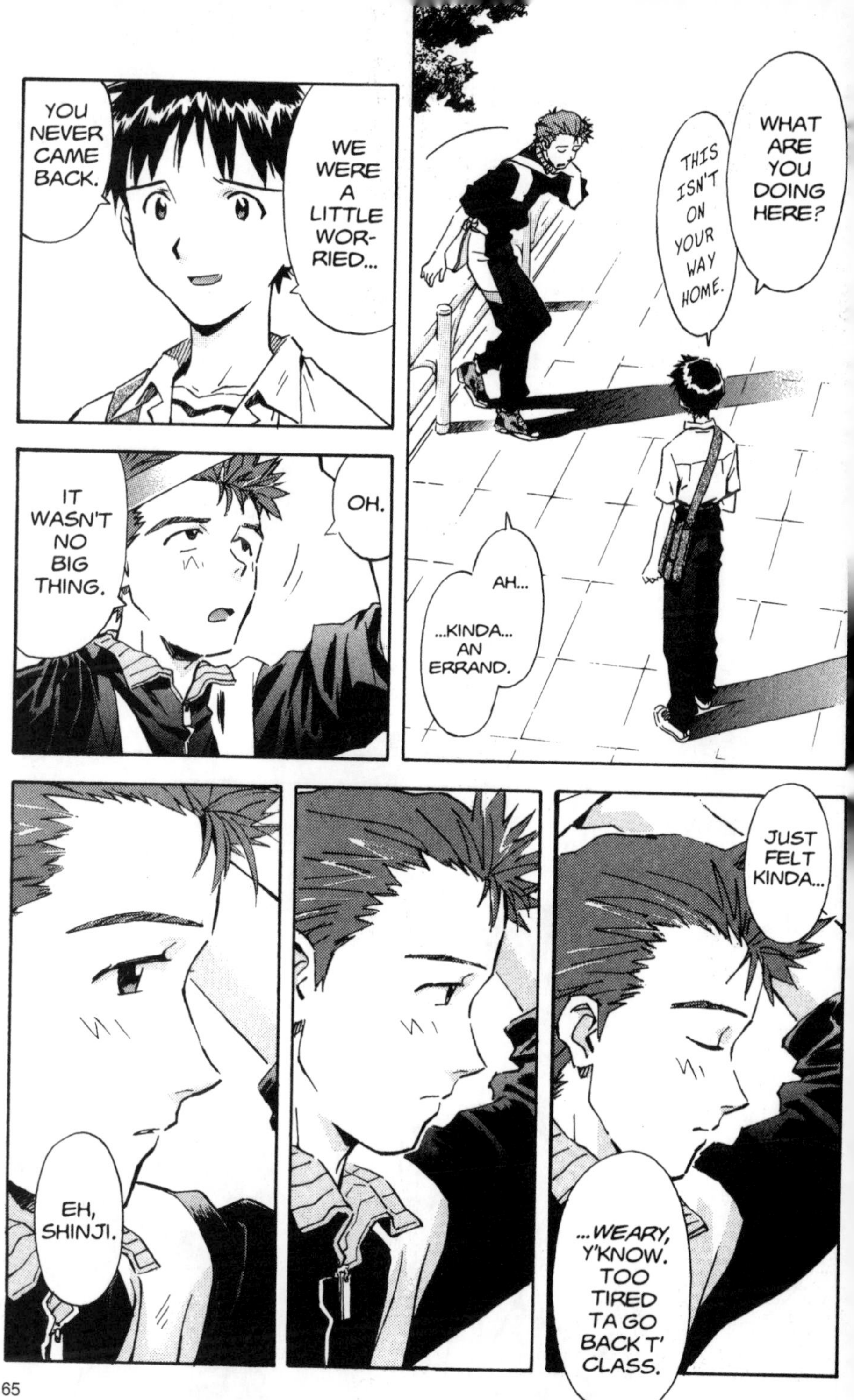
WHAT ARE YOU DOING HERE?
THIS ISN'T ON YOUR WAY HOME.
AH... ...KINDA... AN ERRAND.
WE WERE A LITTLE WOR-RIED...
YOU NEVER CAME BACK.
OH.
IT WASN'T NO BIG THING.
JUST FELT KINDA...
...WEARY, Y'KNOW. TOO TIRED TA GO BACK T' CLASS.
EH, SHINJI.

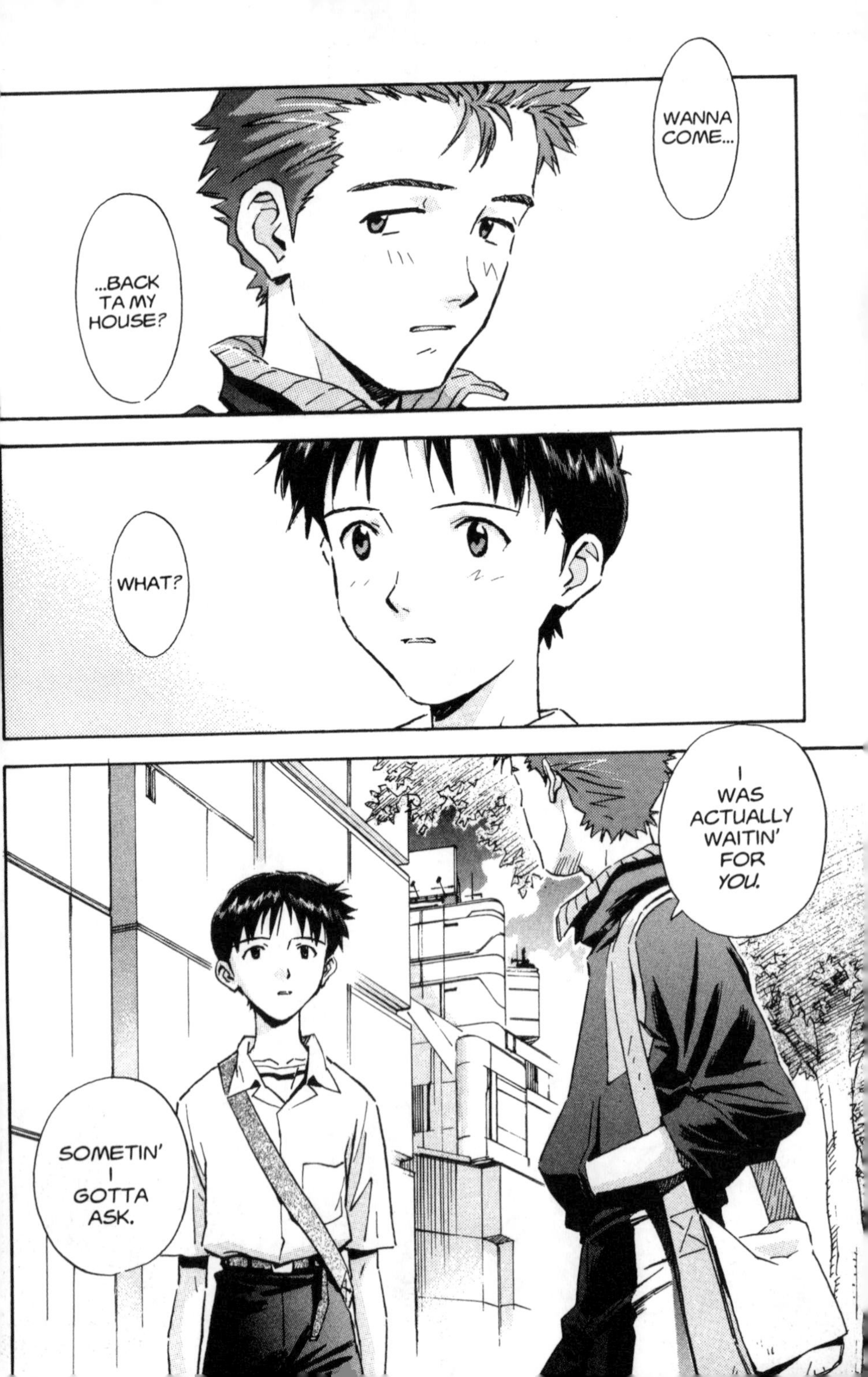
WANNA COME...
...BACK TA MY HOUSE?
WHAT?
I WAS ACTUALLY WAITIN' FOR *YOU*.
SOMETIN' I GOTTA ASK.

Stage 3: CONFESSION

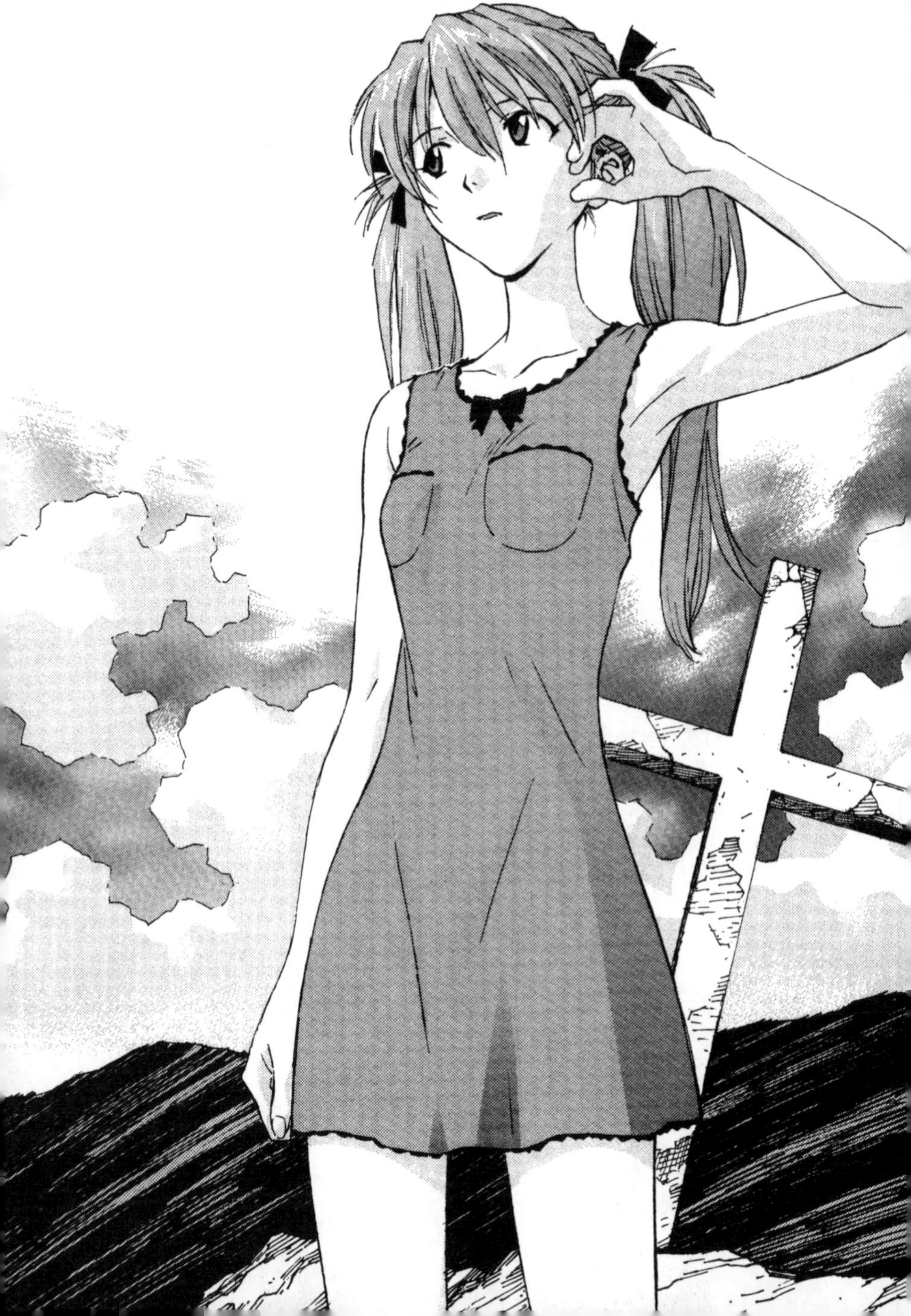

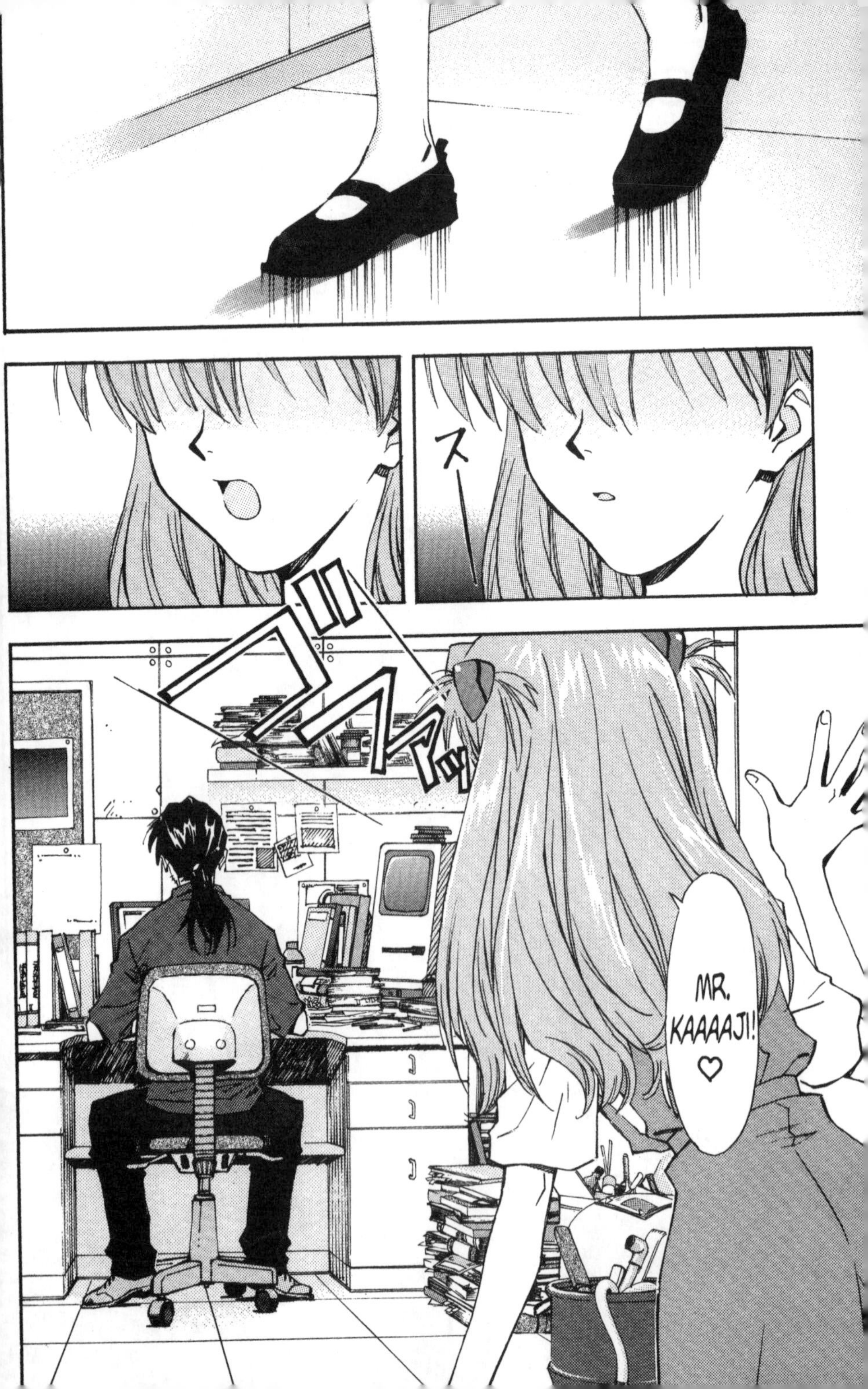
ス
ブンッ
MR. KAAAAJI! ♡

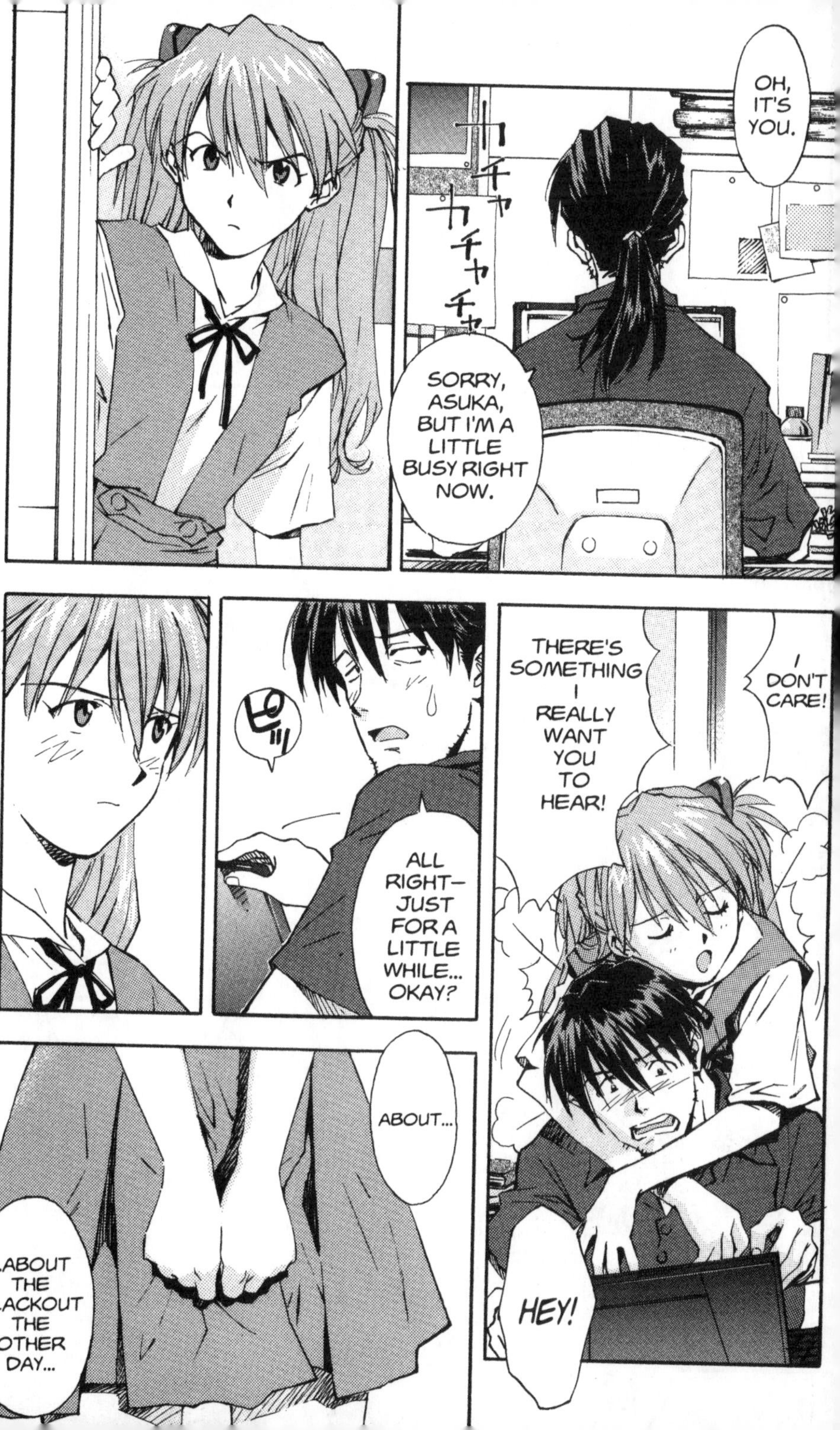
OH, IT'S YOU.
カチャ
カチャ
チャ
SORRY, ASUKA, BUT I'M A LITTLE BUSY RIGHT NOW.
I DON'T CARE!
THERE'S SOMETHING I REALLY WANT YOU TO HEAR!
HEY!
ピッ
ALL RIGHT— JUST FOR A LITTLE WHILE... OKAY?
ABOUT...
...ABOUT THE BLACKOUT THE OTHER DAY...

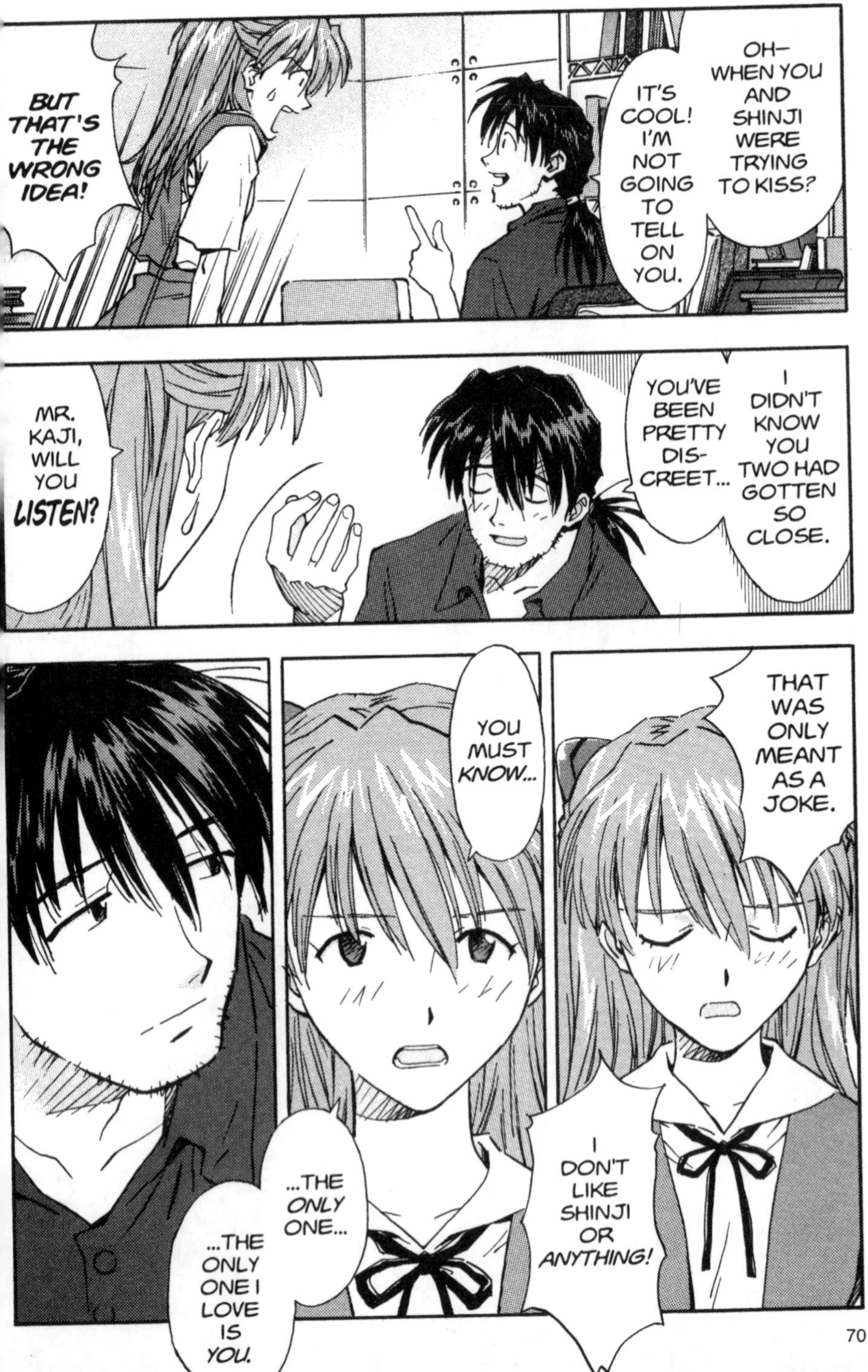
OH— WHEN YOU AND SHINJI WERE TRYING TO KISS?
IT'S COOL! I'M NOT GOING TO TELL ON YOU.
BUT THAT'S THE WRONG IDEA!
I DIDN'T KNOW YOU TWO HAD GOTTEN SO CLOSE.
YOU'VE BEEN PRETTY DIS-CREET...
MR. KAJI, WILL YOU LISTEN?
THAT WAS ONLY MEANT AS A JOKE.
I DON'T LIKE SHINJI OR ANYTHING!
YOU MUST KNOW...
...THE ONLY ONE...
...THE ONLY ONE I LOVE IS YOU.

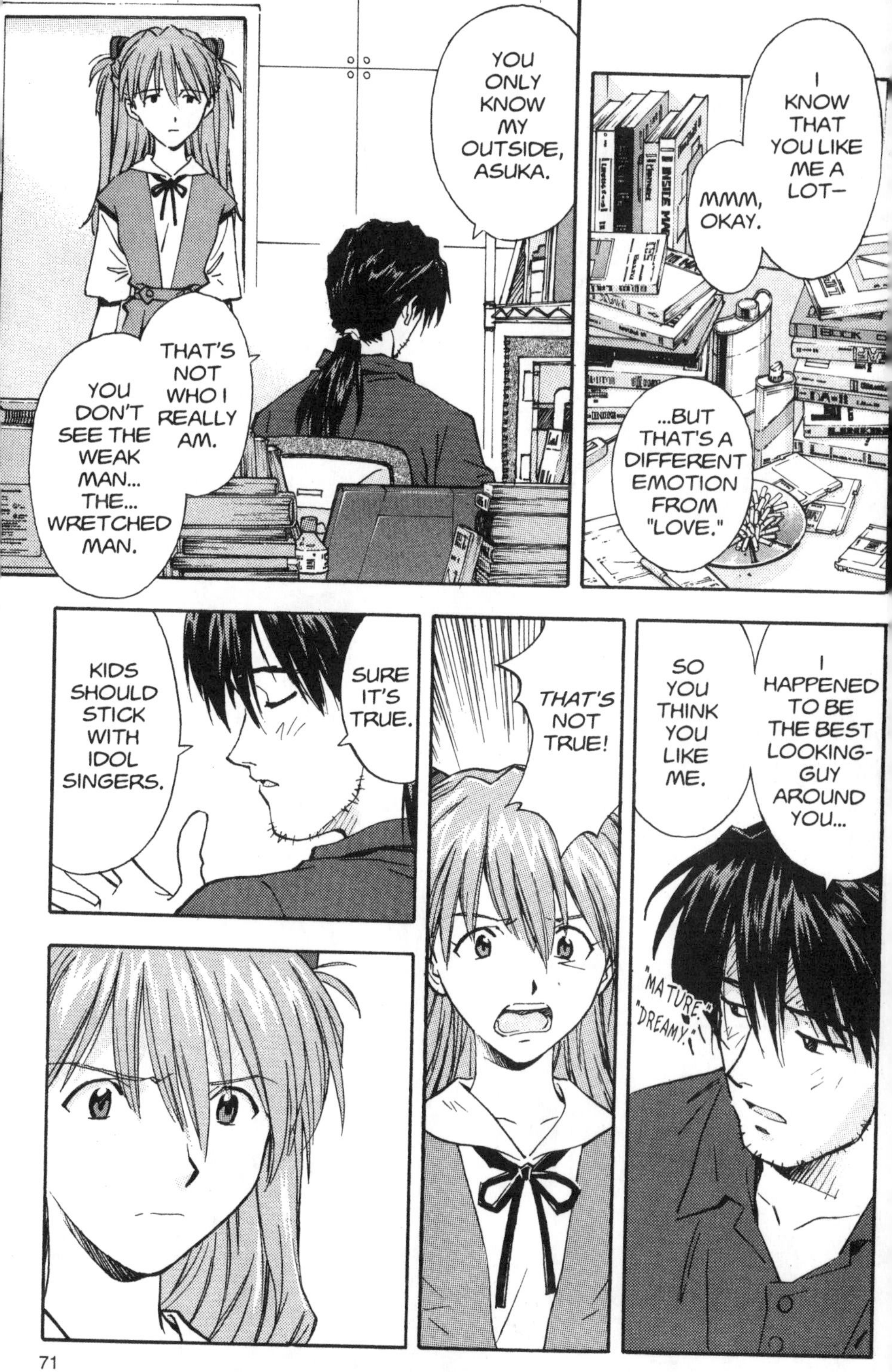
I KNOW THAT YOU LIKE ME A LOT—
MMM, OKAY.
...BUT THAT'S A DIFFERENT EMOTION FROM "LOVE."
YOU ONLY KNOW MY OUTSIDE, ASUKA.
THAT'S NOT WHO I REALLY AM.
YOU DON'T SEE THE WEAK MAN... THE... WRETCHED MAN.
I HAPPENED TO BE THE BEST LOOKING-GUY AROUND YOU...
SO YOU THINK YOU LIKE ME.
"MATURE."
"DREAMY."
THAT'S NOT TRUE!
SURE IT'S TRUE.
KIDS SHOULD STICK WITH IDOL SINGERS.

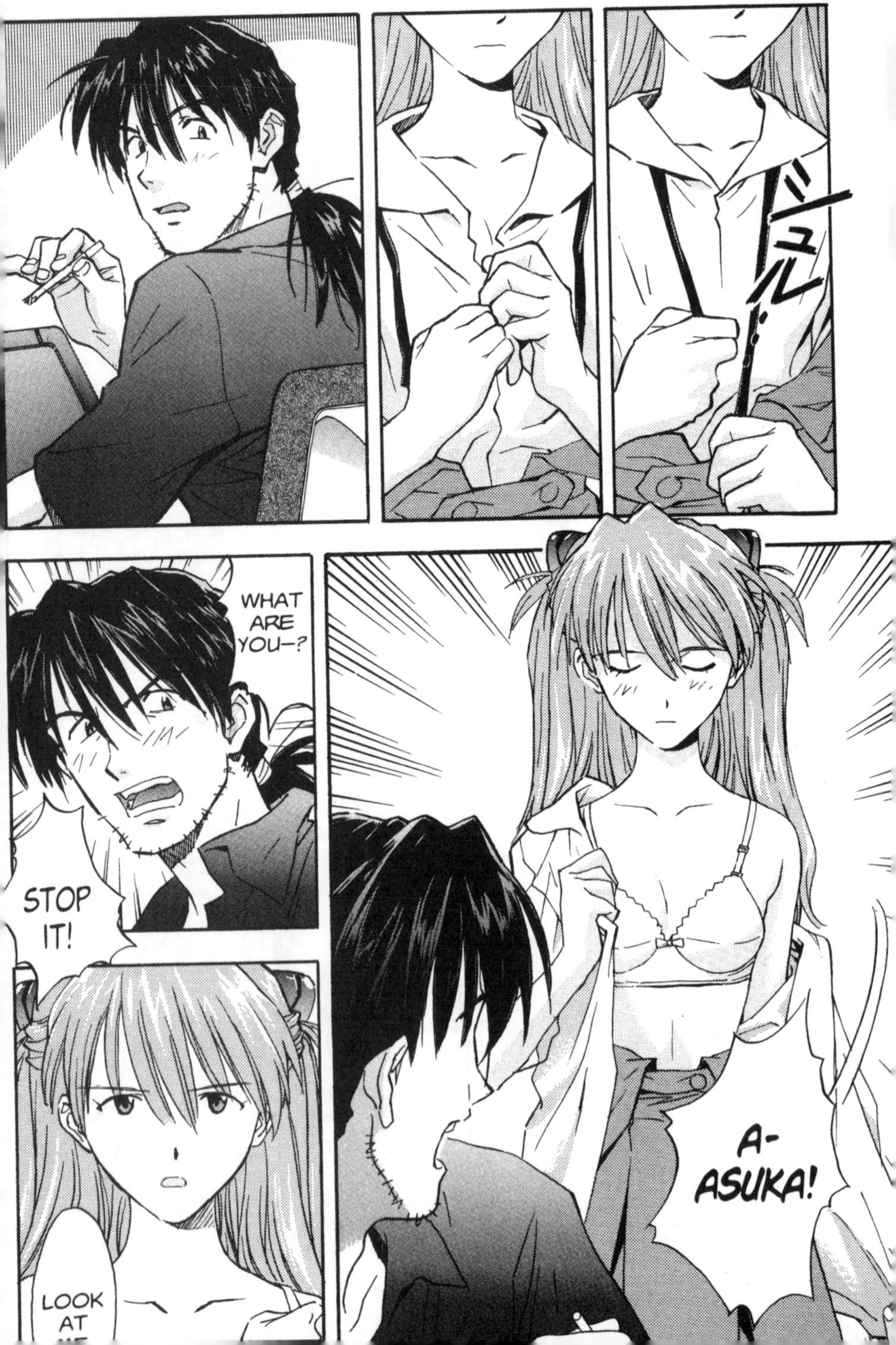
シュル…
A-
ASUKA!
WHAT ARE YOU–?
STOP IT!
LOOK AT

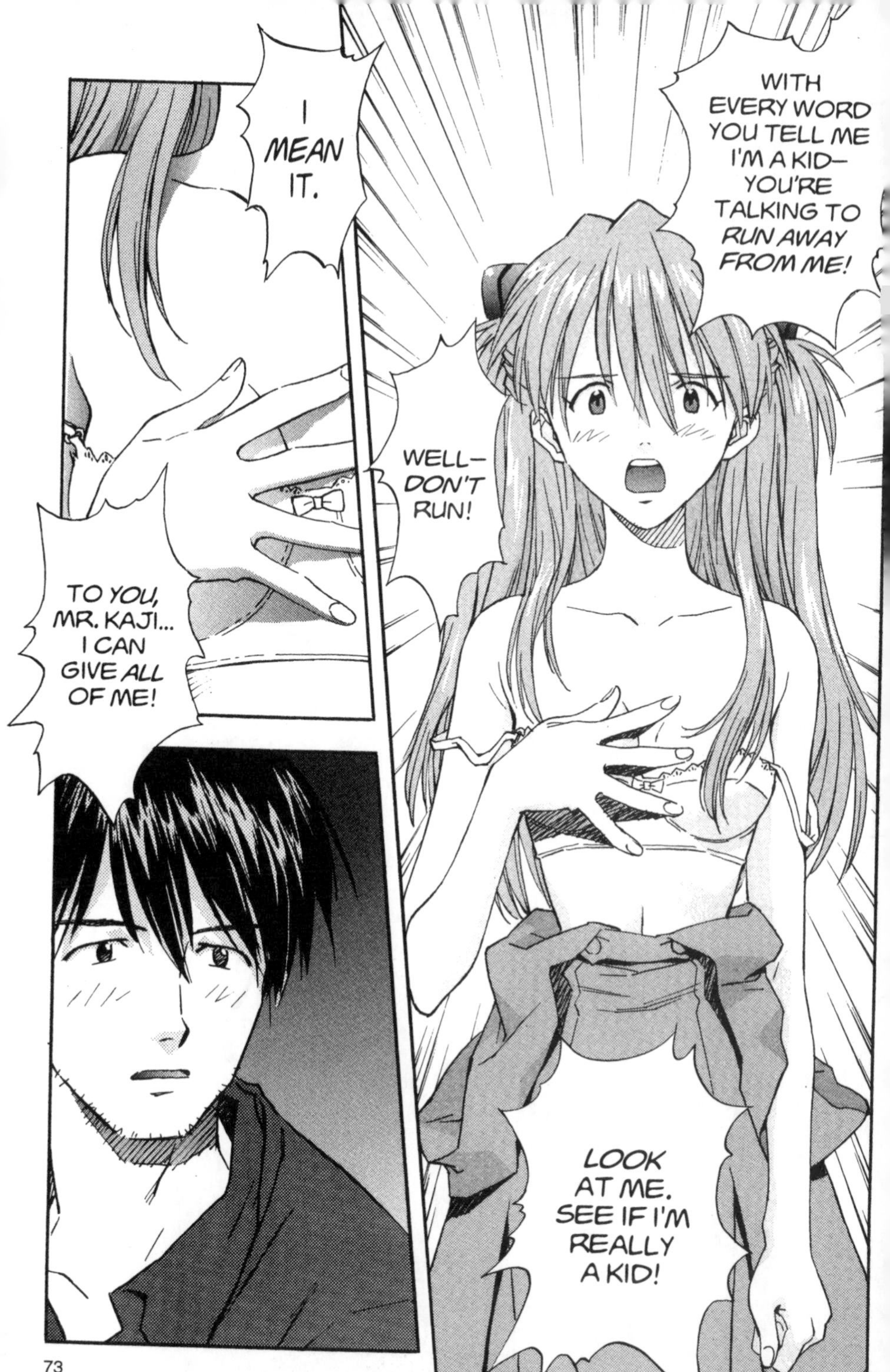
WITH EVERY WORD YOU TELL ME I'M A KID— YOU'RE TALKING TO RUN AWAY FROM ME!
WELL— DON'T RUN!
I MEAN IT.
TO YOU, MR. KAJI... I CAN GIVE ALL OF ME!
LOOK AT ME. SEE IF I'M REALLY A KID!

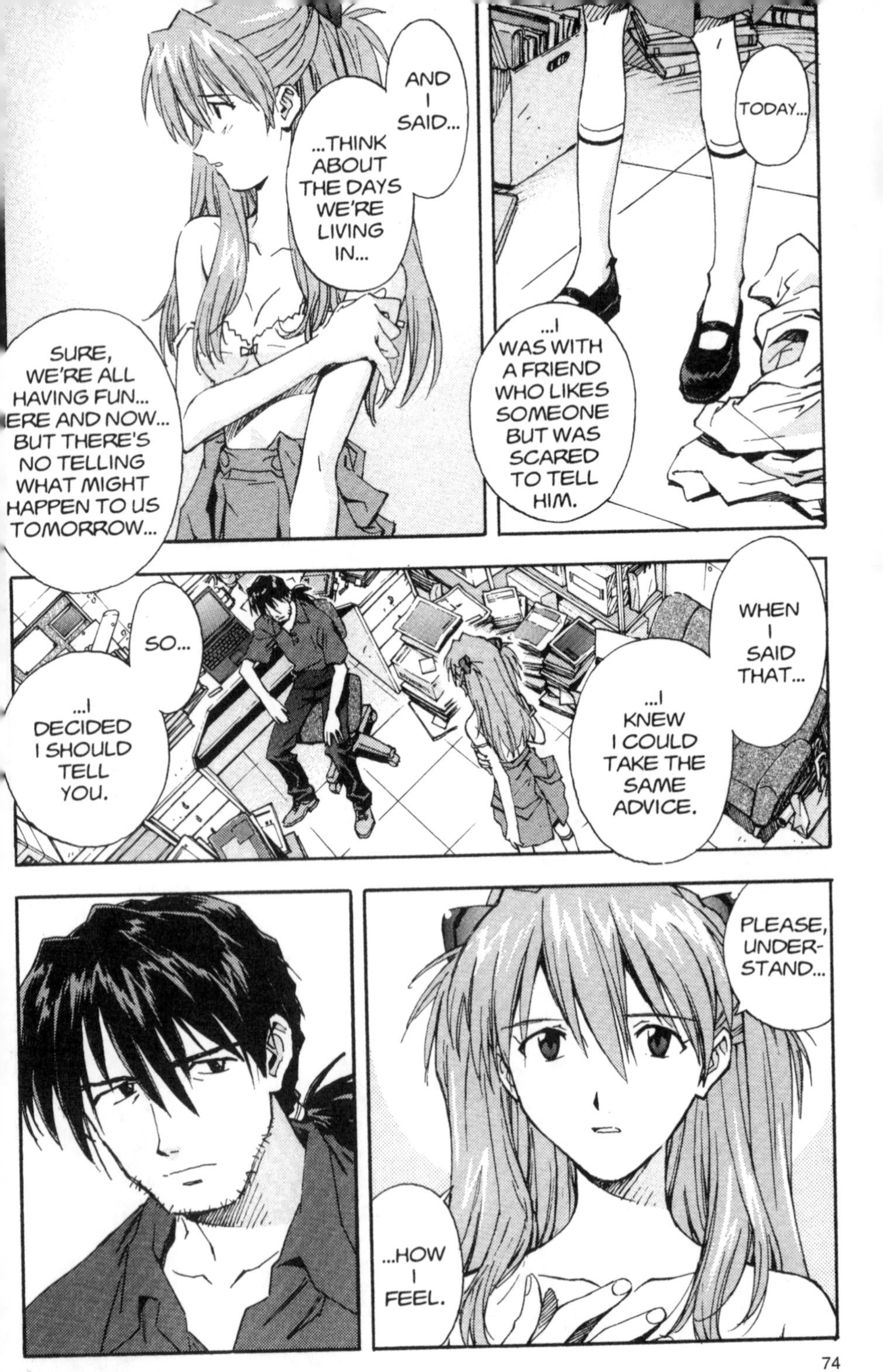
TODAY...
...I WAS WITH A FRIEND WHO LIKES SOMEONE BUT WAS SCARED TO TELL HIM.
AND I SAID...
...THINK ABOUT THE DAYS WE'RE LIVING IN...
SURE, WE'RE ALL HAVING FUN... ERE AND NOW... BUT THERE'S NO TELLING WHAT MIGHT HAPPEN TO US TOMORROW...
WHEN I SAID THAT...
...I KNEW I COULD TAKE THE SAME ADVICE.
SO...
...I DECIDED I SHOULD TELL YOU.
PLEASE, UNDER-STAND...
...HOW I FEEL.

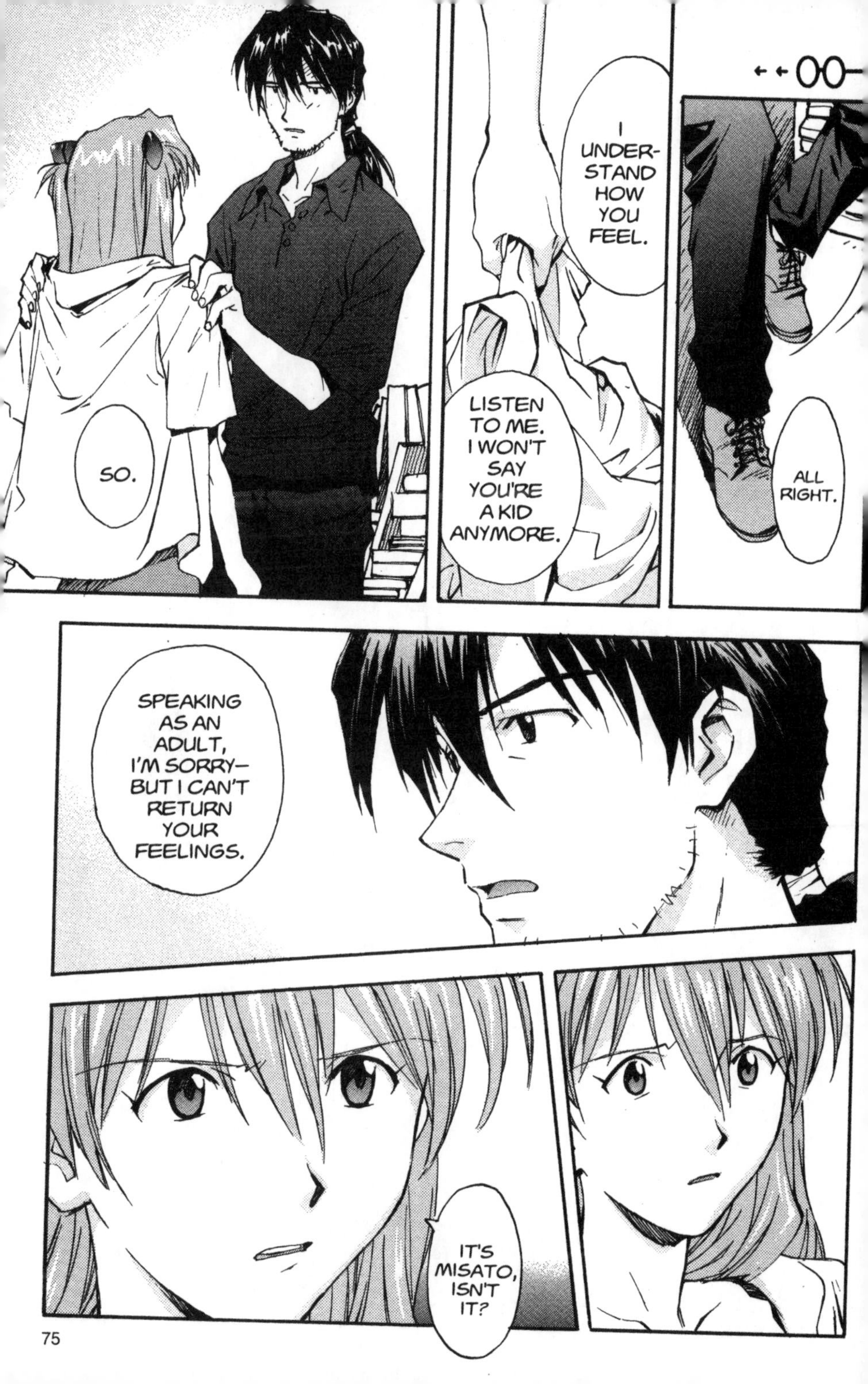
ALL RIGHT.
I UNDERSTAND HOW YOU FEEL.
LISTEN TO ME. I WON'T SAY YOU'RE A KID ANYMORE.
SO.
SPEAKING AS AN ADULT, I'M SORRY— BUT I CAN'T RETURN YOUR FEELINGS.
IT'S MISATO, ISN'T IT?

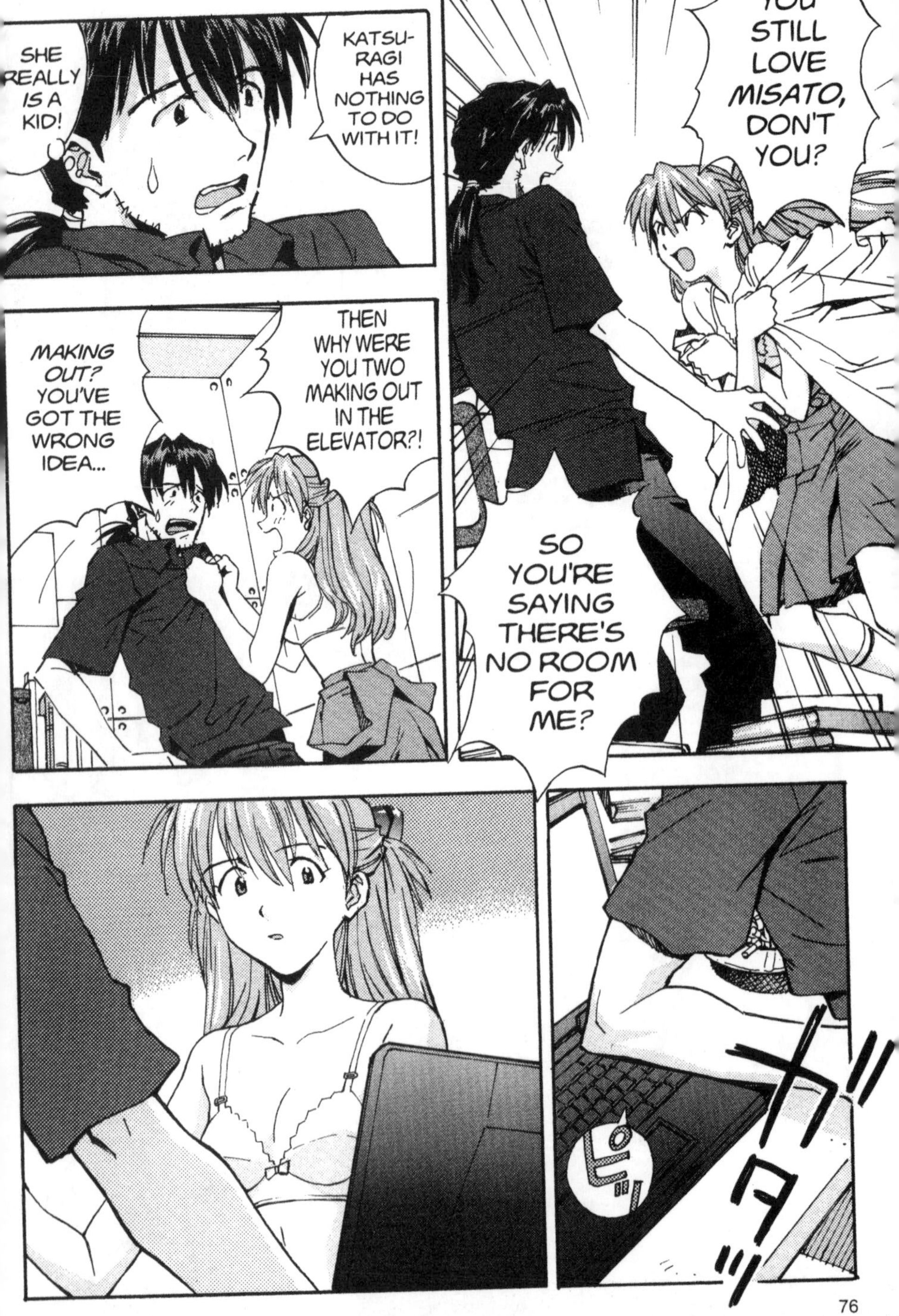
YOU STILL LOVE MISATO, DON'T YOU?
KATSURAGI HAS NOTHING TO DO WITH IT!
SHE REALLY IS A KID!
THEN WHY WERE YOU TWO MAKING OUT IN THE ELEVATOR?!
MAKING OUT? YOU'VE GOT THE WRONG IDEA...
SO YOU'RE SAYING THERE'S NO ROOM FOR ME?
ガタッ
ピッ

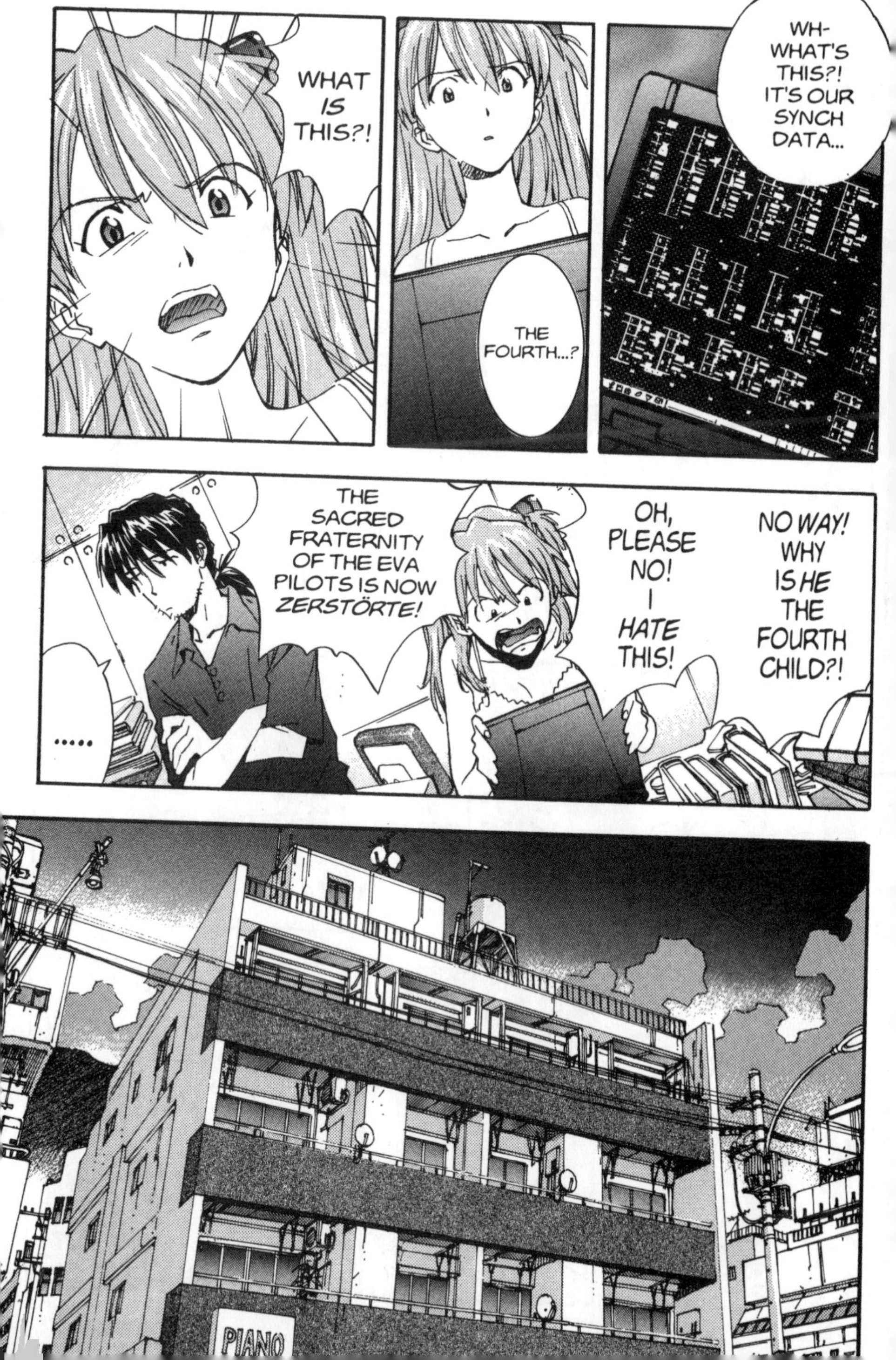
WH- WHAT'S THIS?! IT'S OUR SYNCH DATA...
THE FOURTH...?
WHAT *IS* THIS?!
NO *WAY!* WHY IS *HE* THE FOURTH CHILD?!
OH, PLEASE NO! I *HATE* THIS!
THE SACRED FRATERNITY OF THE EVA PILOTS IS NOW *ZERSTÖRTE!*
.....
PIANO

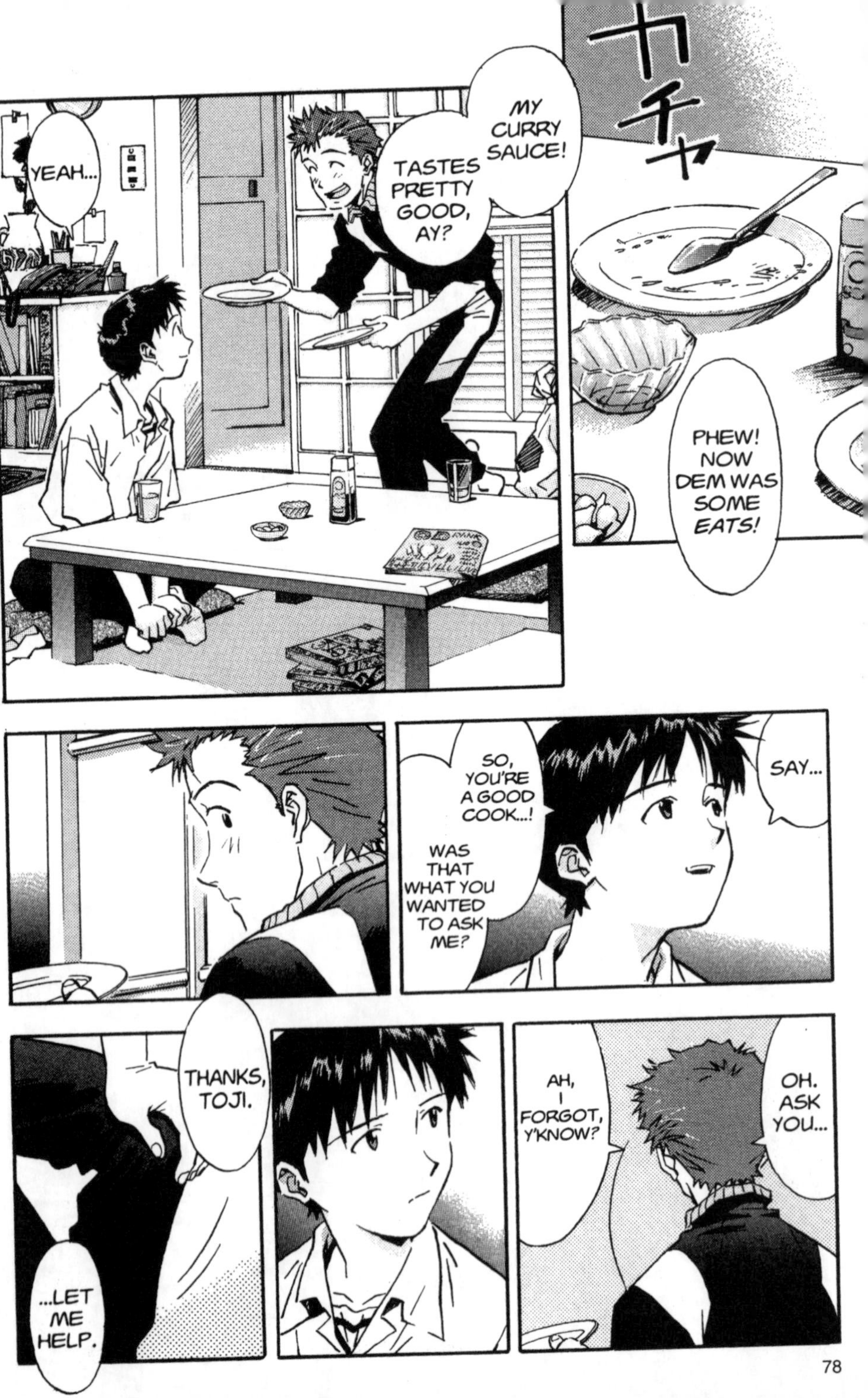
カチャ
PHEW! NOW DEM WAS SOME EATS!
MY CURRY SAUCE!
TASTES PRETTY GOOD, AY?
YEAH...
SAY...
SO, YOU'RE A GOOD COOK...!
WAS THAT WHAT YOU WANTED TO ASK ME?
OH. ASK YOU...
AH, I FORGOT, Y'KNOW?
THANKS, TOJI.
...LET ME HELP.

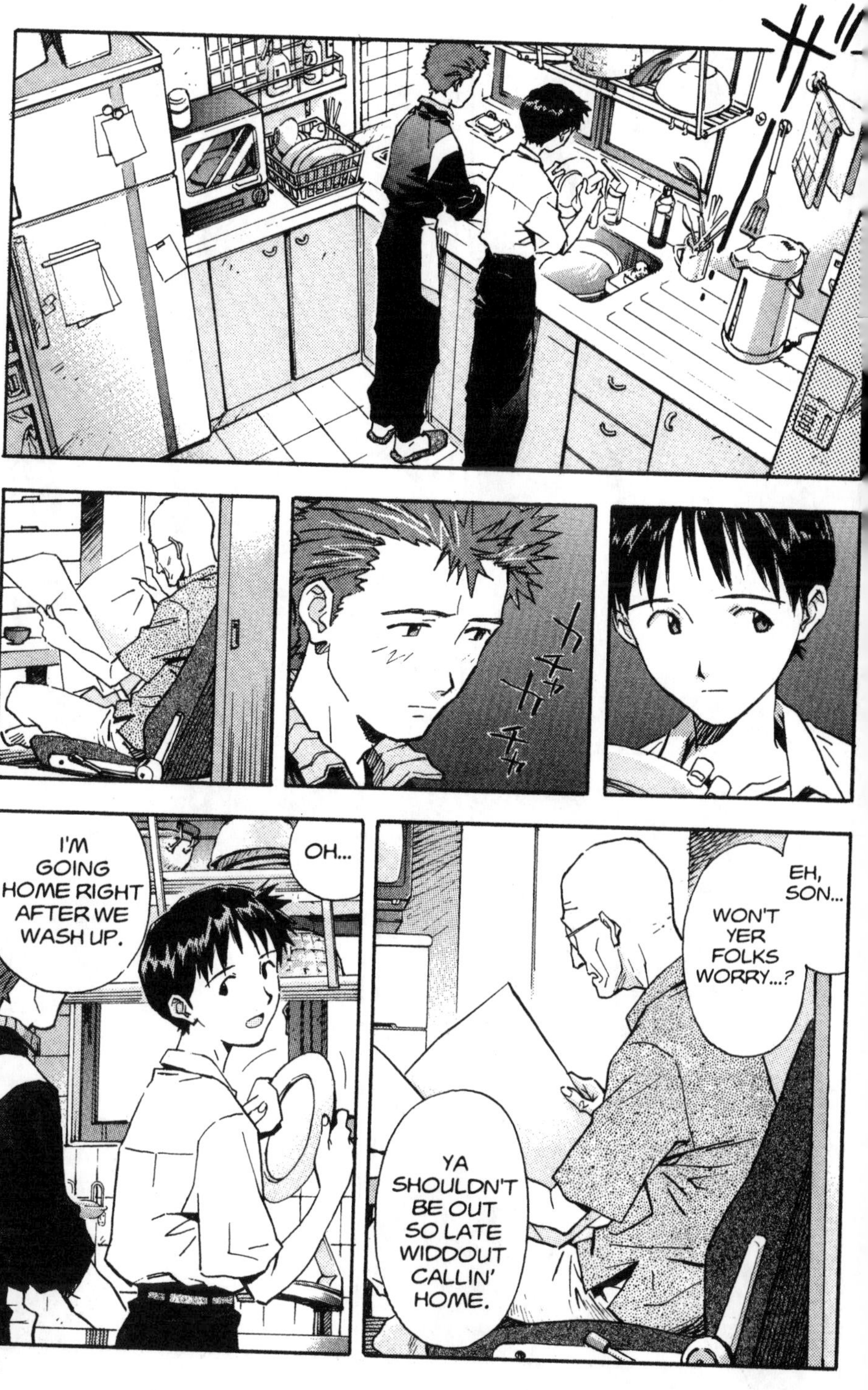
EH, SON...
WON'T YER FOLKS WORRY...?
YA SHOULDN'T BE OUT SO LATE WIDDOUT CALLIN' HOME.
OH...
I'M GOING HOME RIGHT AFTER WE WASH UP.

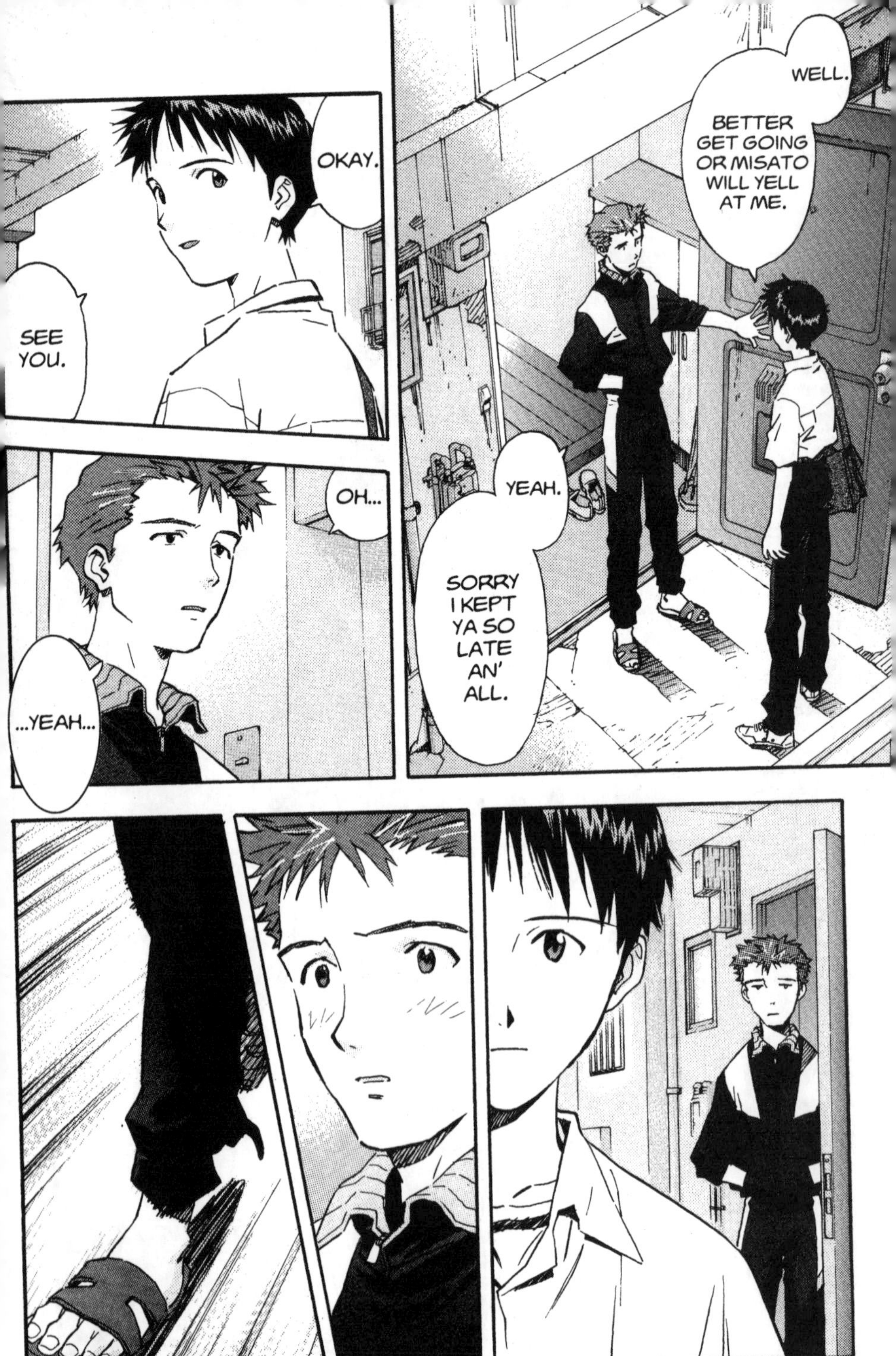
WELL.
BETTER GET GOING OR MISATO WILL YELL AT ME.
YEAH.
SORRY I KEPT YA SO LATE AN' ALL.
OKAY.
SEE YOU.
OH...
...YEAH...

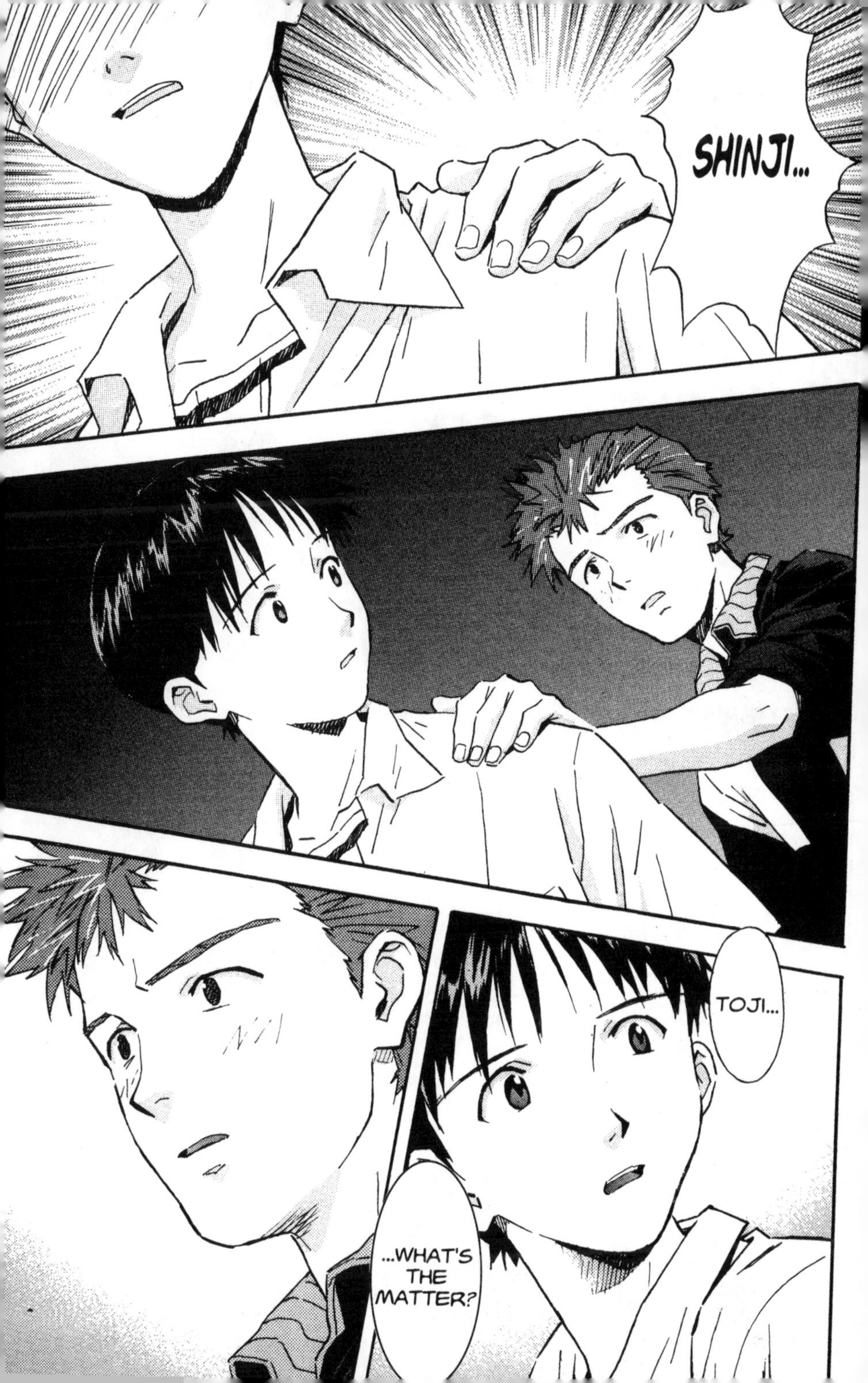
SHINJI...
TOJI...
...WHAT'S THE MATTER?

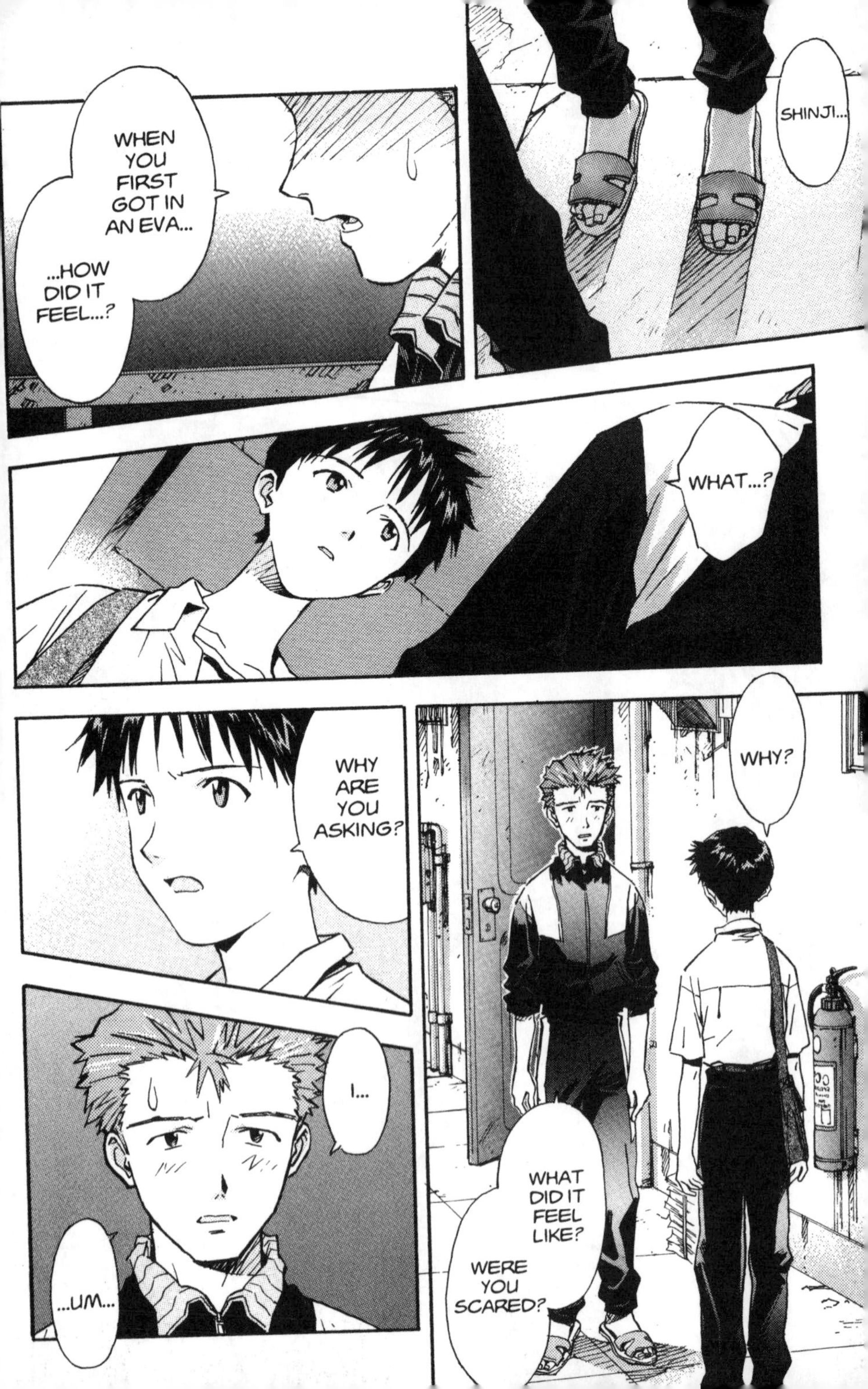
SHINJI...
WHEN YOU FIRST GOT IN AN EVA...
...HOW DID IT FEEL...?
WHAT...?
WHY?
WHAT DID IT FEEL LIKE?
WERE YOU SCARED?
WHY ARE YOU ASKING?
I...
...UM...

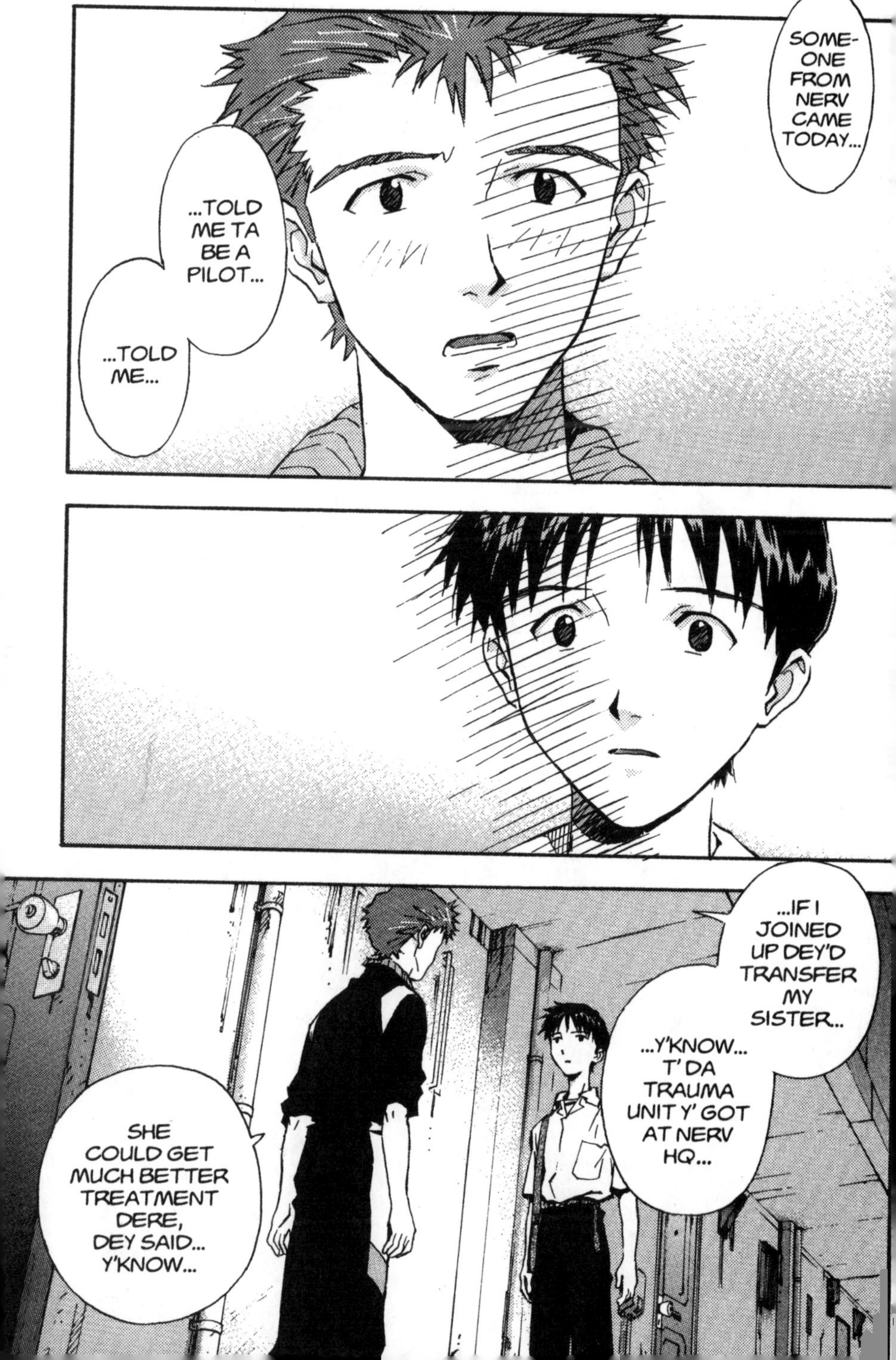
SOME-ONE FROM NERV CAME TODAY...
...TOLD ME TA BE A PILOT...
...TOLD ME...
...IF I JOINED UP DEY'D TRANSFER MY SISTER...
...Y'KNOW... T' DA TRAUMA UNIT Y' GOT AT NERV HQ...
SHE COULD GET MUCH BETTER TREATMENT DERE, DEY SAID... Y'KNOW...

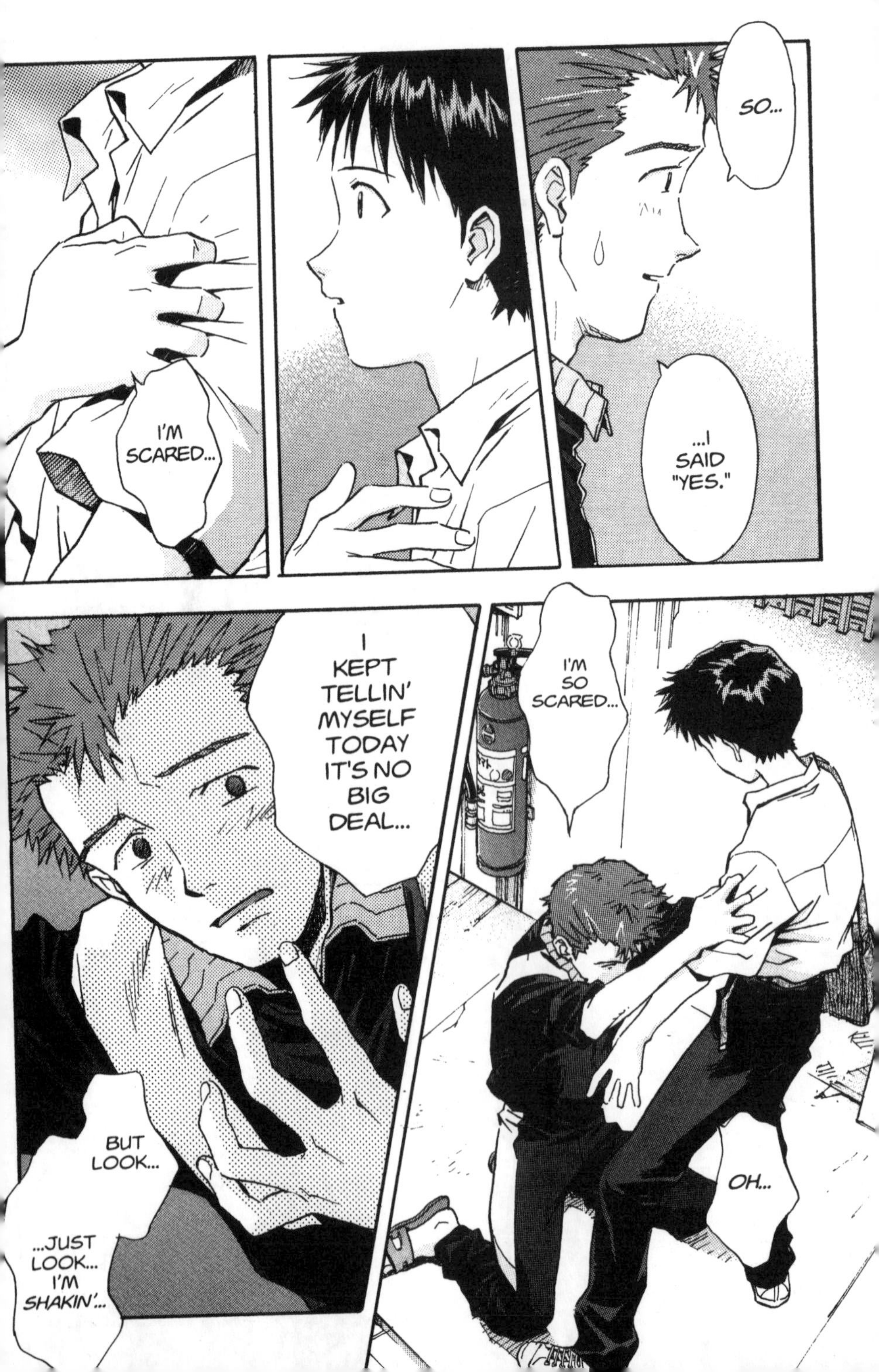
SO...
...I SAID "YES."
I'M SCARED...
I'M SO SCARED...
OH...
I KEPT TELLIN' MYSELF TODAY IT'S NO BIG DEAL...
BUT LOOK...
...JUST LOOK... I'M SHAKIN'...

85

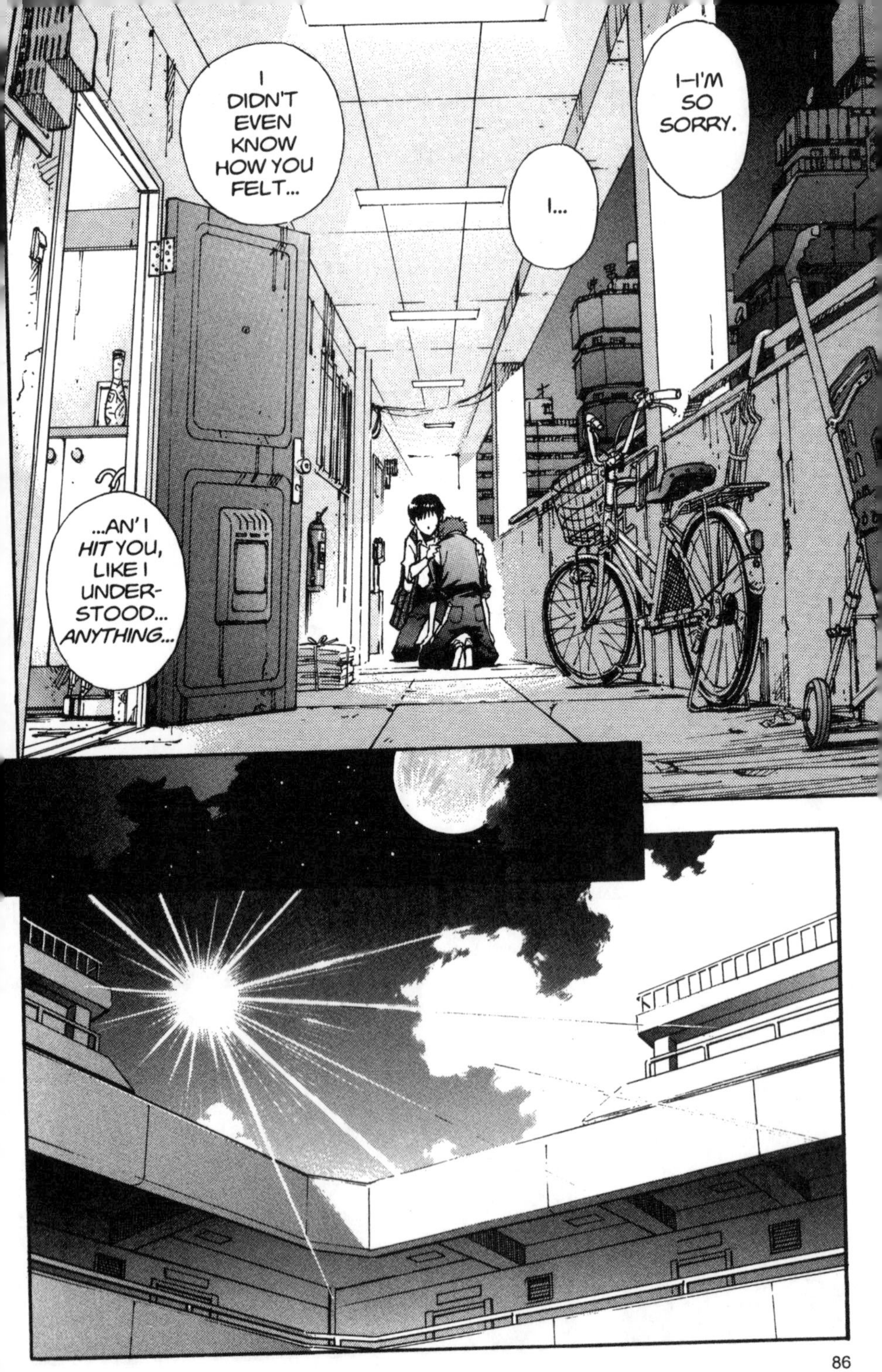
I-I'M SO SORRY.
I...
I DIDN'T EVEN KNOW HOW YOU FELT...
...AN' I HIT YOU, LIKE I UNDERSTOOD... ANYTHING...

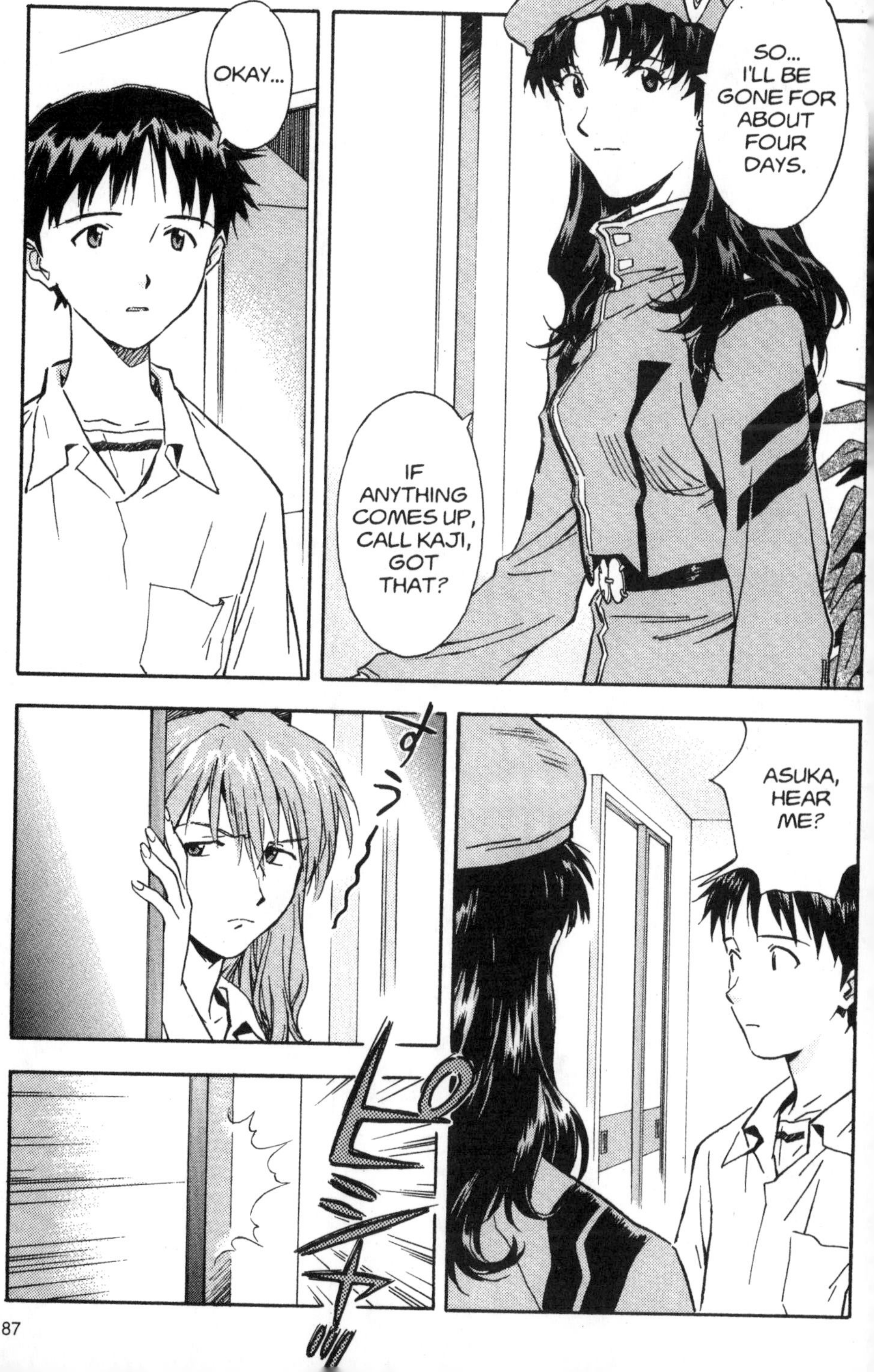
SO... I'LL BE GONE FOR ABOUT FOUR DAYS.
IF ANYTHING COMES UP, CALL KAJI, GOT THAT?
OKAY...
ASUKA, HEAR ME?

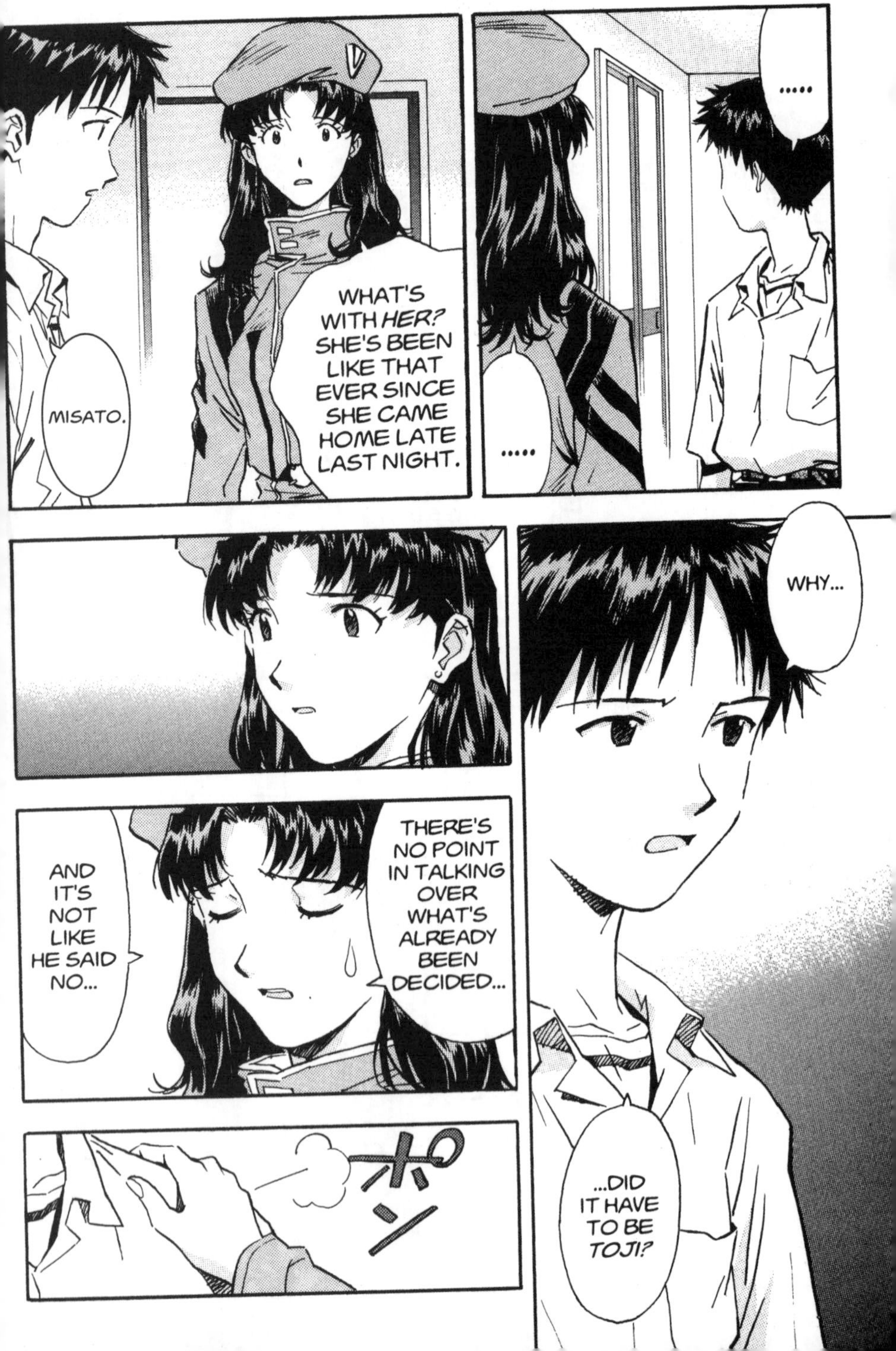
.....
.....
WHAT'S WITH *HER?* SHE'S BEEN LIKE THAT EVER SINCE SHE CAME HOME LATE LAST NIGHT.
MISATO.
WHY...
...DID IT HAVE TO BE *TOJI?*
THERE'S NO POINT IN TALKING OVER WHAT'S ALREADY BEEN DECIDED...
AND IT'S NOT LIKE HE SAID NO...
ポン

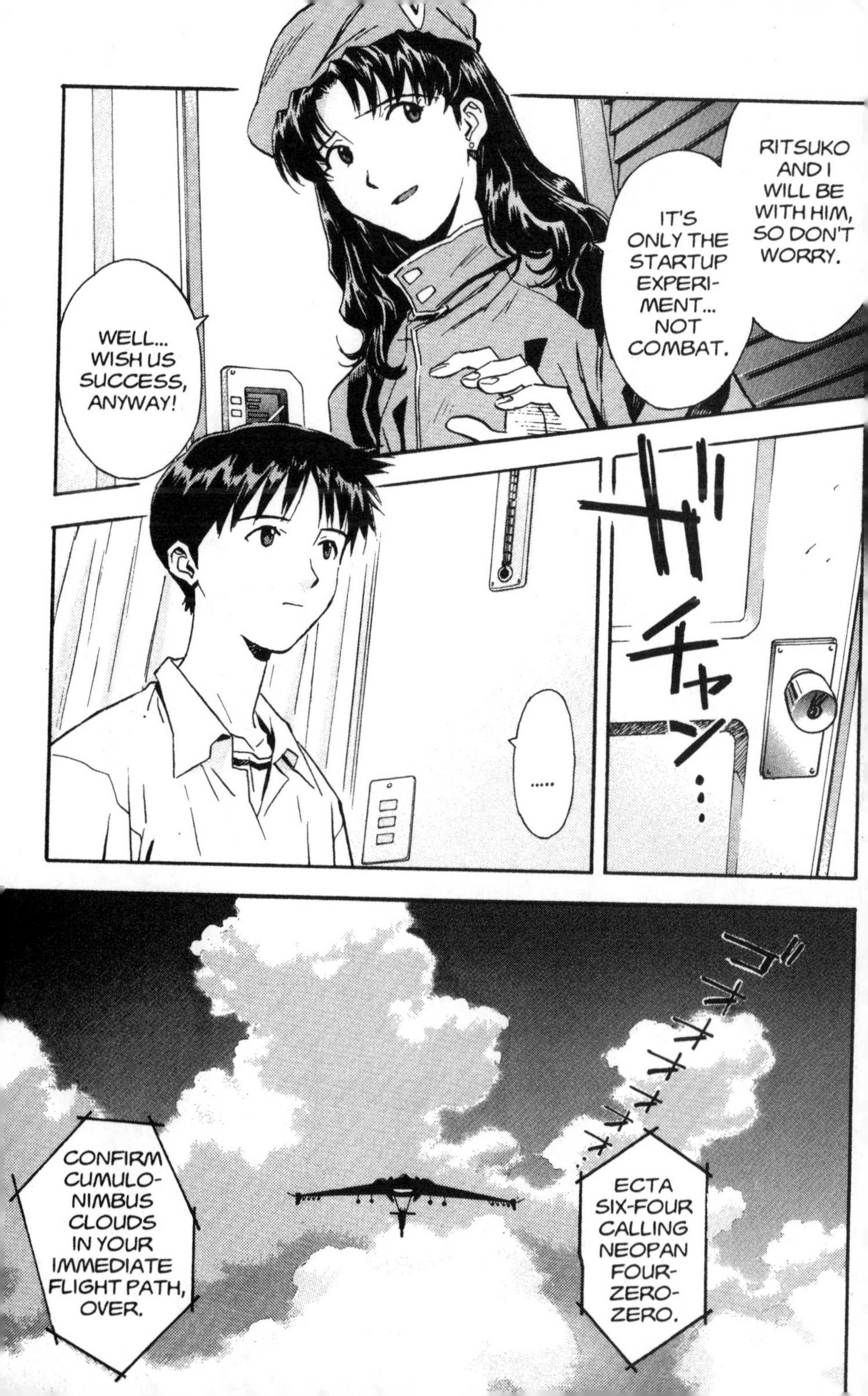
RITSUKO AND I WILL BE WITH HIM, SO DON'T WORRY.
IT'S ONLY THE STARTUP EXPERIMENT... NOT COMBAT.
WELL... WISH US SUCCESS, ANYWAY!
ガチャン…
......
ゴオオオオオ…
ECTA SIX-FOUR CALLING NEOPAN FOUR-ZERO-ZERO.
CONFIRM CUMULONIMBUS CLOUDS IN YOUR IMMEDIATE FLIGHT PATH, OVER.

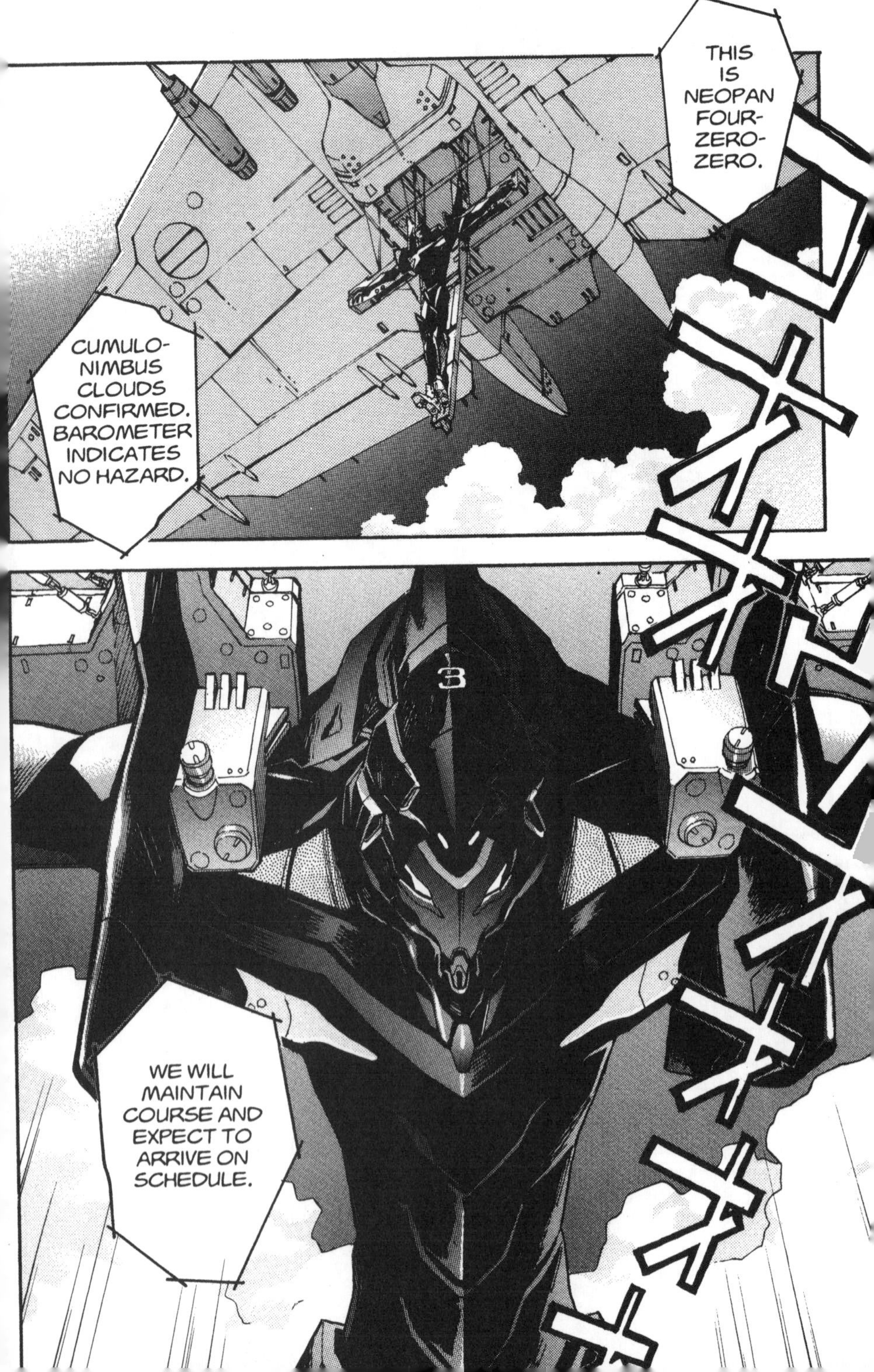
THIS IS NEOPAN FOUR-ZERO-ZERO.
CUMULO-NIMBUS CLOUDS CONFIRMED. BAROMETER INDICATES NO HAZARD.
WE WILL MAINTAIN COURSE AND EXPECT TO ARRIVE ON SCHEDULE.

Stage 4:
THE GIFT

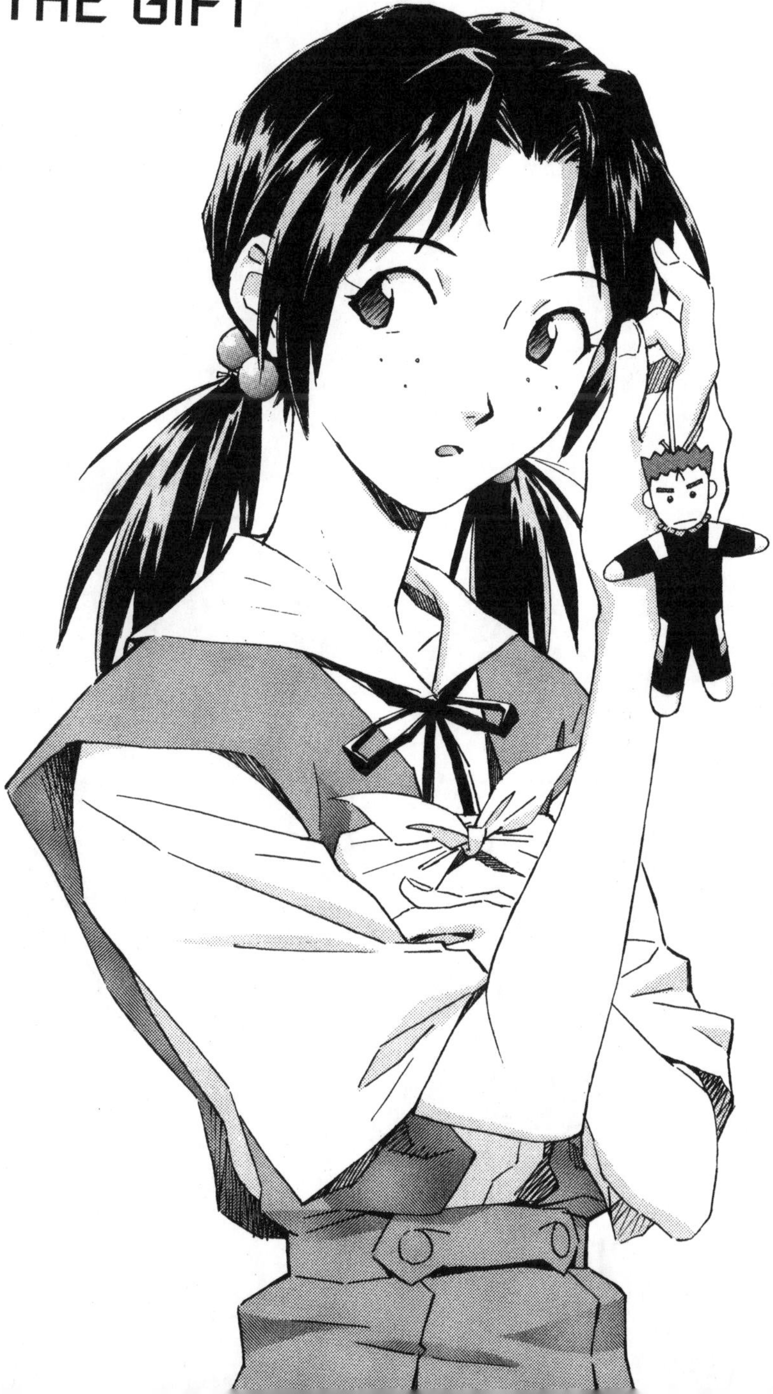

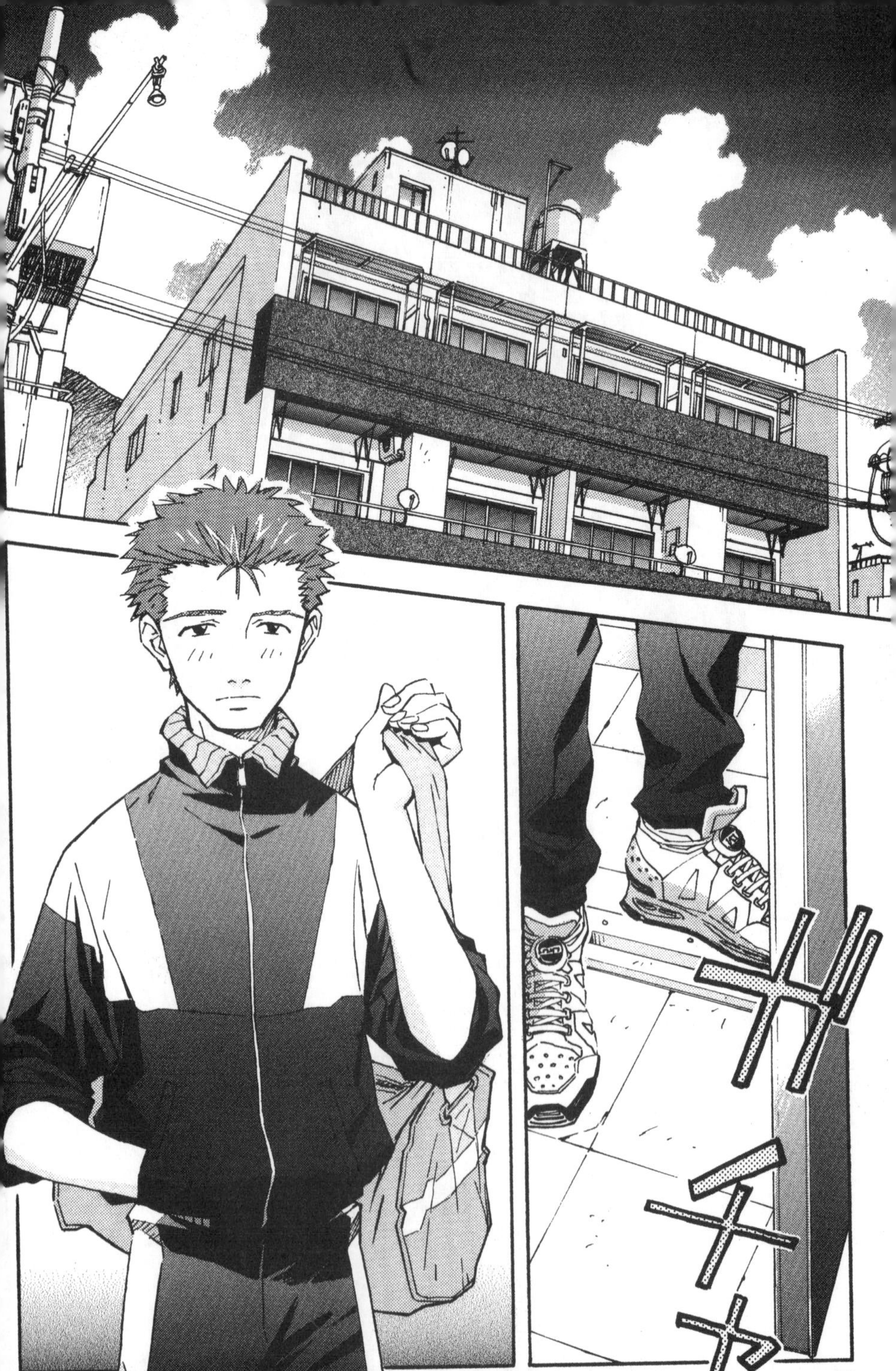

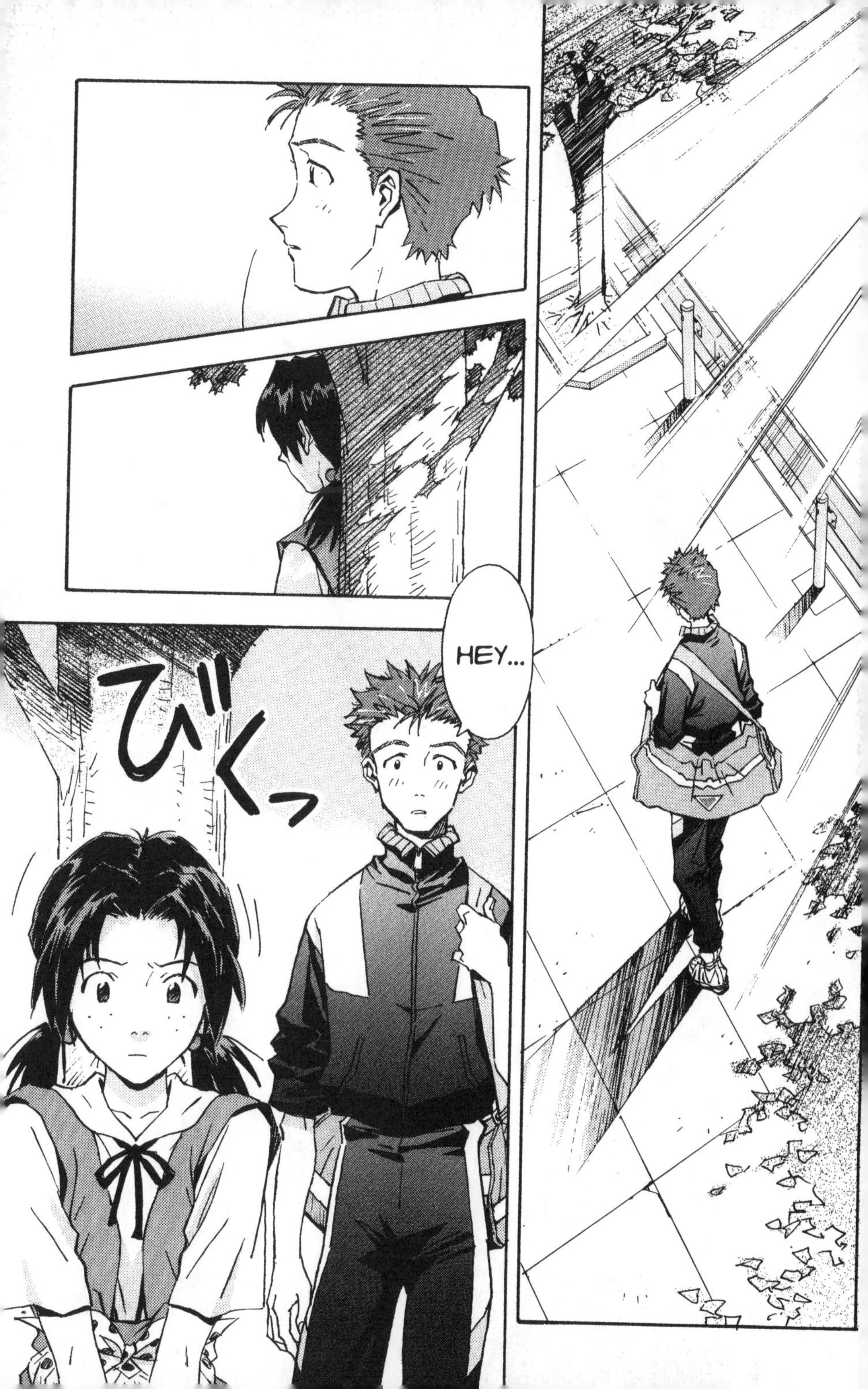
...
HEY...
びくっ

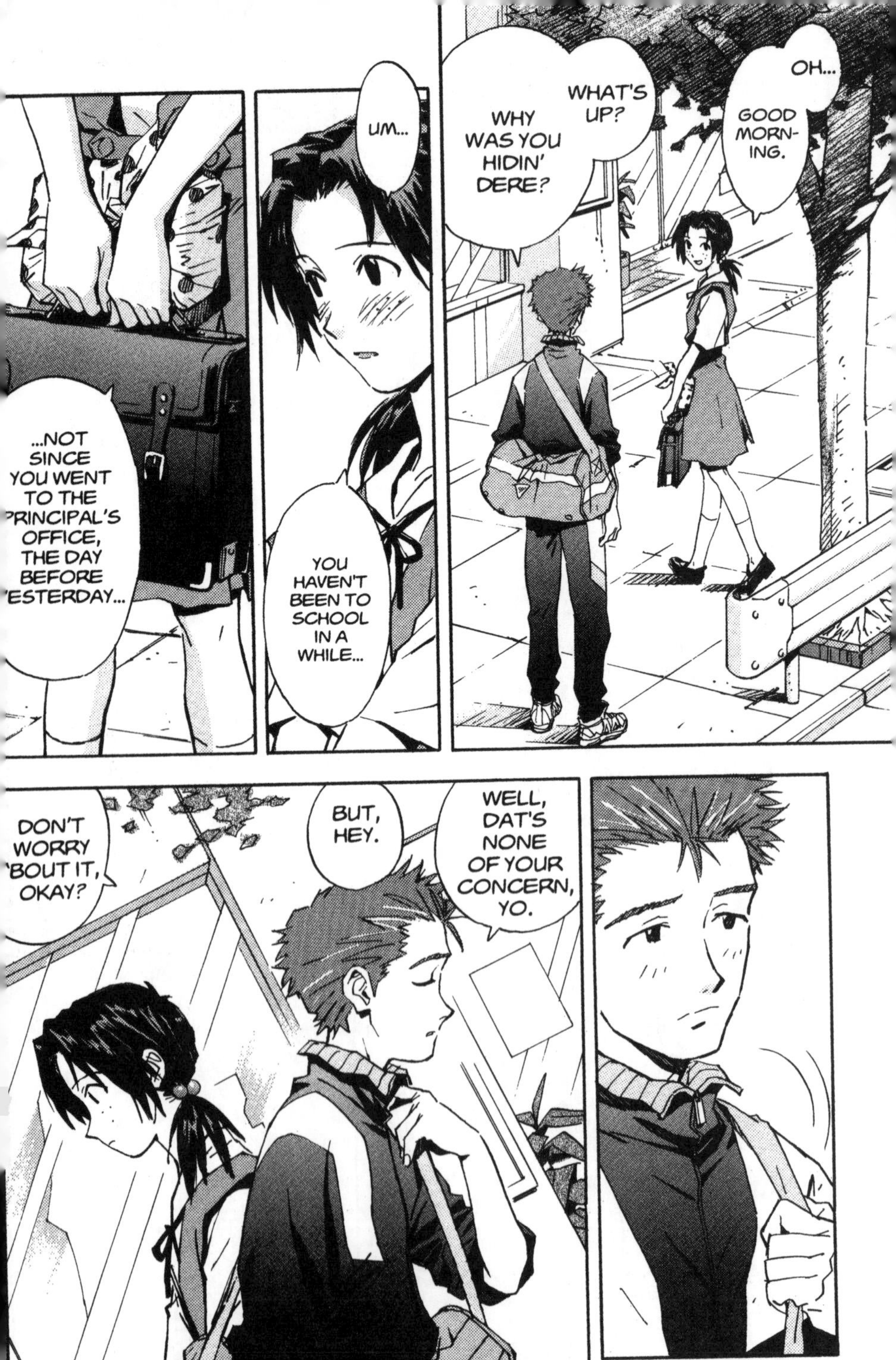
OH...
GOOD MORN-ING.
WHAT'S UP?
WHY WAS YOU HIDIN' DERE?
UM...
YOU HAVEN'T BEEN TO SCHOOL IN A WHILE...
...NOT SINCE YOU WENT TO THE PRINCIPAL'S OFFICE, THE DAY BEFORE YESTERDAY...
WELL, DAT'S NONE OF YOUR CONCERN, YO.
BUT, HEY.
DON'T WORRY 'BOUT IT, OKAY?

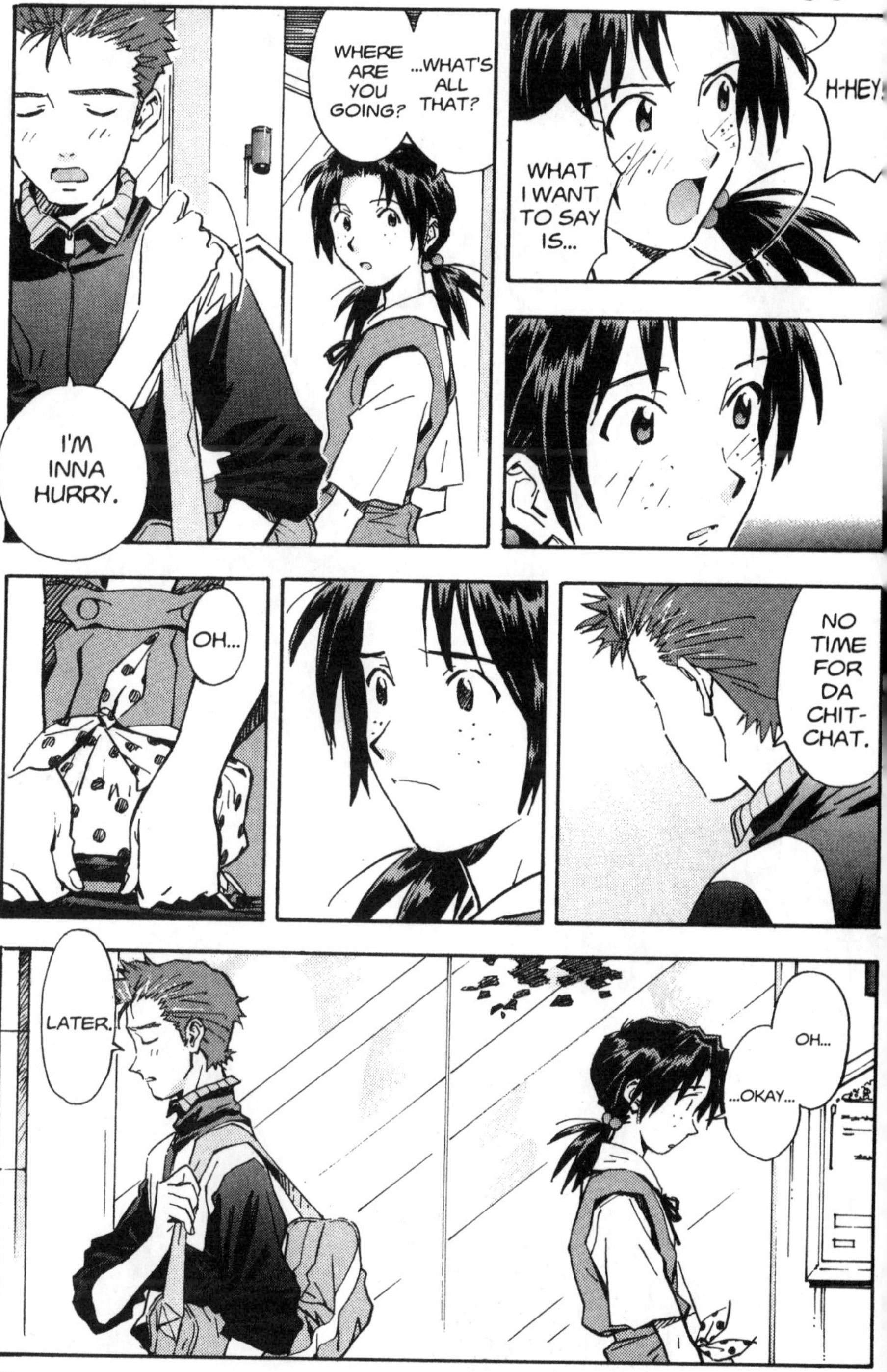
H-HEY!
WHAT I WANT TO SAY IS...
WHERE ARE YOU GOING?
...WHAT'S ALL THAT?
I'M INNA HURRY.
NO TIME FOR DA CHIT-CHAT.
OH...
OH...
...OKAY...
LATER.

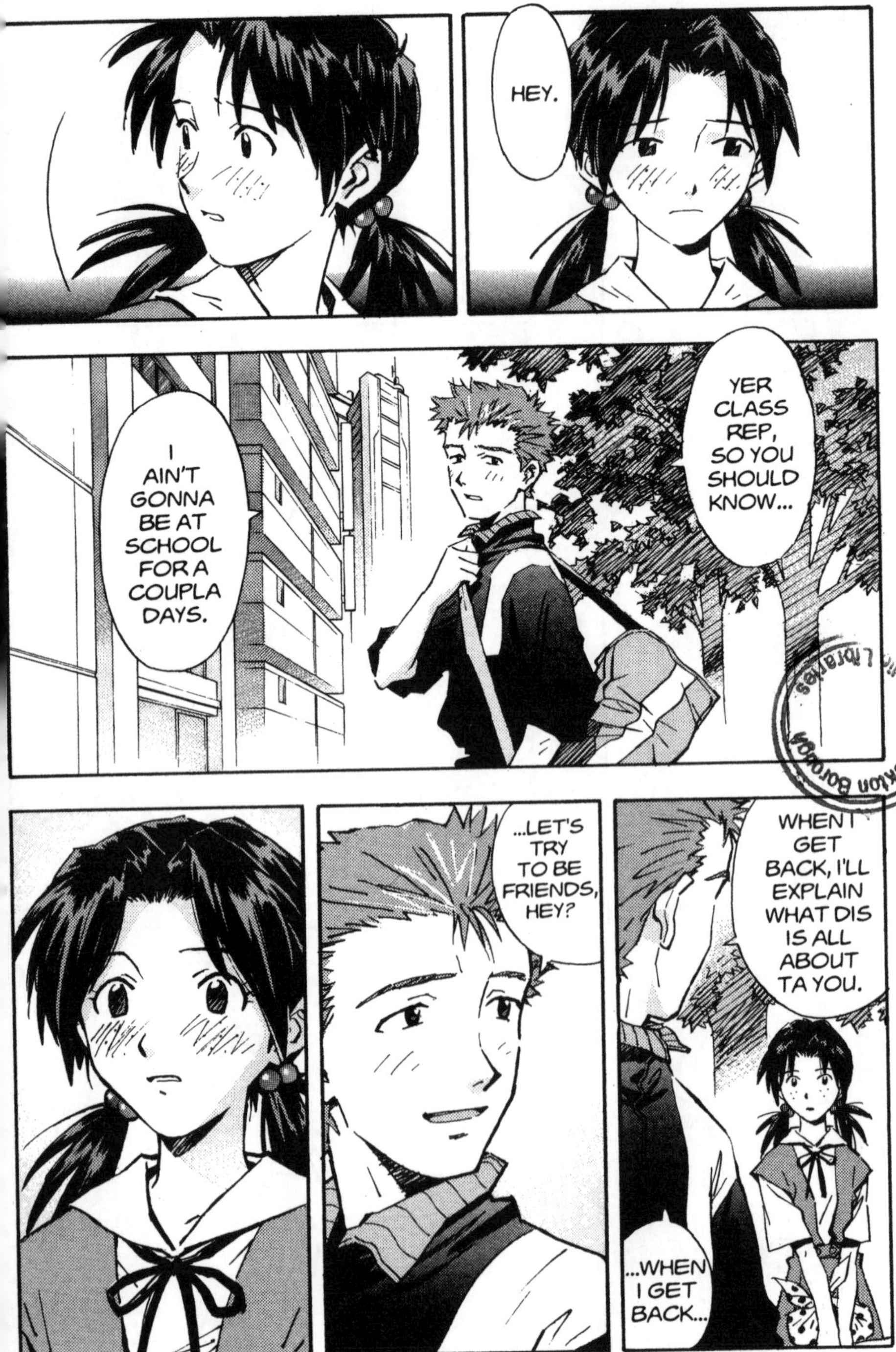
HEY.
YER CLASS REP, SO YOU SHOULD KNOW...
I AIN'T GONNA BE AT SCHOOL FOR A COUPLA DAYS.
WHEN I GET BACK, I'LL EXPLAIN WHAT DIS IS ALL ABOUT TA YOU.
...WHEN I GET BACK...
...LET'S TRY TO BE FRIENDS, HEY?

YEAH

SURE.

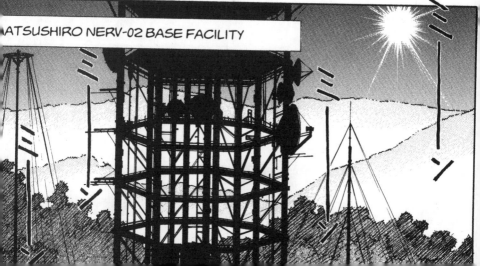

ATSUSHIRO NERV-02 BASE FACILITY

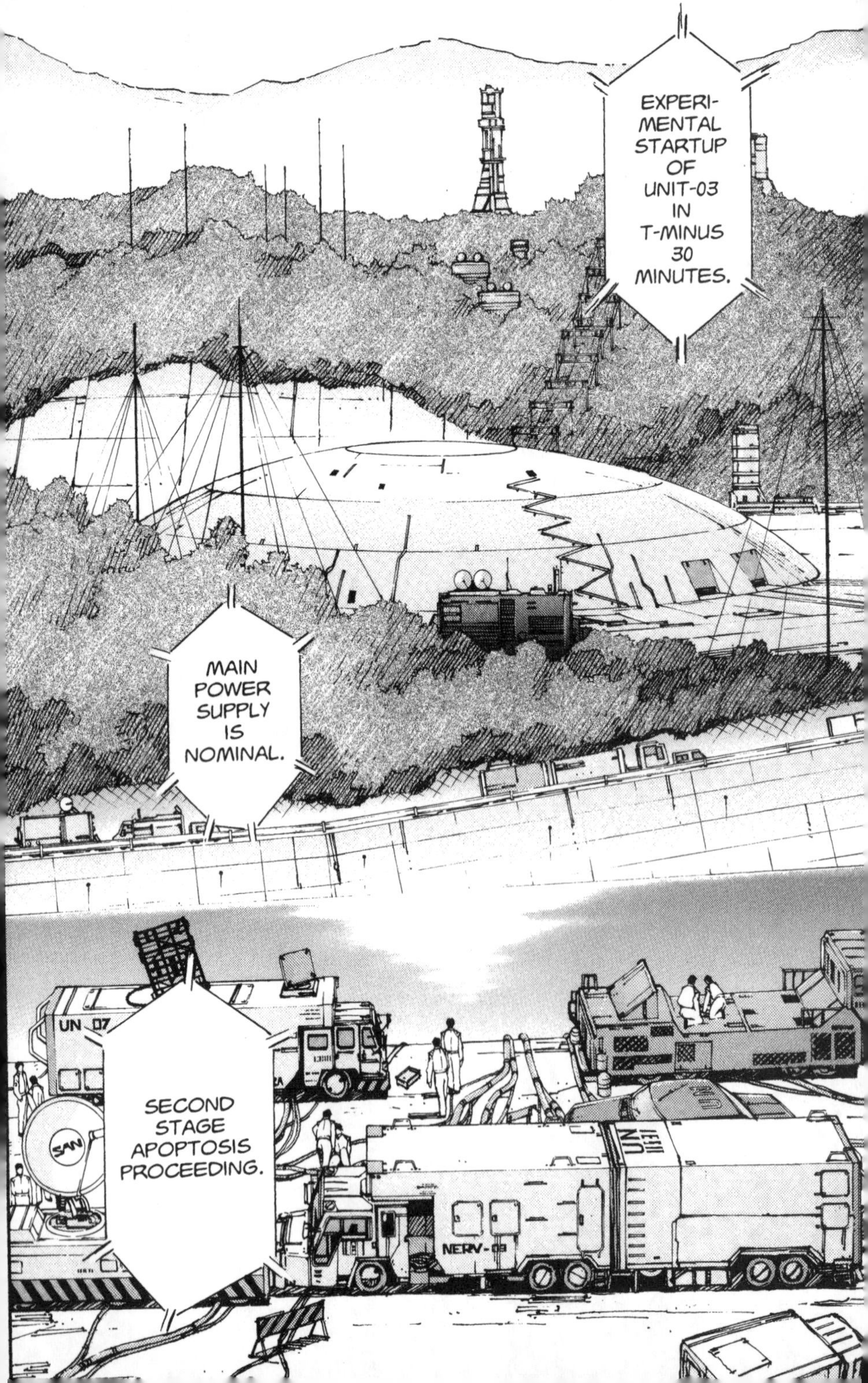
EXPERI-
MENTAL
STARTUP
OF
UNIT-03
IN
T-MINUS
30
MINUTES.
MAIN
POWER
SUPPLY
IS
NOMINAL.
SECOND
STAGE
APOPTOSIS
PROCEEDING.
NERV-03

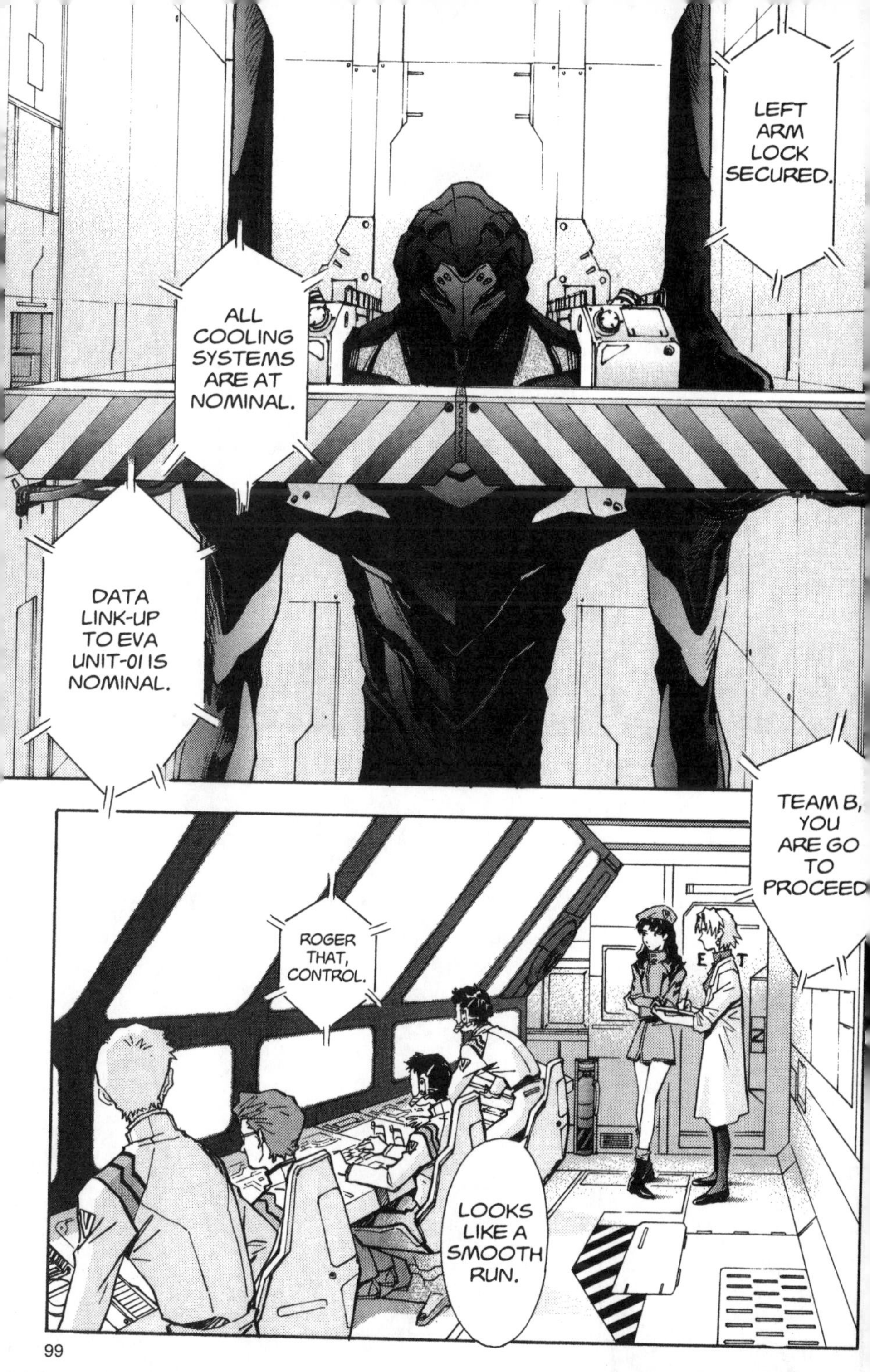
LEFT ARM LOCK SECURED.
ALL COOLING SYSTEMS ARE AT NOMINAL.
DATA LINK-UP TO EVA UNIT-01 IS NOMINAL.
TEAM B, YOU ARE GO TO PROCEED
ROGER THAT, CONTROL.
LOOKS LIKE A SMOOTH RUN.

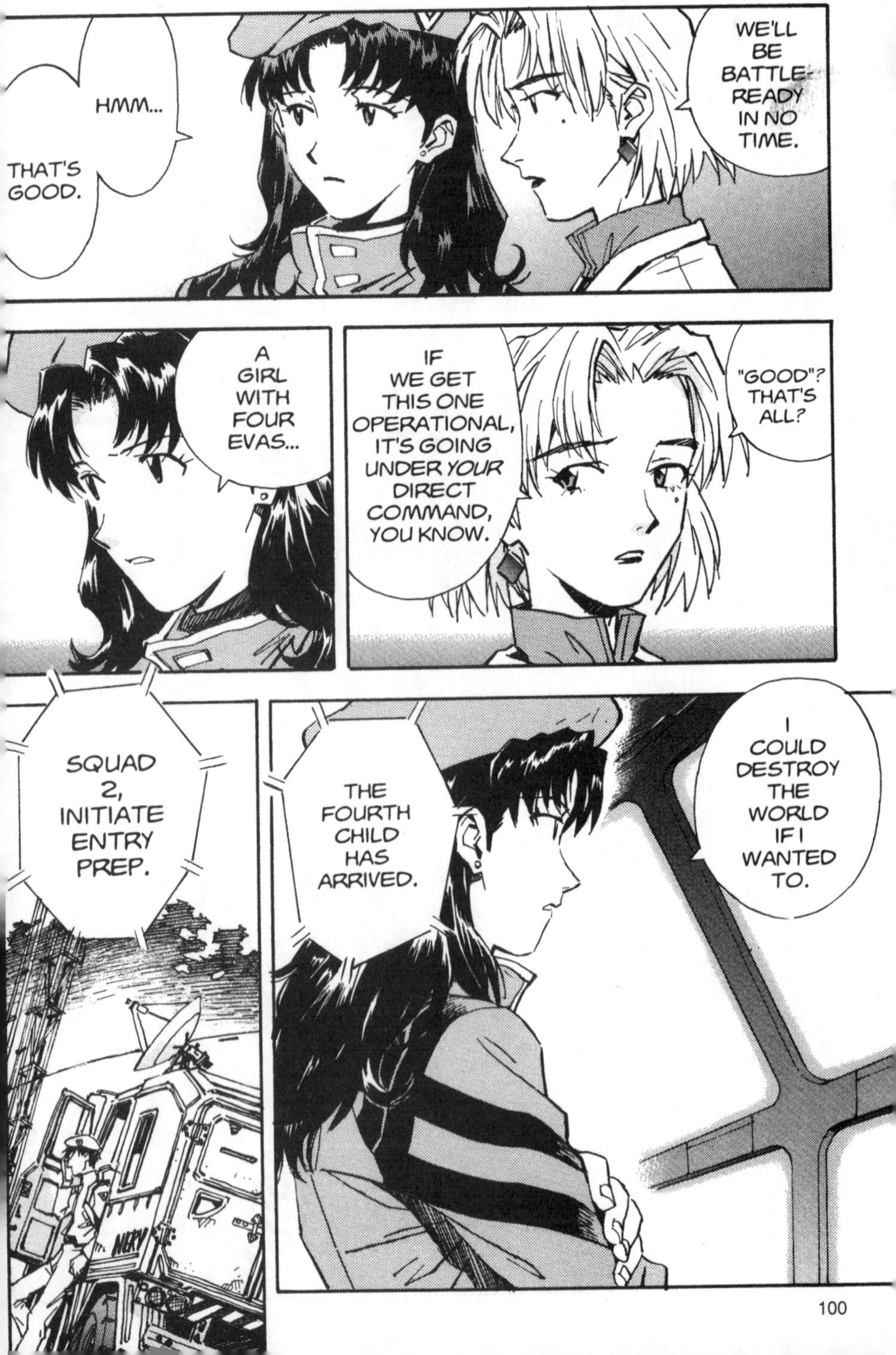
WE'LL BE BATTLE-READY IN NO TIME.
HMM...
THAT'S GOOD.
"GOOD"? THAT'S ALL?
IF WE GET THIS ONE OPERATIONAL, IT'S GOING UNDER *YOUR* DIRECT COMMAND, YOU KNOW.
A GIRL WITH FOUR EVAS...
I COULD DESTROY THE WORLD IF I WANTED TO.
THE FOURTH CHILD HAS ARRIVED.
SQUAD 2, INITIATE ENTRY PREP.
NERV

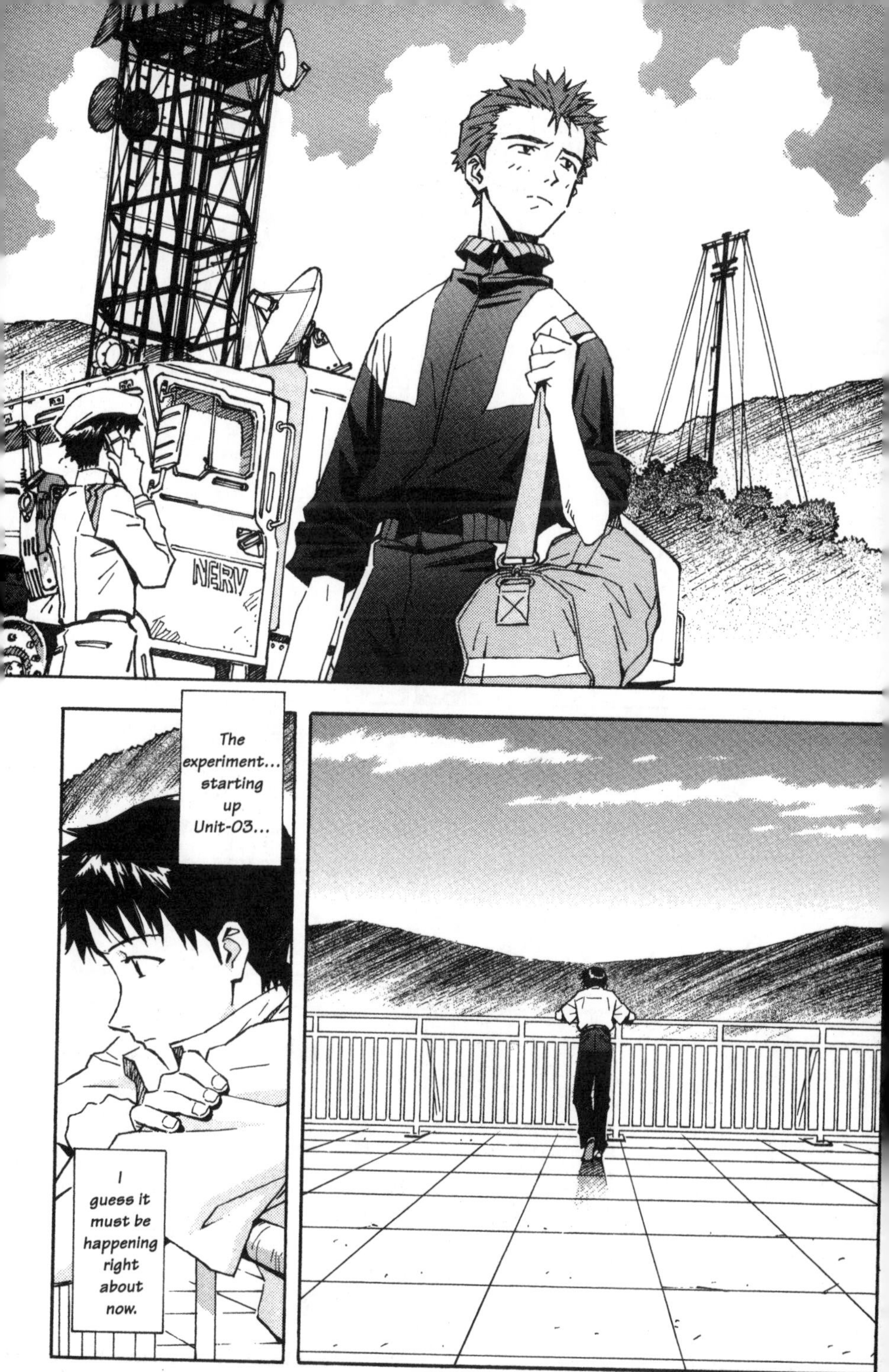
NERV
The experiment... starting up Unit-03...
I guess it must be happening right about now.

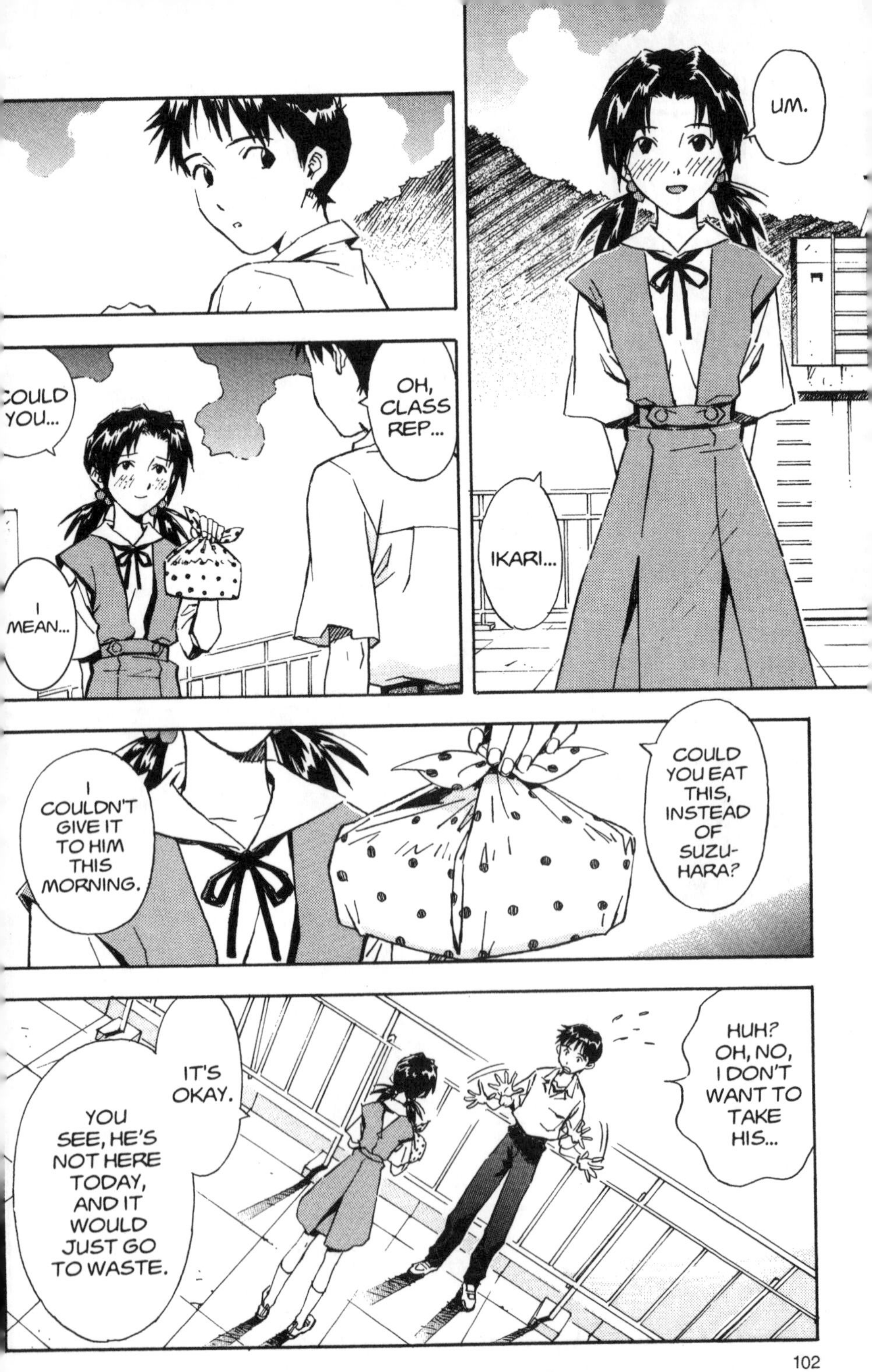
UM.
IKARI...
OH, CLASS REP...
COULD YOU...
I MEAN...
COULD YOU EAT THIS, INSTEAD OF SUZU-HARA?
I COULDN'T GIVE IT TO HIM THIS MORNING.
HUH? OH, NO, I DON'T WANT TO TAKE HIS...
IT'S OKAY.
YOU SEE, HE'S NOT HERE TODAY, AND IT WOULD JUST GO TO WASTE.

HUH?

TEE-
HEE!

LATER.

I COULDN'T GIVE IT TO HIM...

...BUT SOME-THING GOOD HAPPENED ANYWAY.

LOOKED THE SAME AS ALWAYS TO ME.

Y-YOU THINK SO?

SHE HAD THIS CREEPY GRIN ON HER FACE.

OH. YEAH.

THAT WAS ...RIGHT? THE CLASS REP...

!?

LET'S JUST EAT, OKAY?

NOW....?

REEEEAALLY

IT'S ASUKA'S! SHE WASN'T HUNGRY TODAY— THAT'S ALL.

OH, THIS?

THAT—

THAT AIN'T NO MAN'S LUNCH BOX!

DON'T GET THE WRONG IDEA.

THE LUCKY PILOT...

WHO IS IT?

UNIT -03.

IT'S MADE IT TO JAPAN, RIGHT?

YEAH.

MISATO LEFT FOR MATSUSHIRO YESTERDAY— FOR THE STARTUP EXPERIMENT.

MAYBE IT'S HIM.

TOJI HASN'T BEEN TO SCHOOL SINCE YESTERDAY.

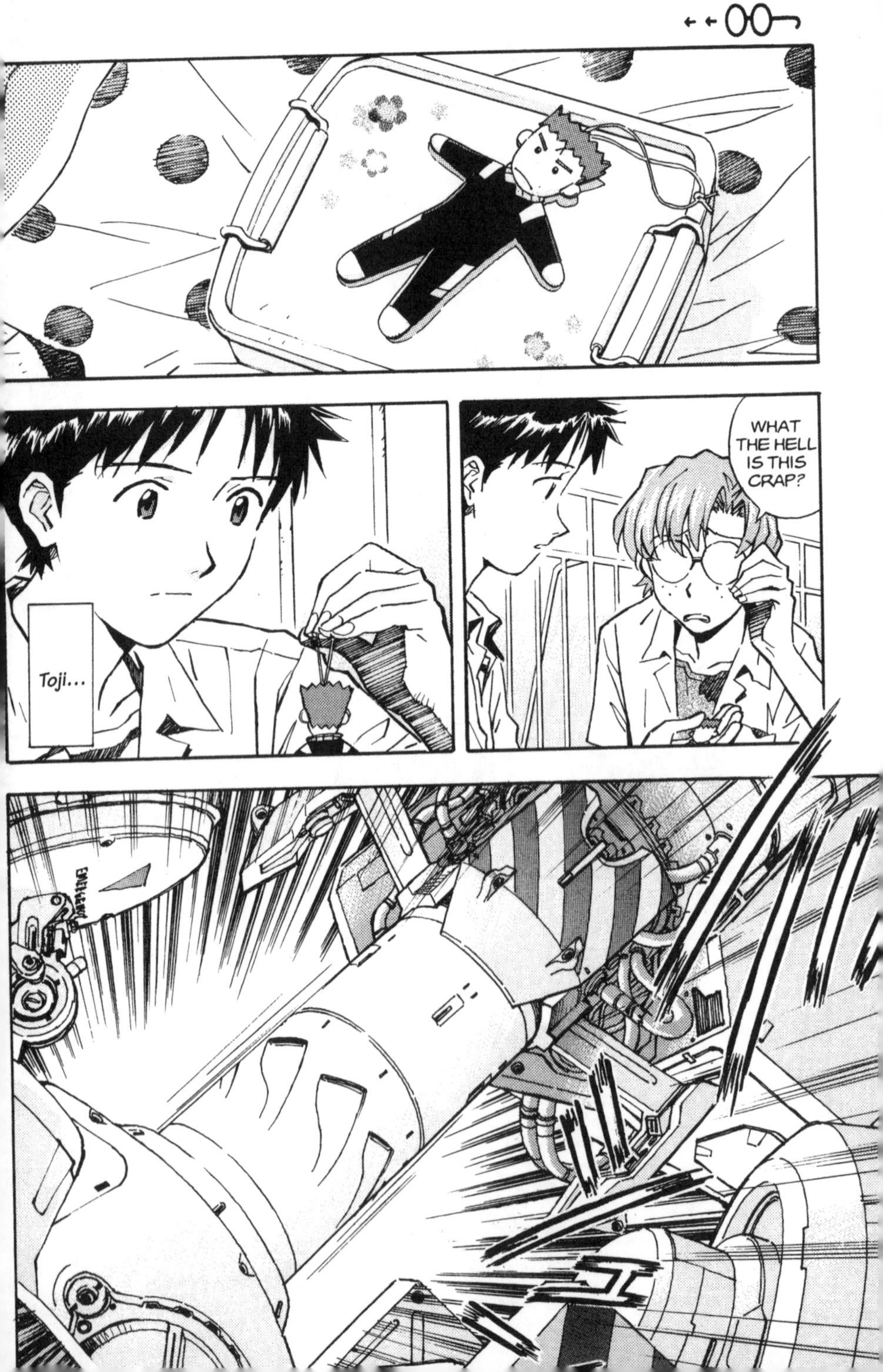
WHAT THE HELL IS THIS CRAP?
Toji...

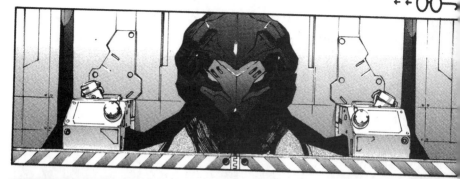

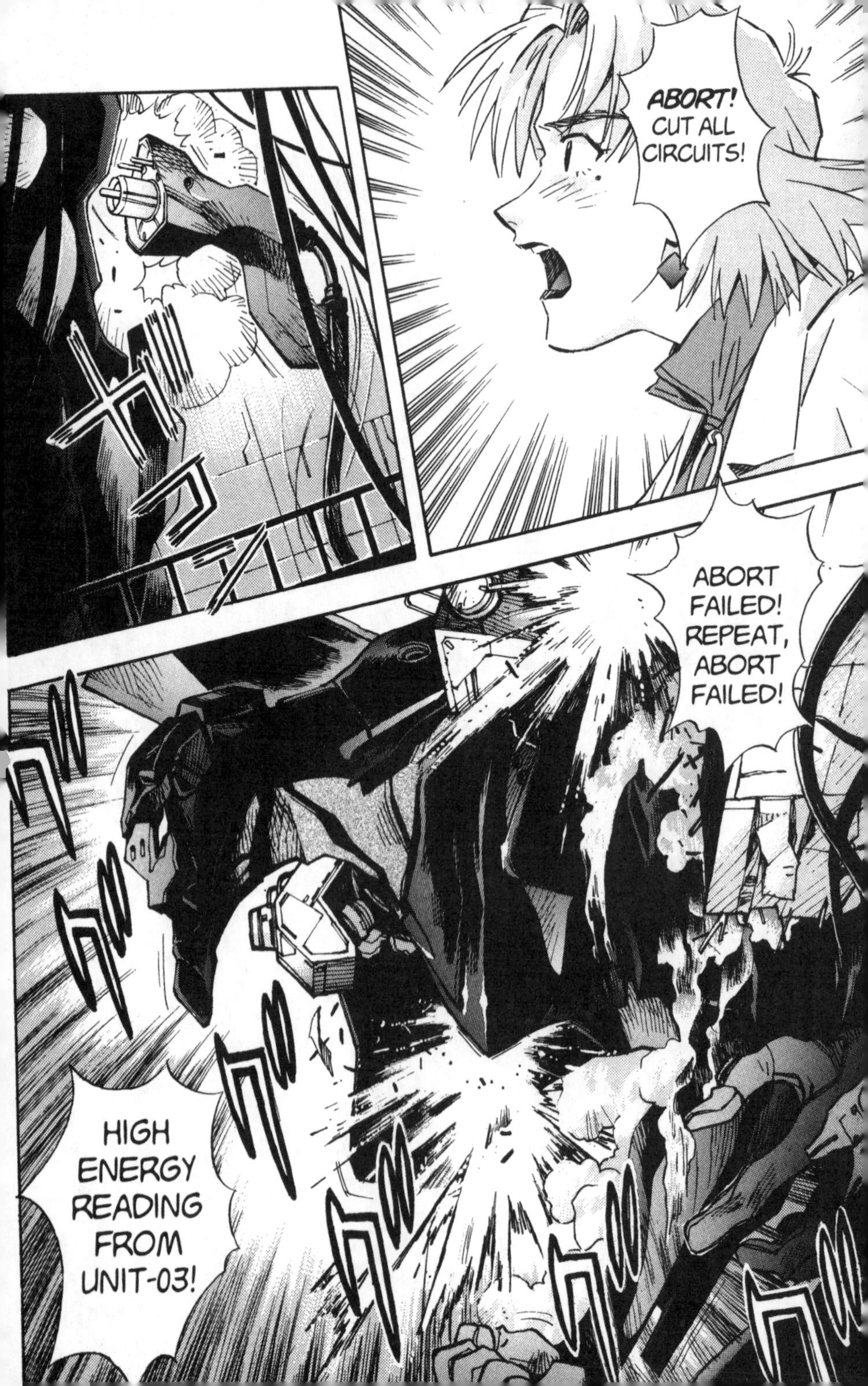
ABORT! CUT ALL CIRCUITS!
ABORT FAILED! REPEAT, ABORT FAILED!
HIGH ENERGY READING FROM UNIT-03!

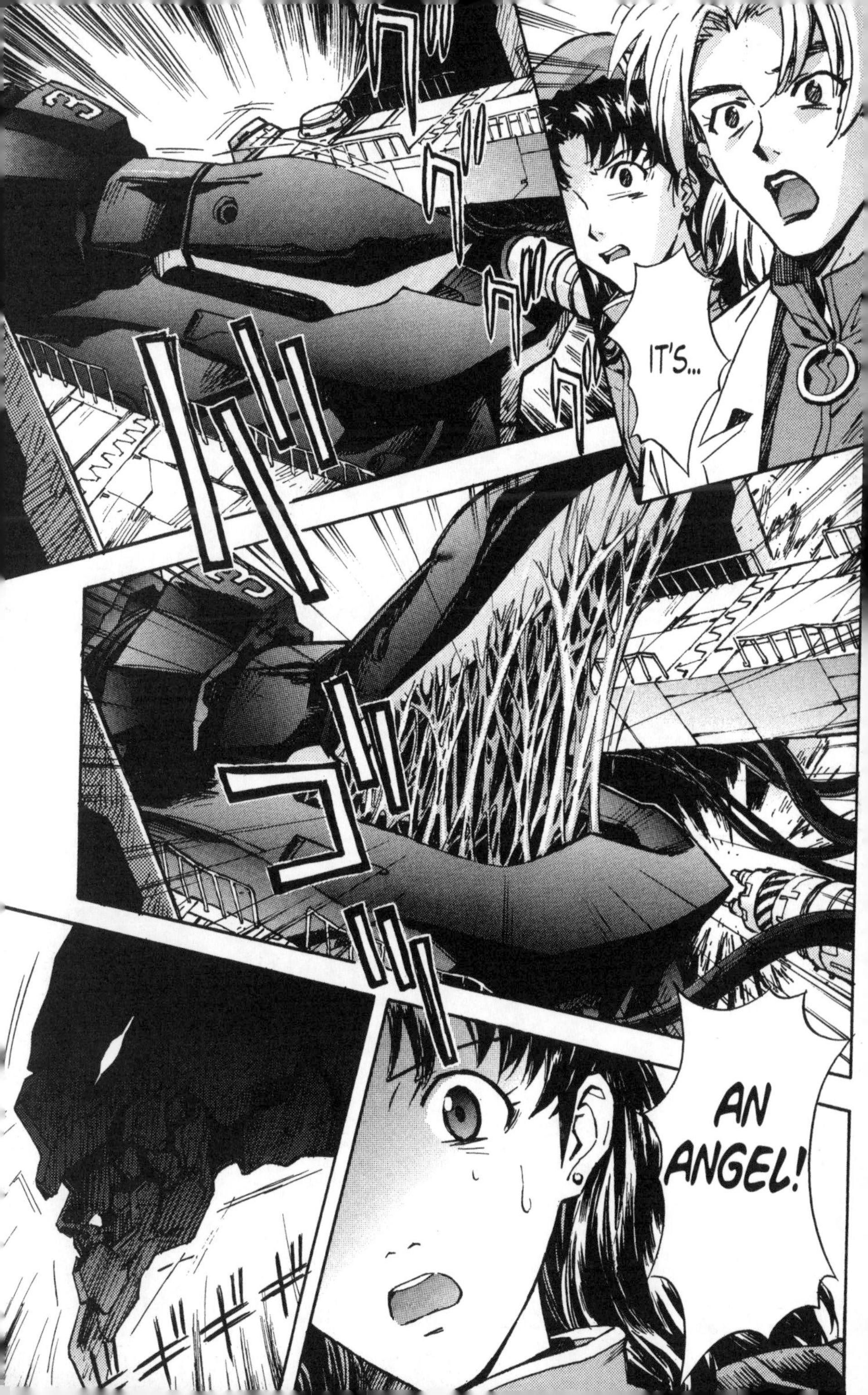
IT'S...
AN ANGEL!

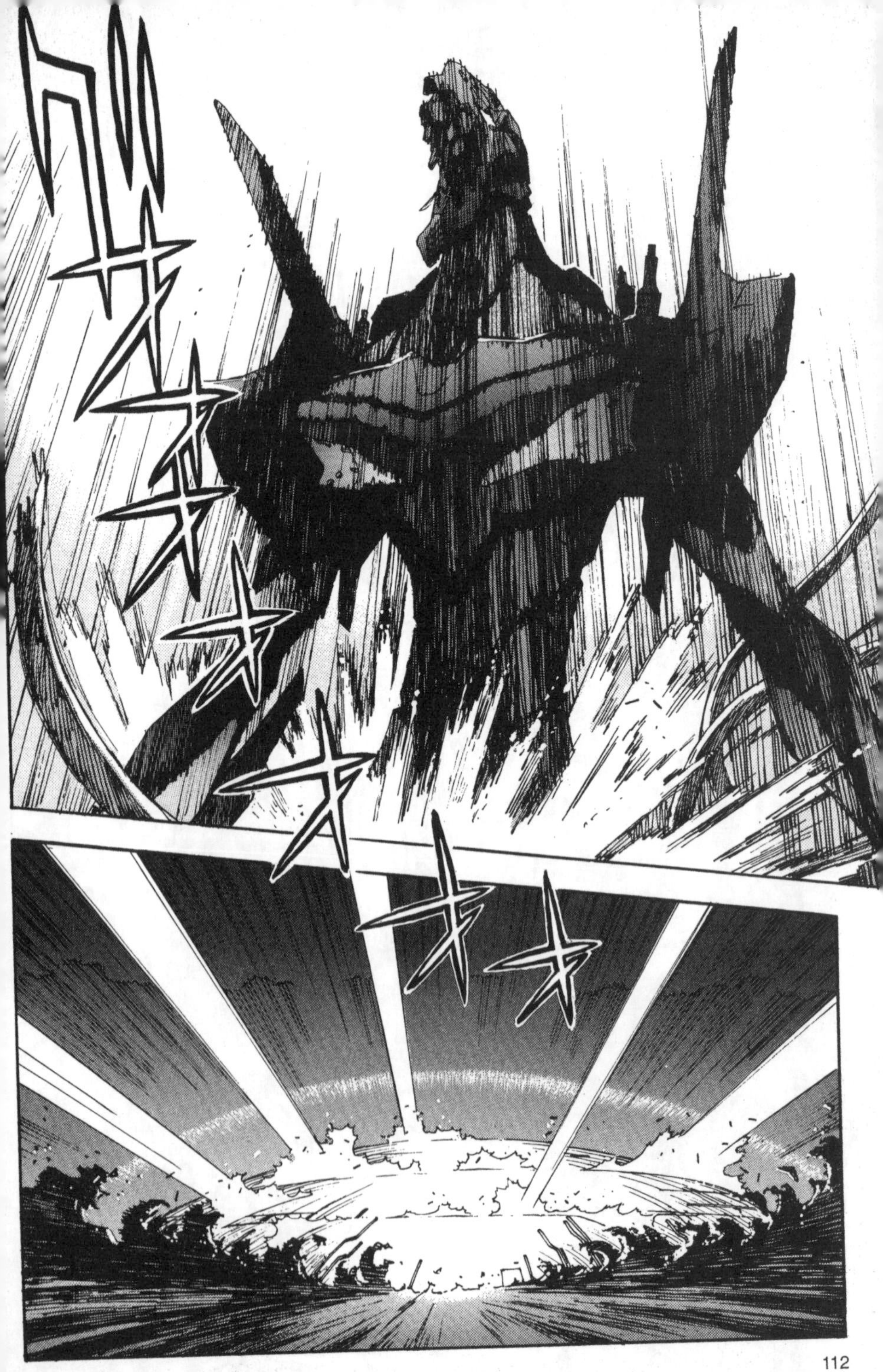
カッ

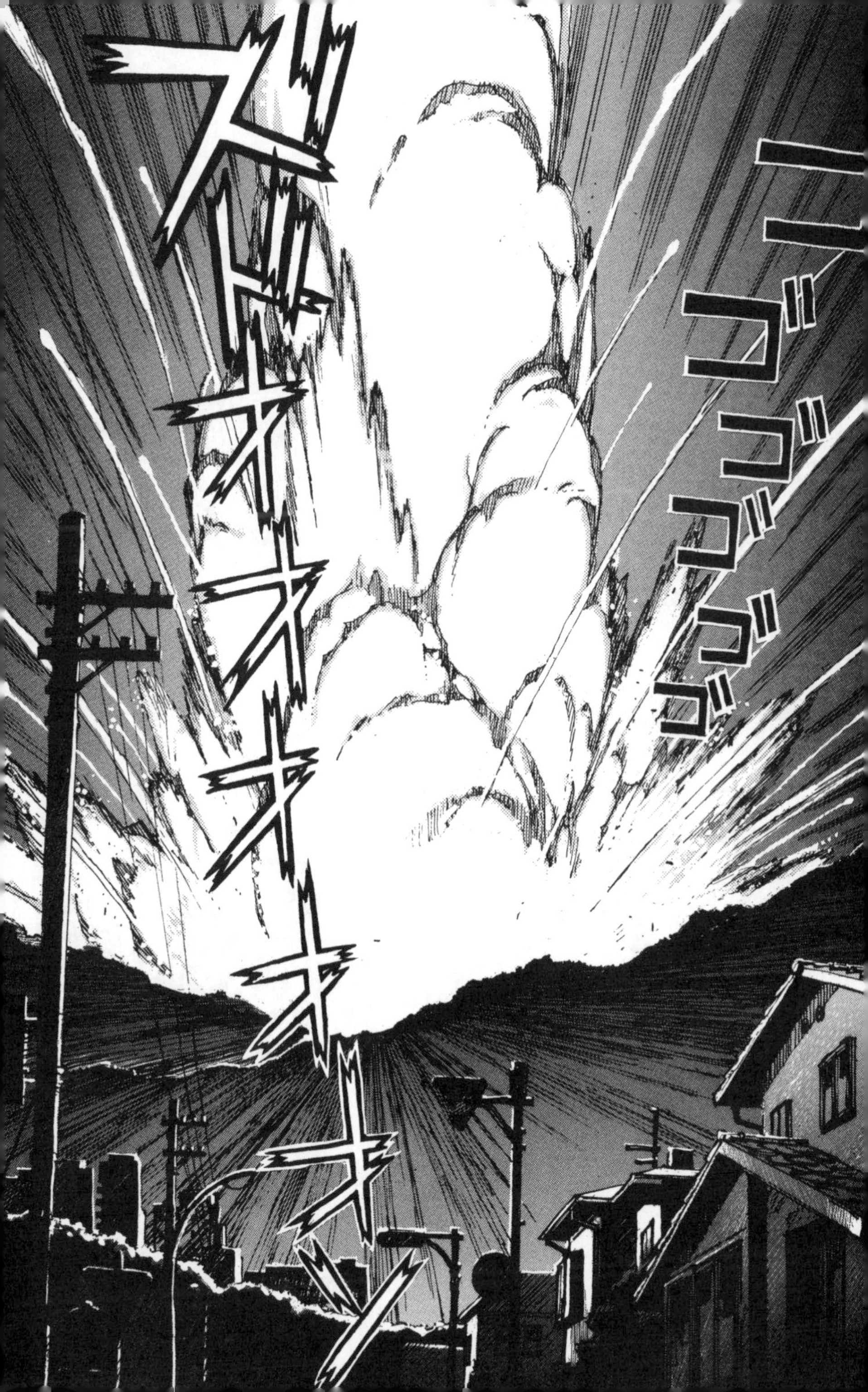
ゴゴゴゴゴゴ
ズドオオオオオン

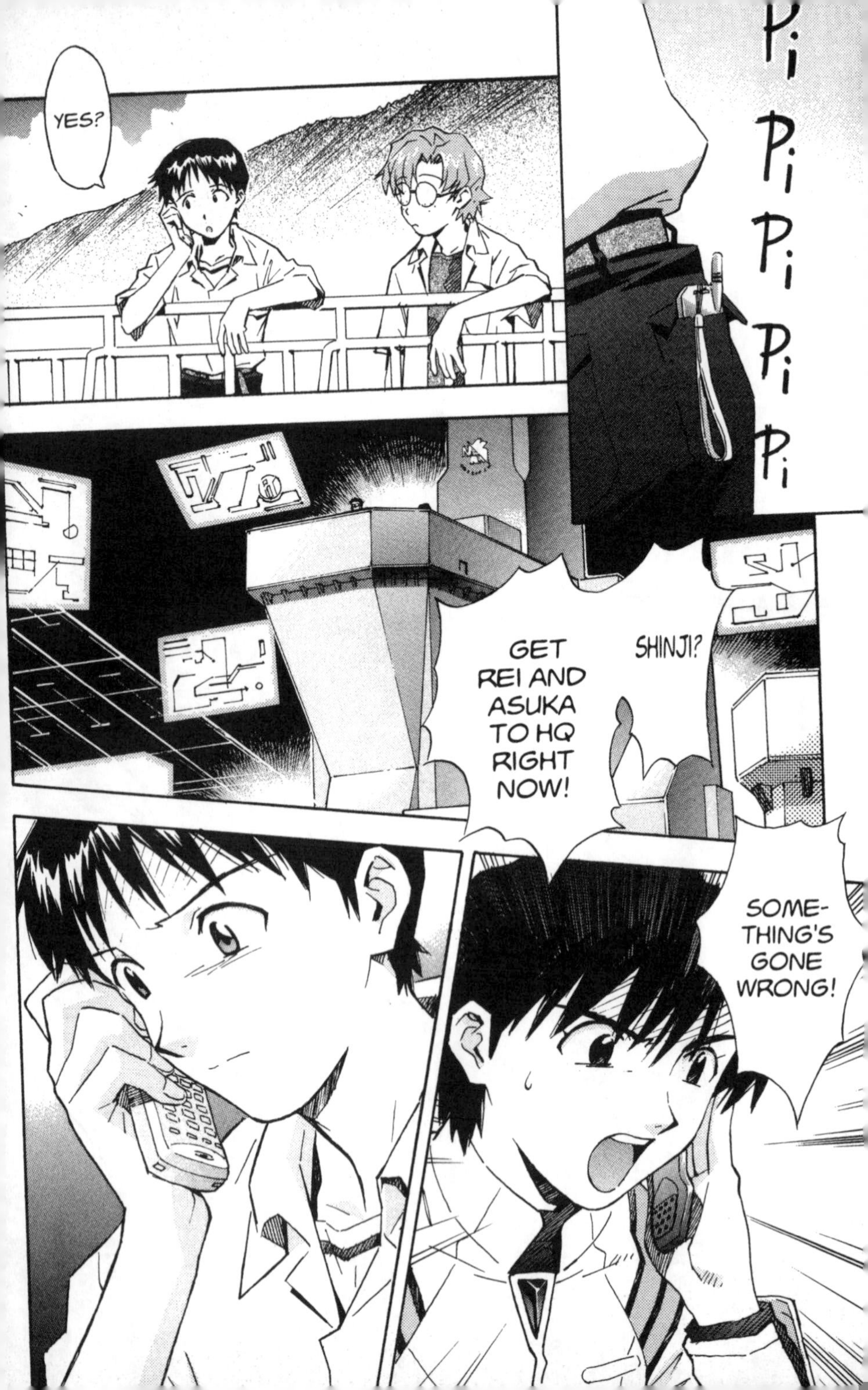
Pi Pi Pi Pi Pi
YES?
SHINJI?
GET REI AND ASUKA TO HQ RIGHT NOW!
SOMETHING'S GONE WRONG!

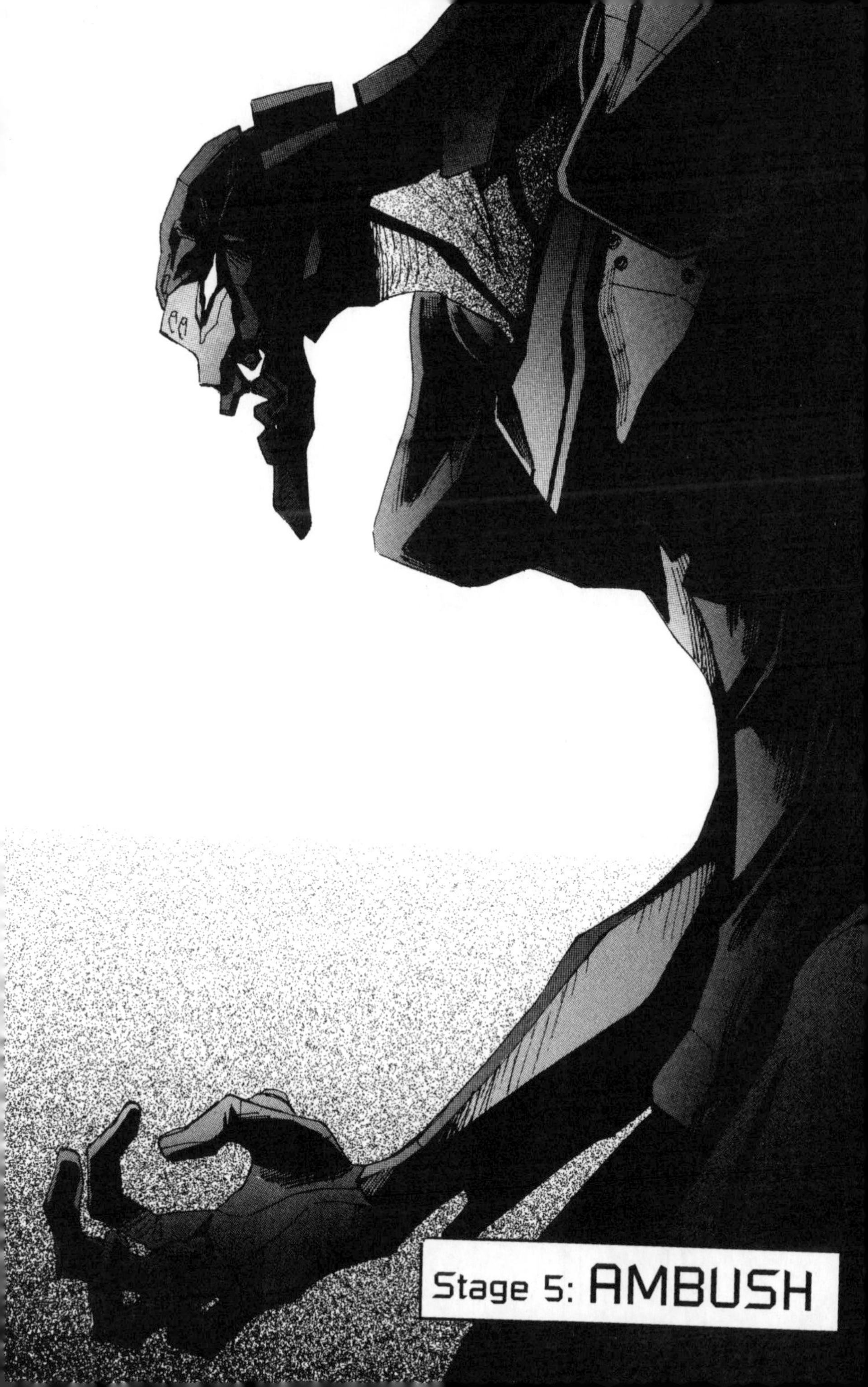
Stage 5: AMBUSH

WE'VE DETECTED AN UNIDENTIFIED OBJECT MOVING AWAY FROM THE SITE...

WE THINK IT'S AN ANGEL!

NO WORD YET FROM THE SITE, SIR!

DAMAGE REPORT?

GET THIS UNDER CONTROL BEFORE THE SDF INTERVENES!

DISPATCH A RESCUE SQUAD AND THE THIRD DETACHMENT!

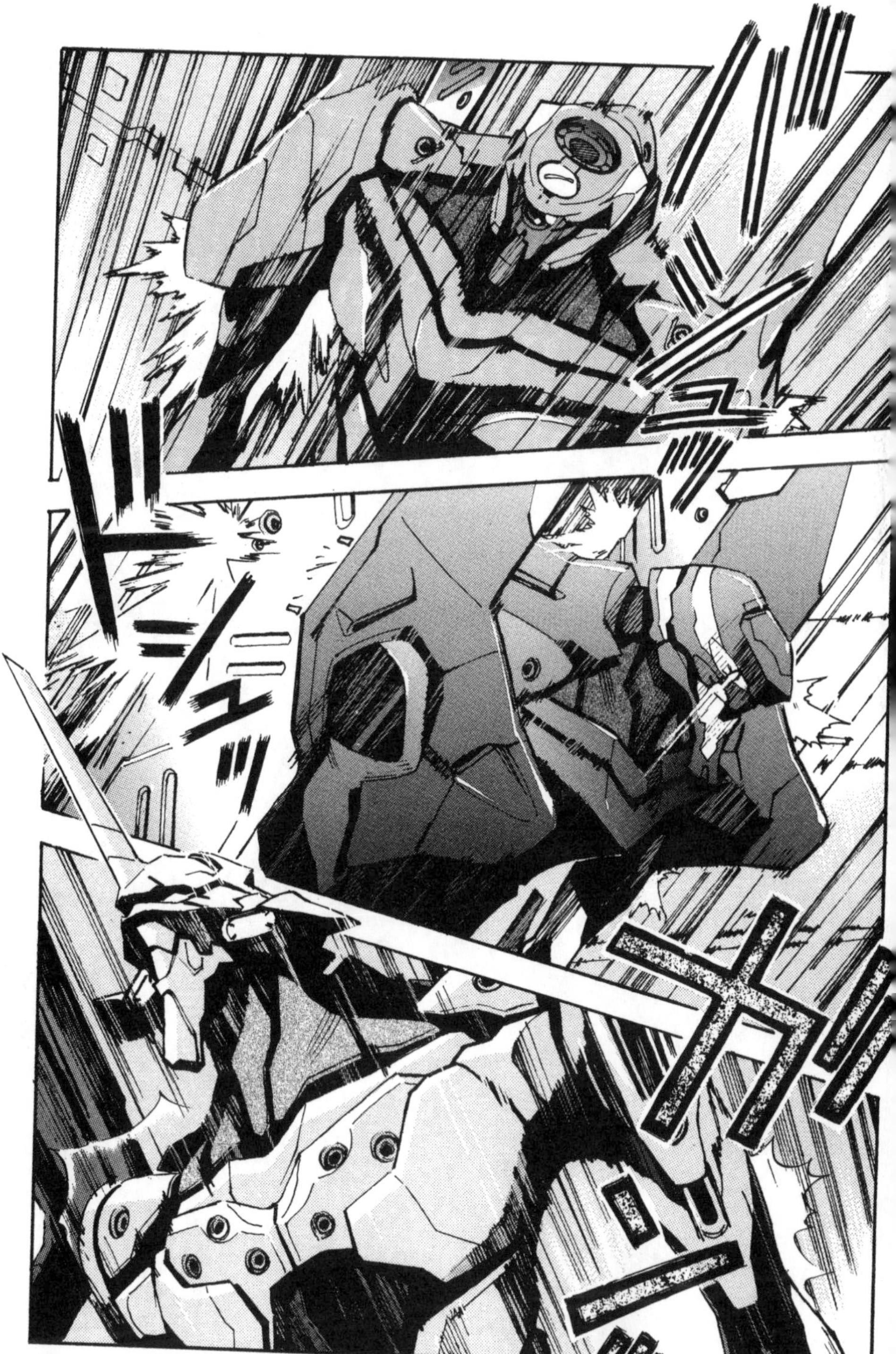

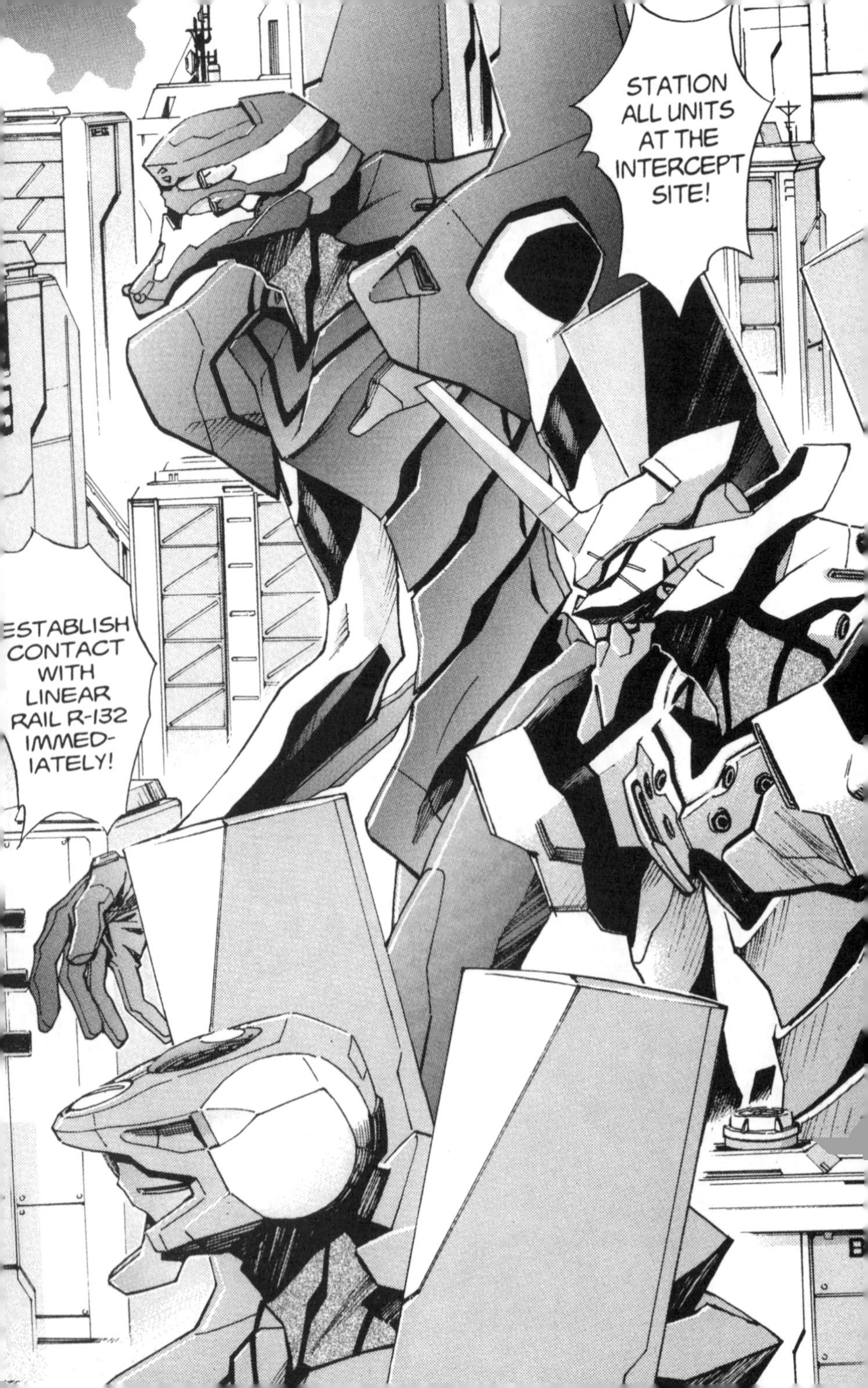
STATION ALL UNITS AT THE INTERCEPT SITE!
ESTABLISH CONTACT WITH LINEAR RAIL R-132 IMMED-IATELY!

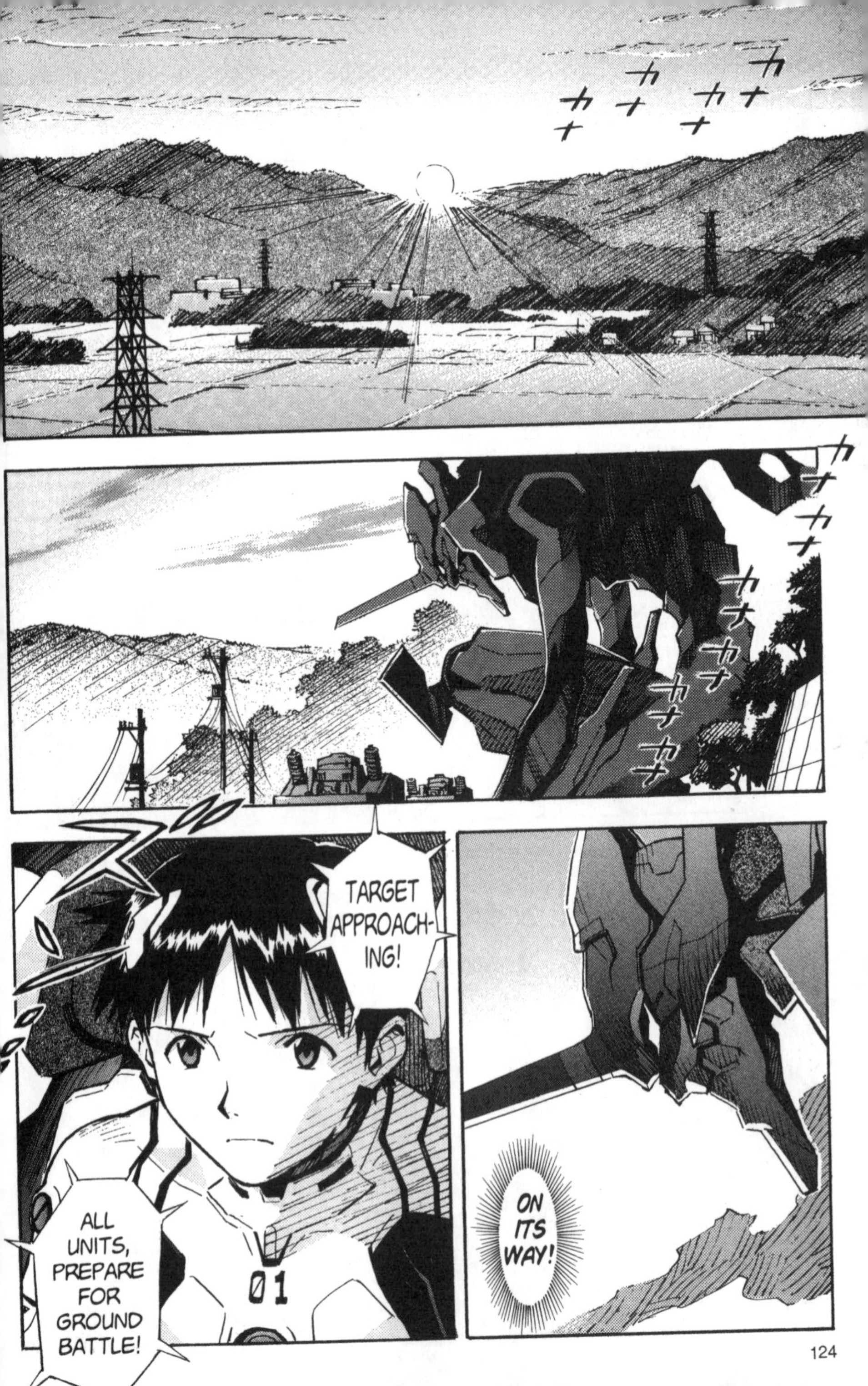
カナ カナ
カナ カナ
ON ITS WAY!
TARGET APPROACHING!
ALL UNITS, PREPARE FOR GROUND BATTLE!

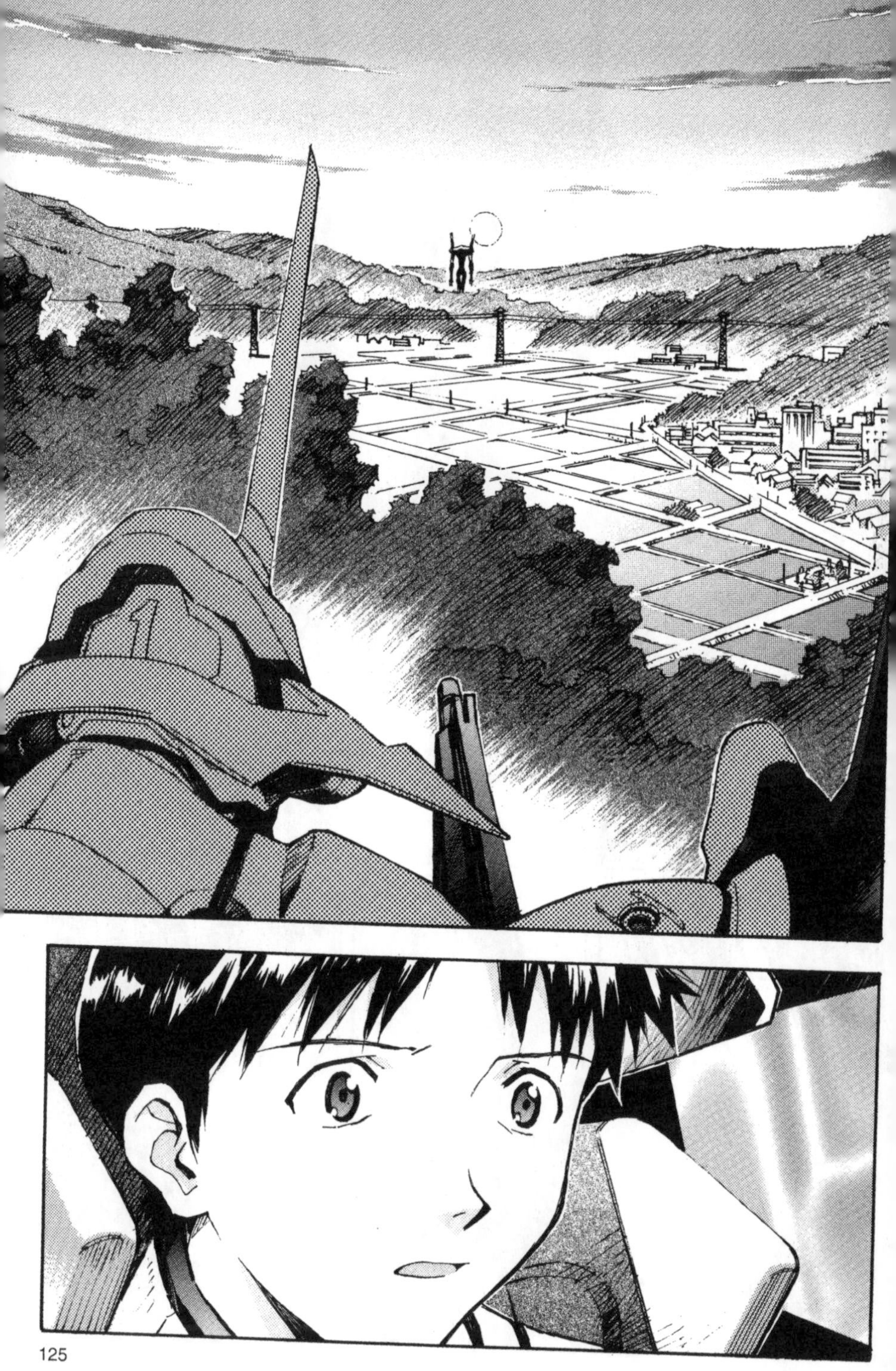

THE TARGET...

THAT'S THE TARGET?

BUT... BUT...

...IT'S AN EVA!

IT'S AN ANGEL NOW.

SHINJI.

IT'S NO LONGER AN EVA UNIT.

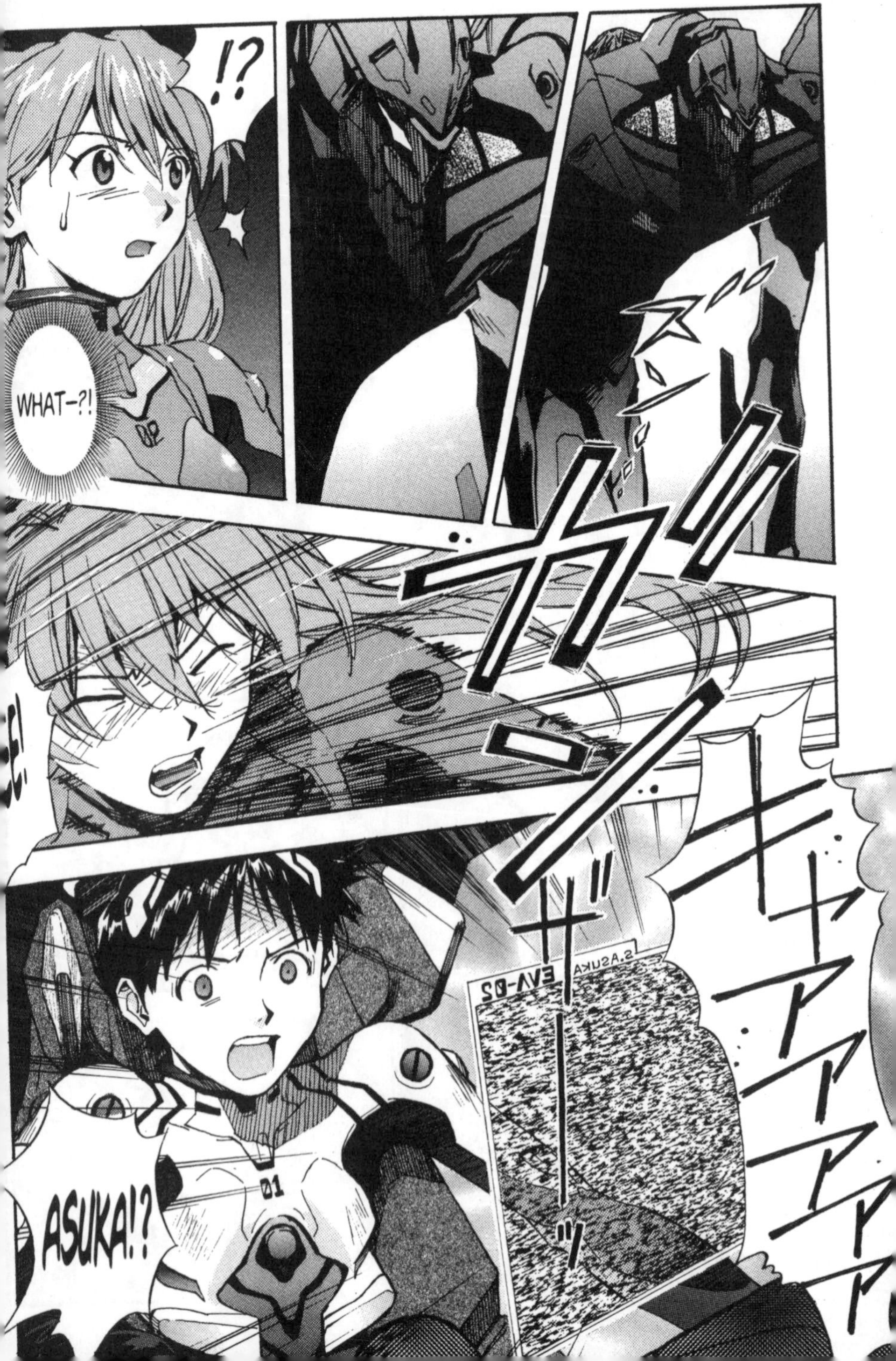
!?
WHAT-?!
ASUKA!?

UNIT -00!

YES, SIR.

AVOID CLOSE COMBAT AND DELAY THE TARGET.

REI.

AYANAMI!

SHINJI! DID YOU HEAR ME?

HURRY TO UNIT -00!

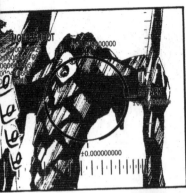

THERE **IS** SOME-ONE IN THERE.

HE'S RIGHT.

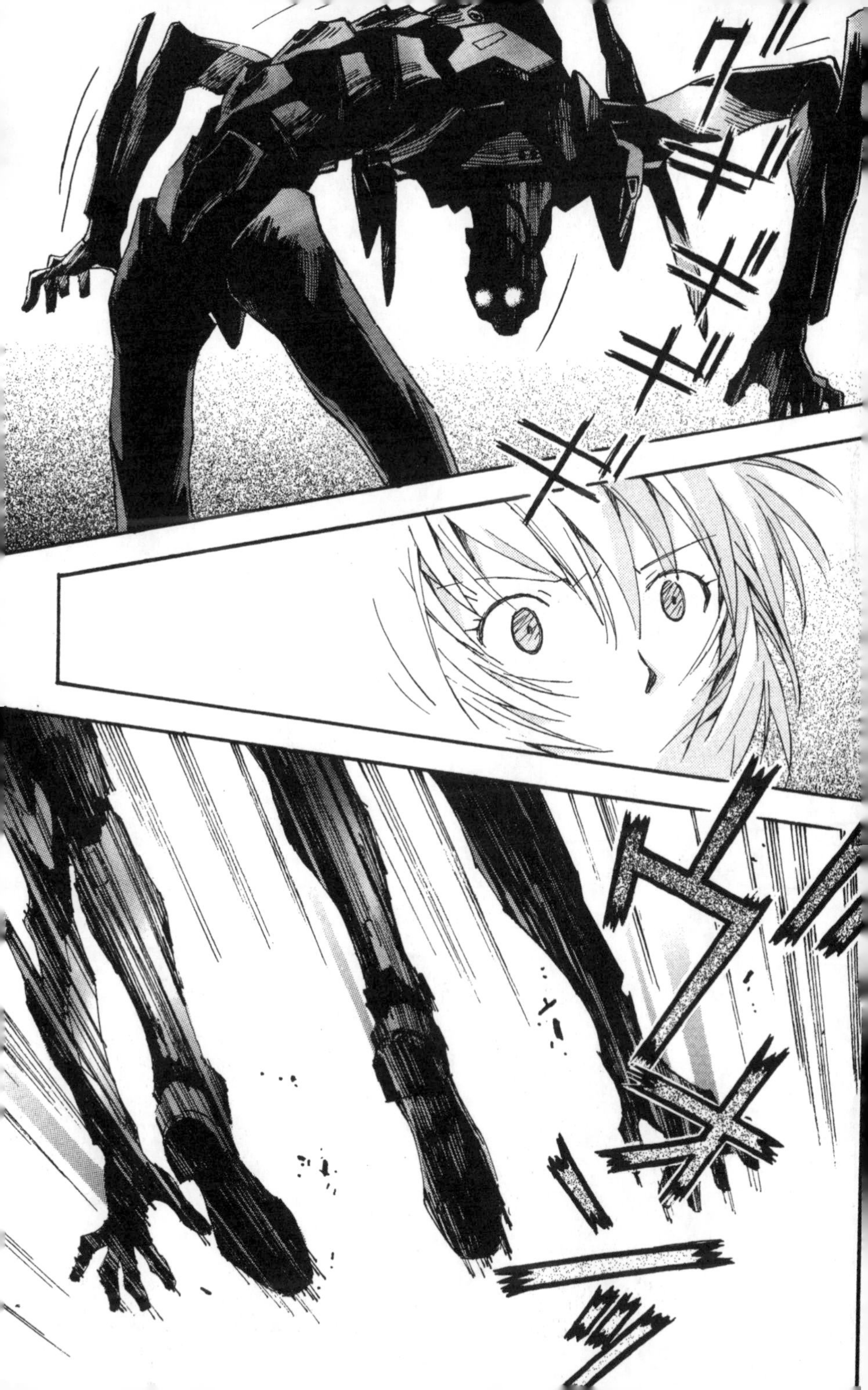
グギギギギ

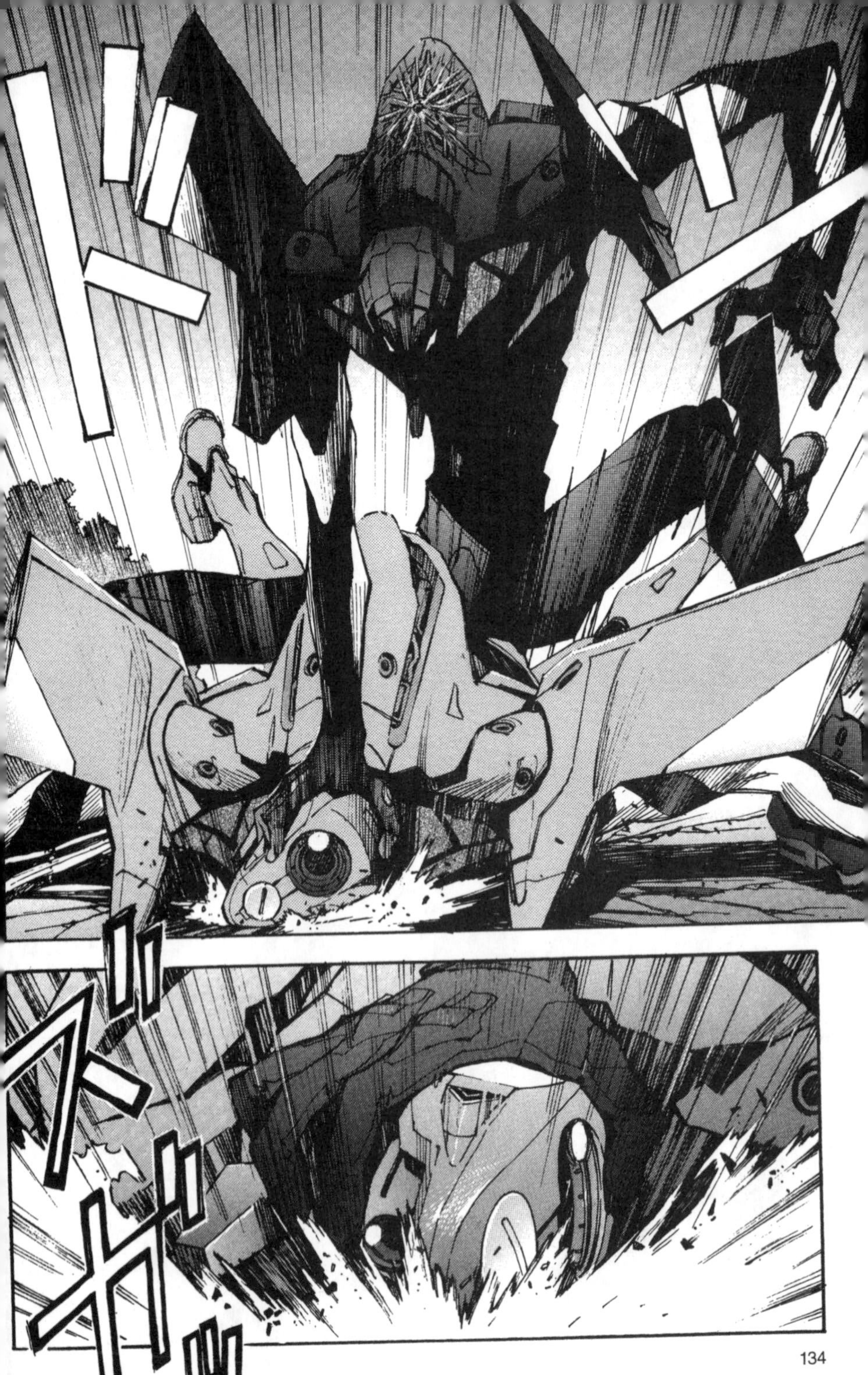
ズガッ

AH...?!

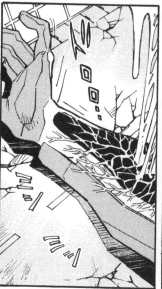

AH...

THE ANGEL HAS INVADED UNIT-00'S LEFT ARM!

PENE-TRATING NEURAL NODES!

AAAAAAARGH!

CUT IT!

I DON'T CARE.

THE NEURAL LINK'S IN PLACE!

BUT...!

SEVER UNIT-00'S LEFT ARM!

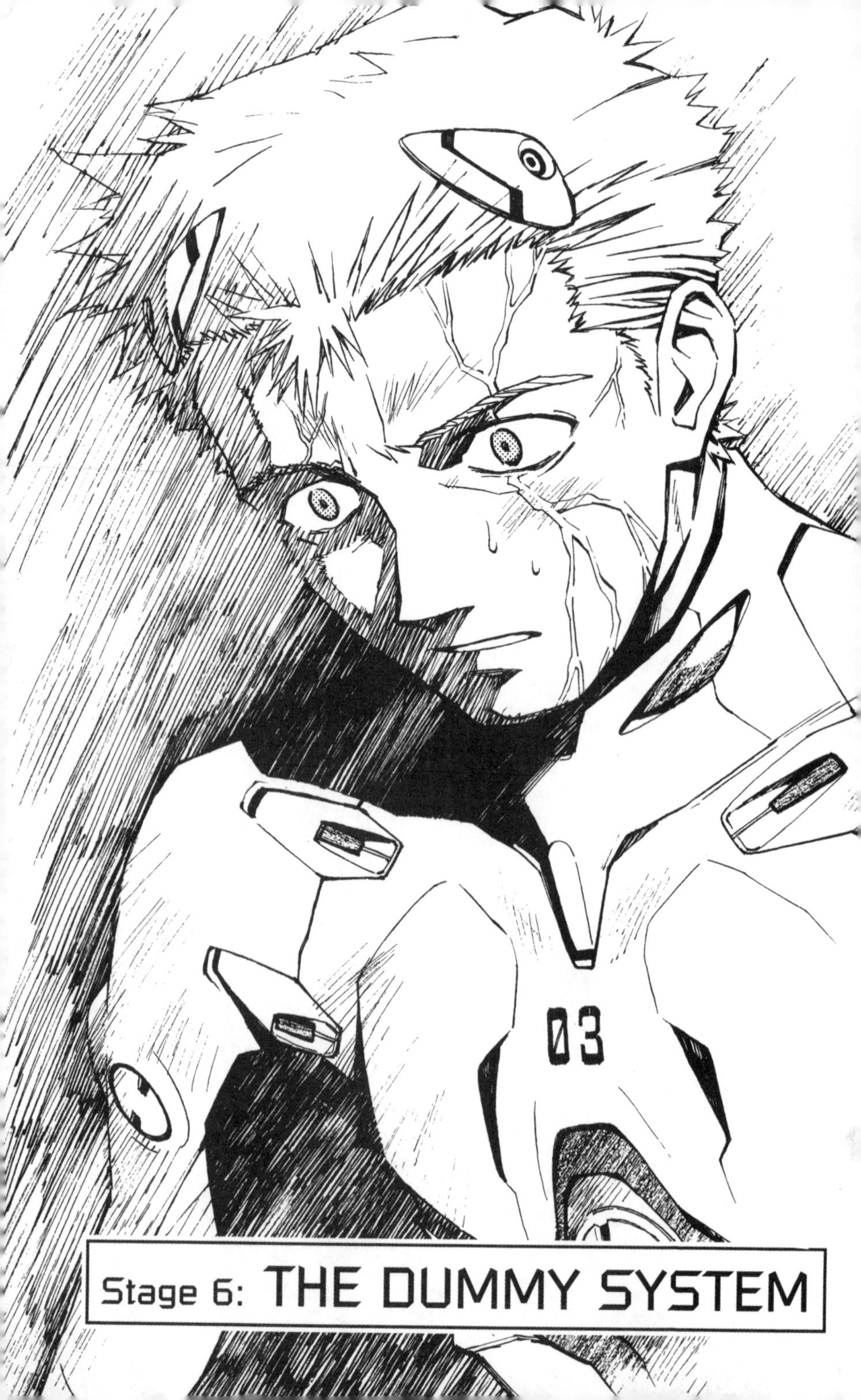
03

Stage 6: THE DUMMY SYSTEM

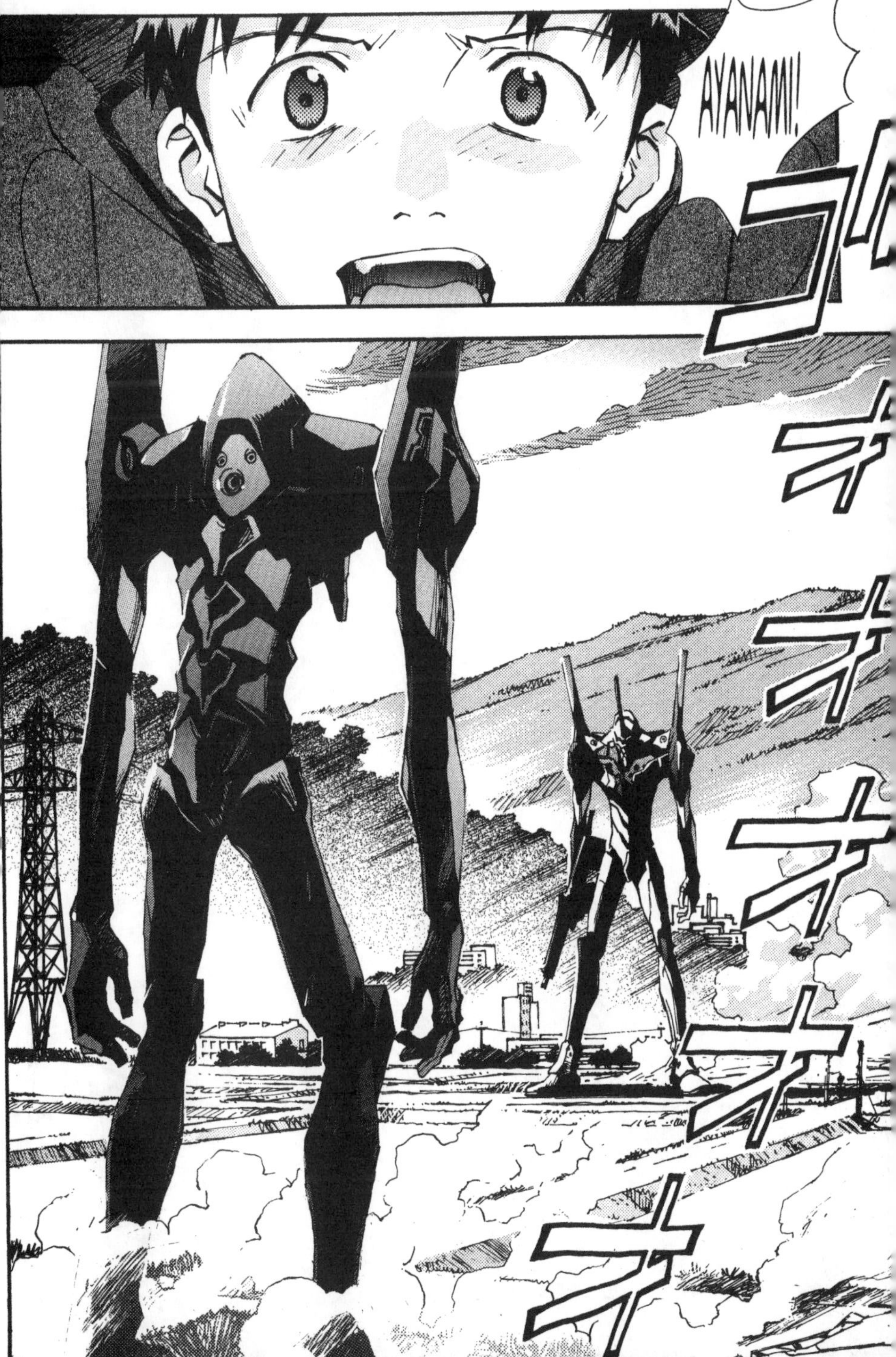
AYANAMI!
ゴオオオオオ

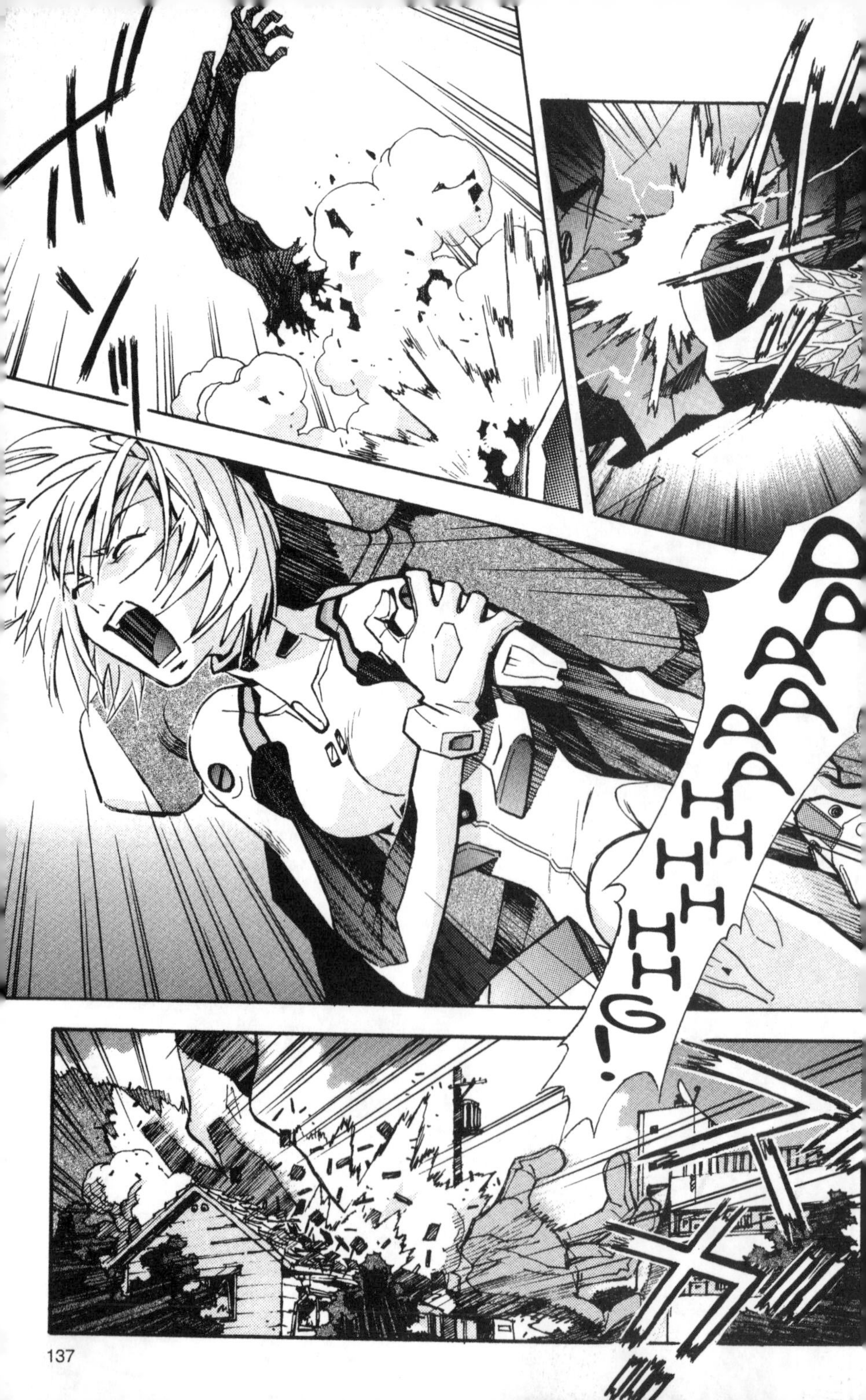
AAAAAAHHHHHHG!

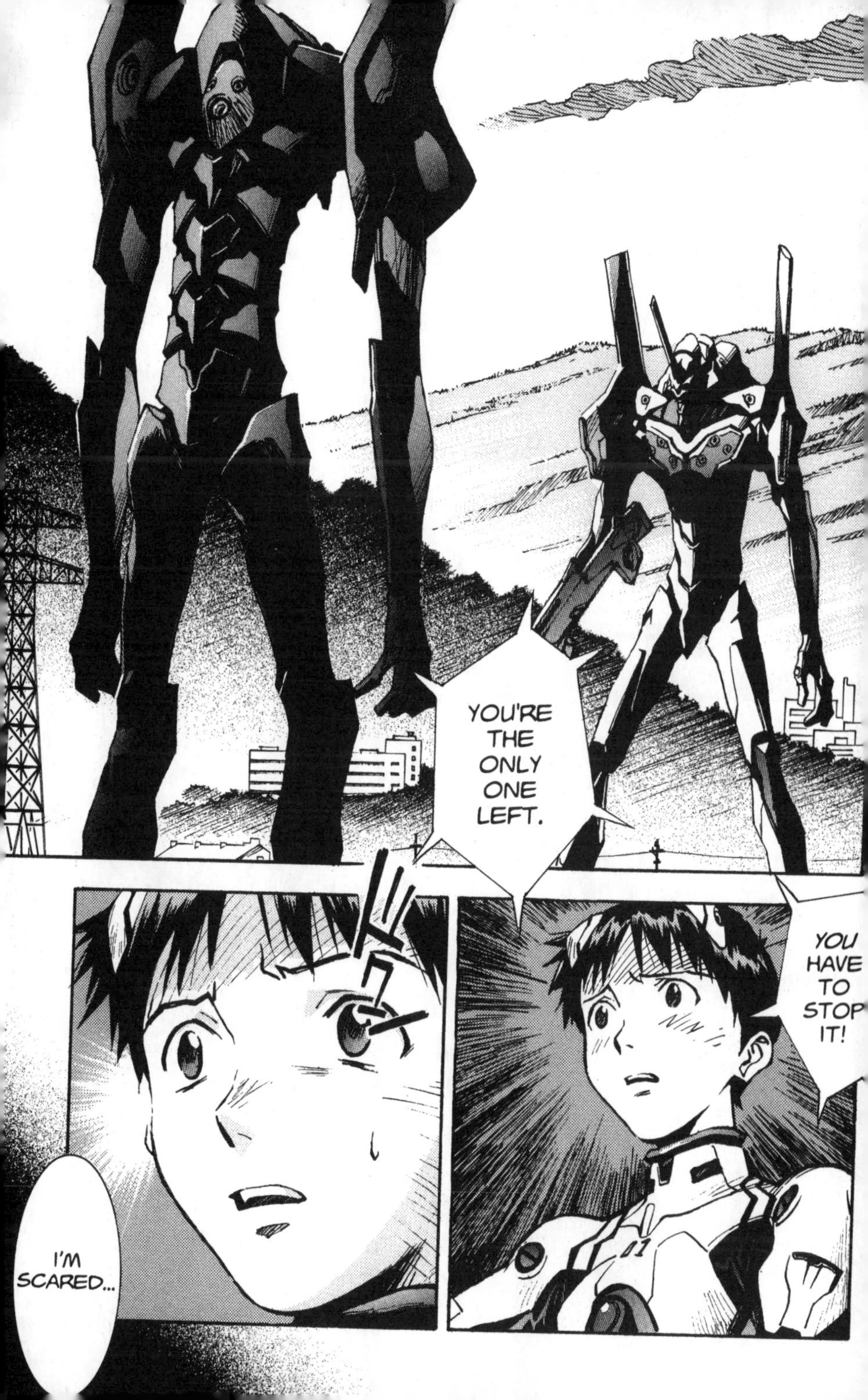
YOU'RE THE ONLY ONE LEFT.
YOU HAVE TO STOP IT!
I'M SCARED...

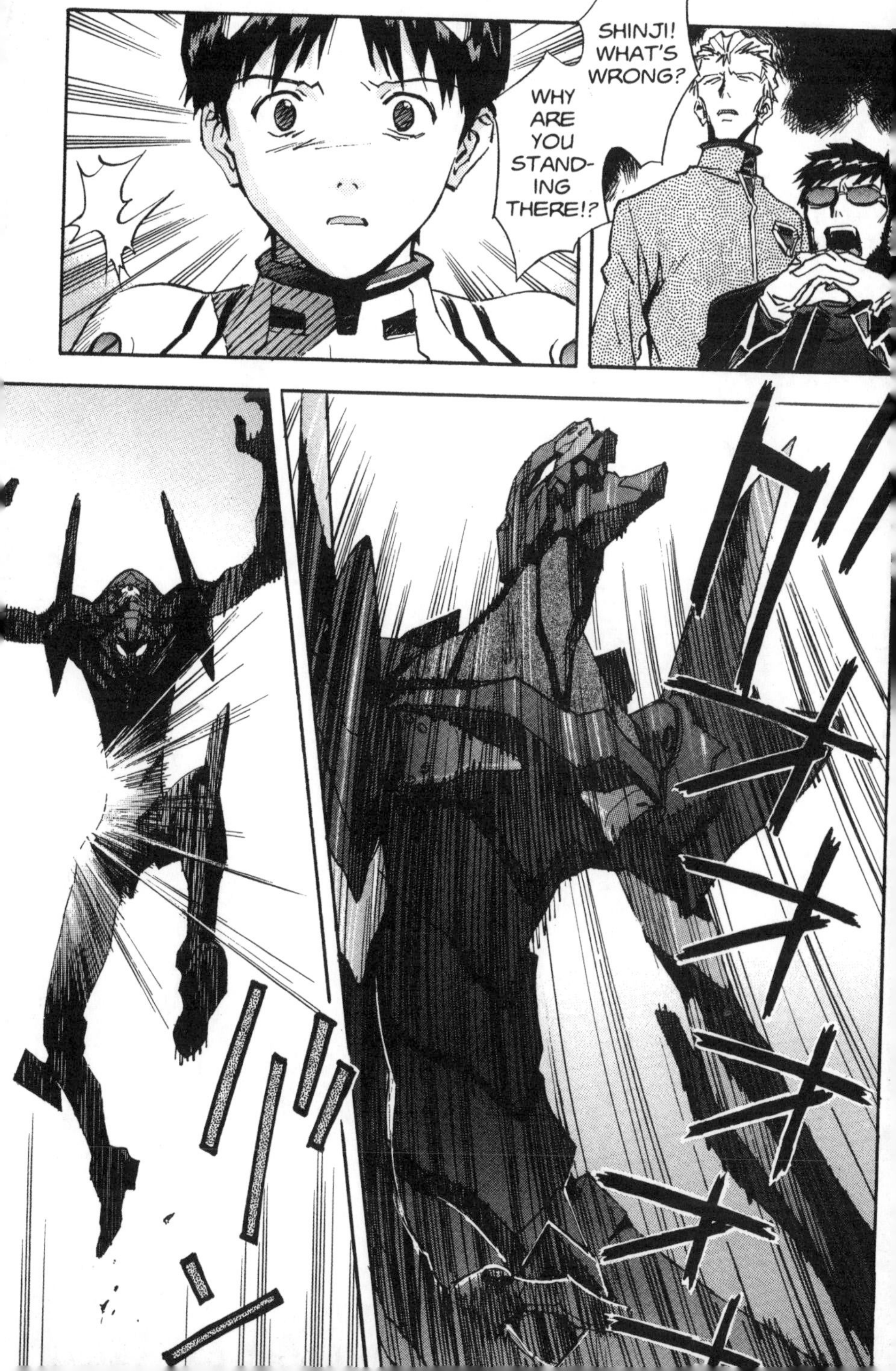
SHINJI! WHAT'S WRONG?
WHY ARE YOU STAND-ING THERE!?

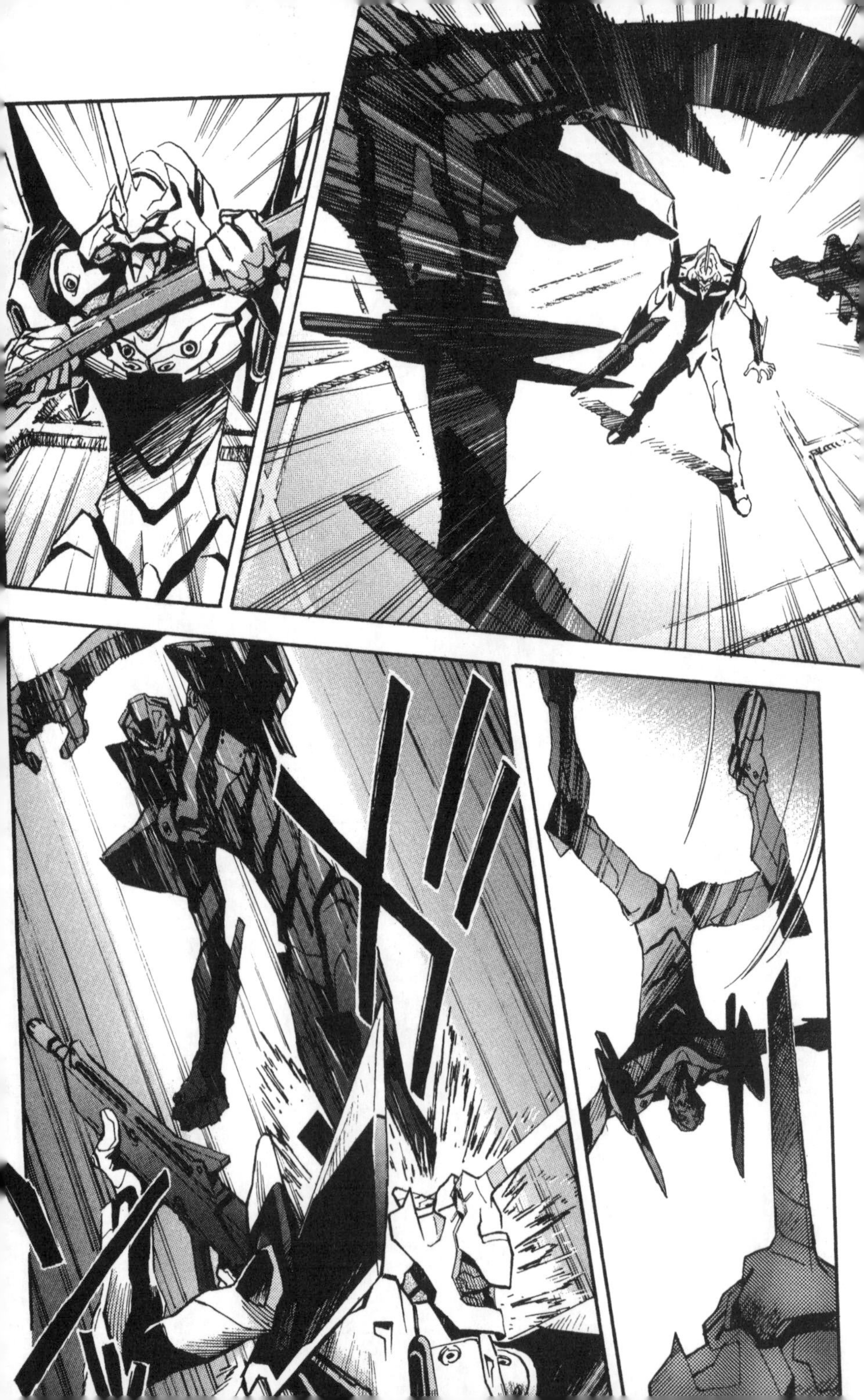

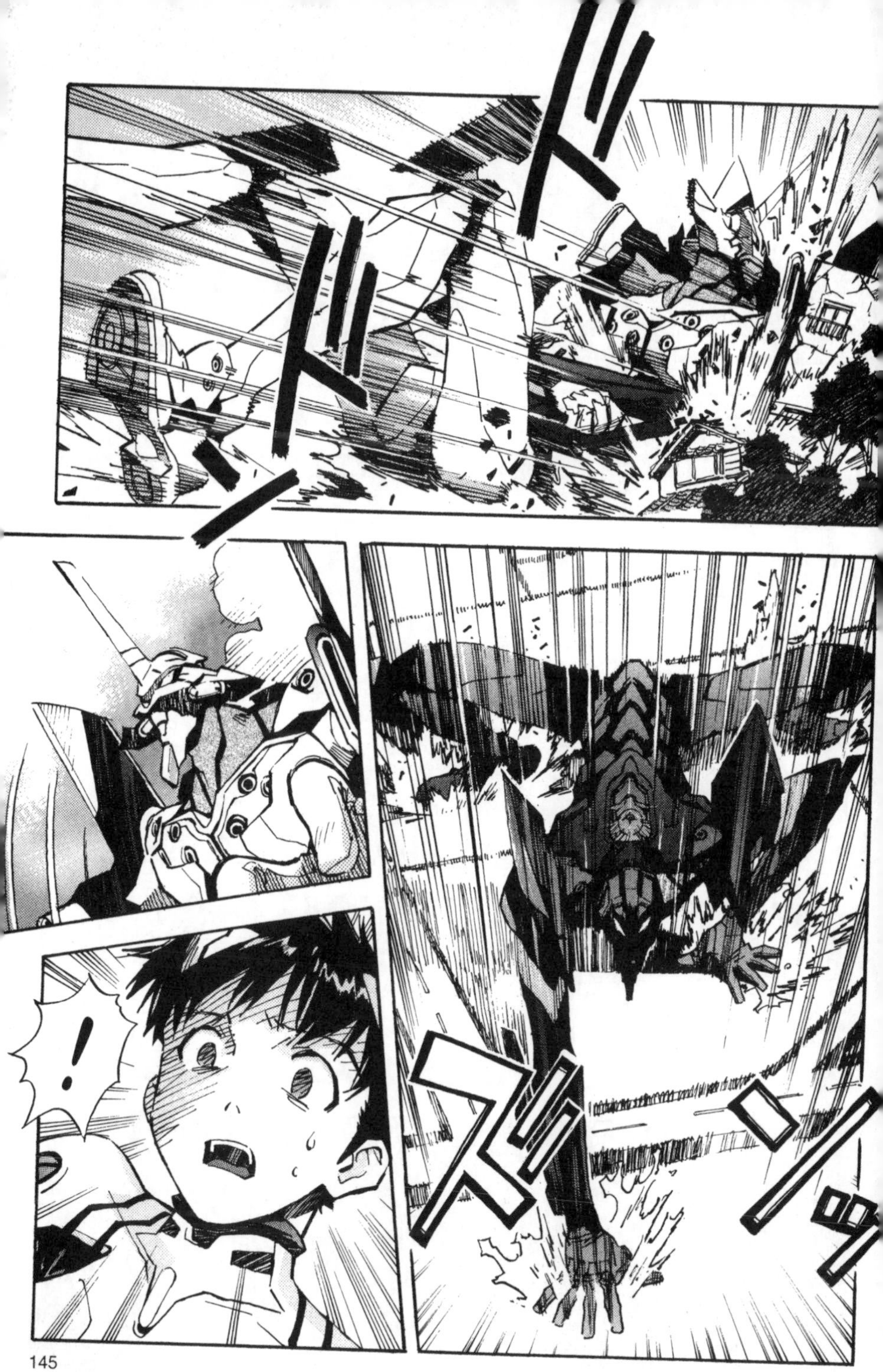
ドド
ズシーンッ
!

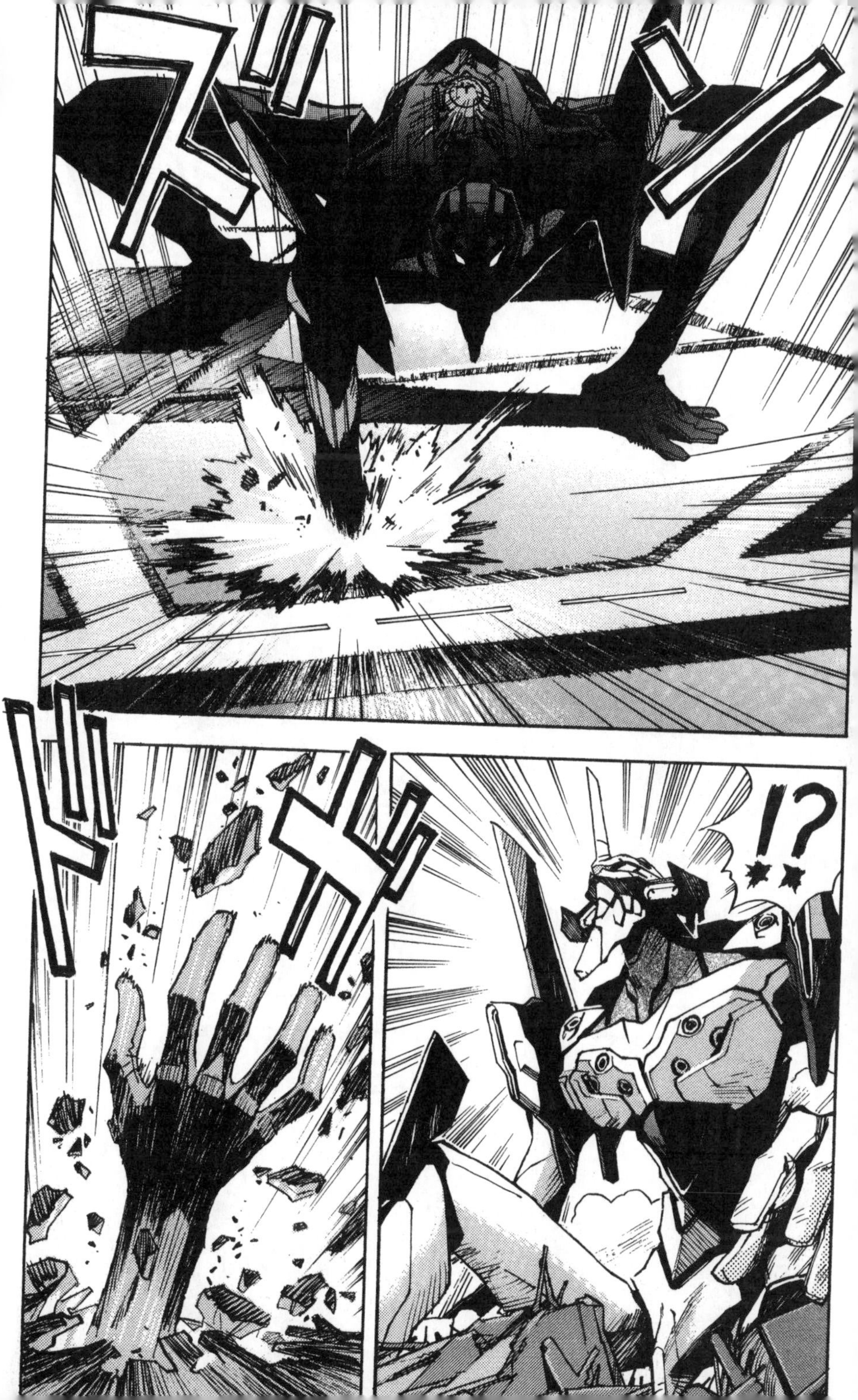
!?

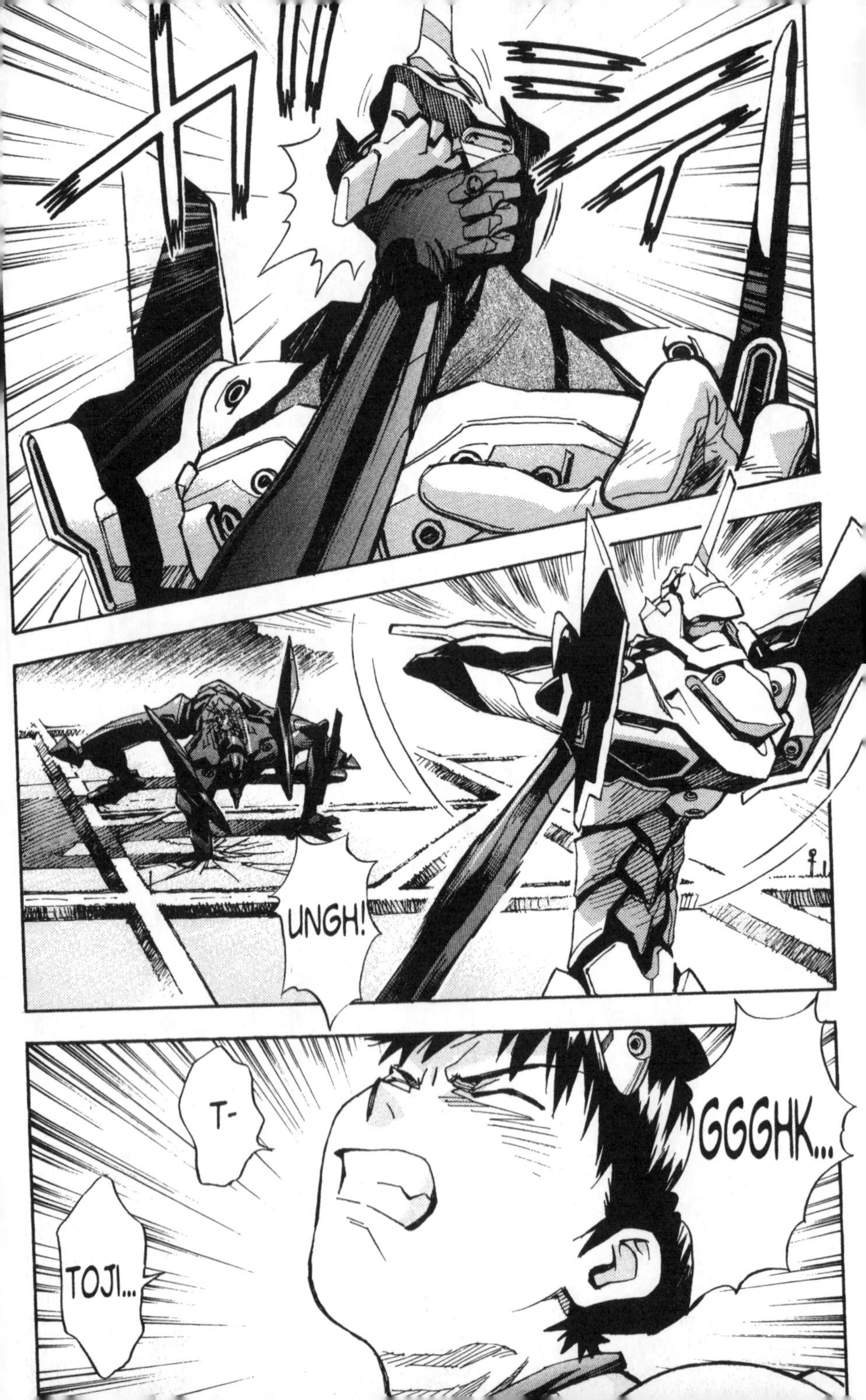
UNGH!
GGGHK...
T-
TOJI...

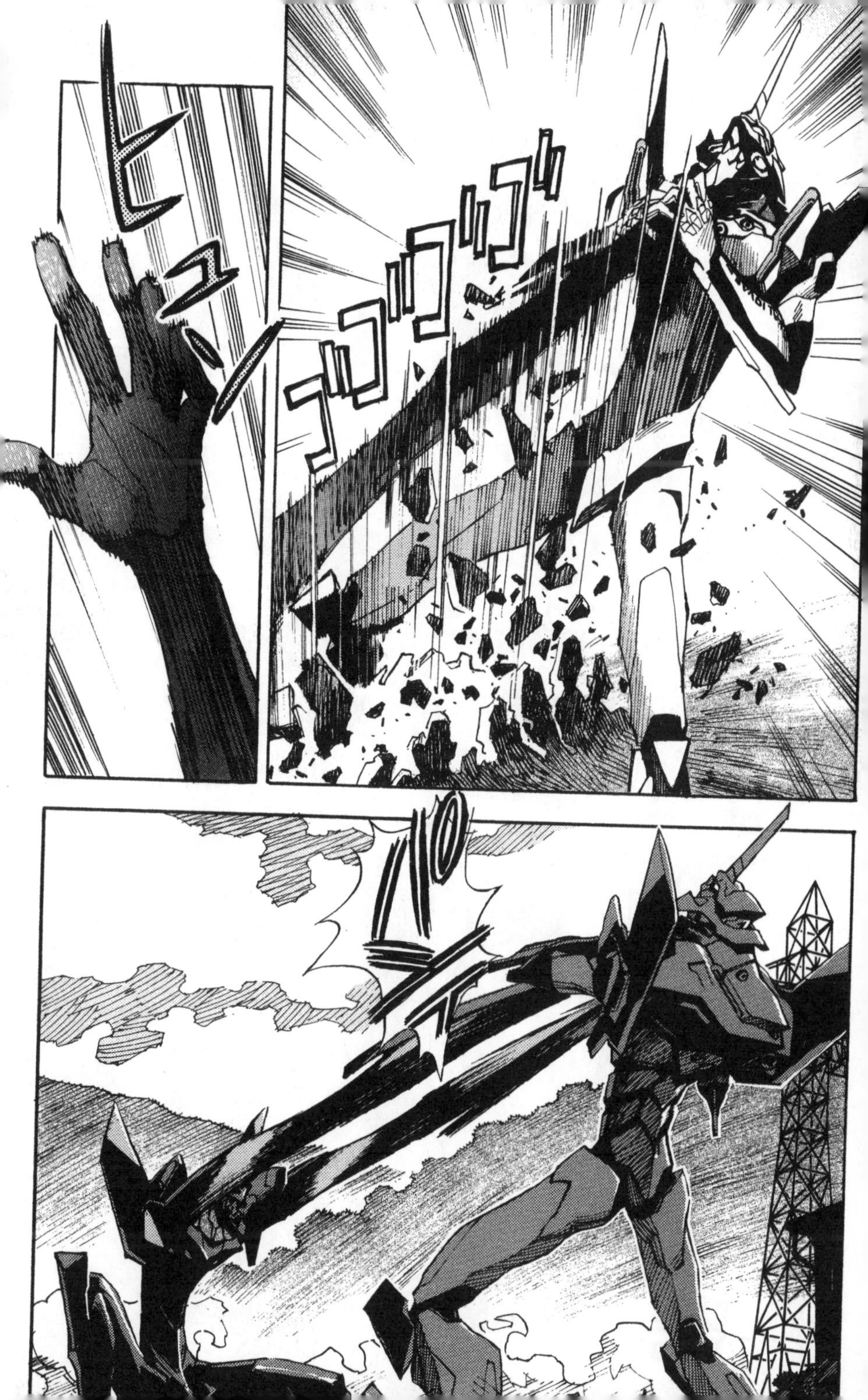
ゴゴゴゴゴ
ヒュッ
パッ

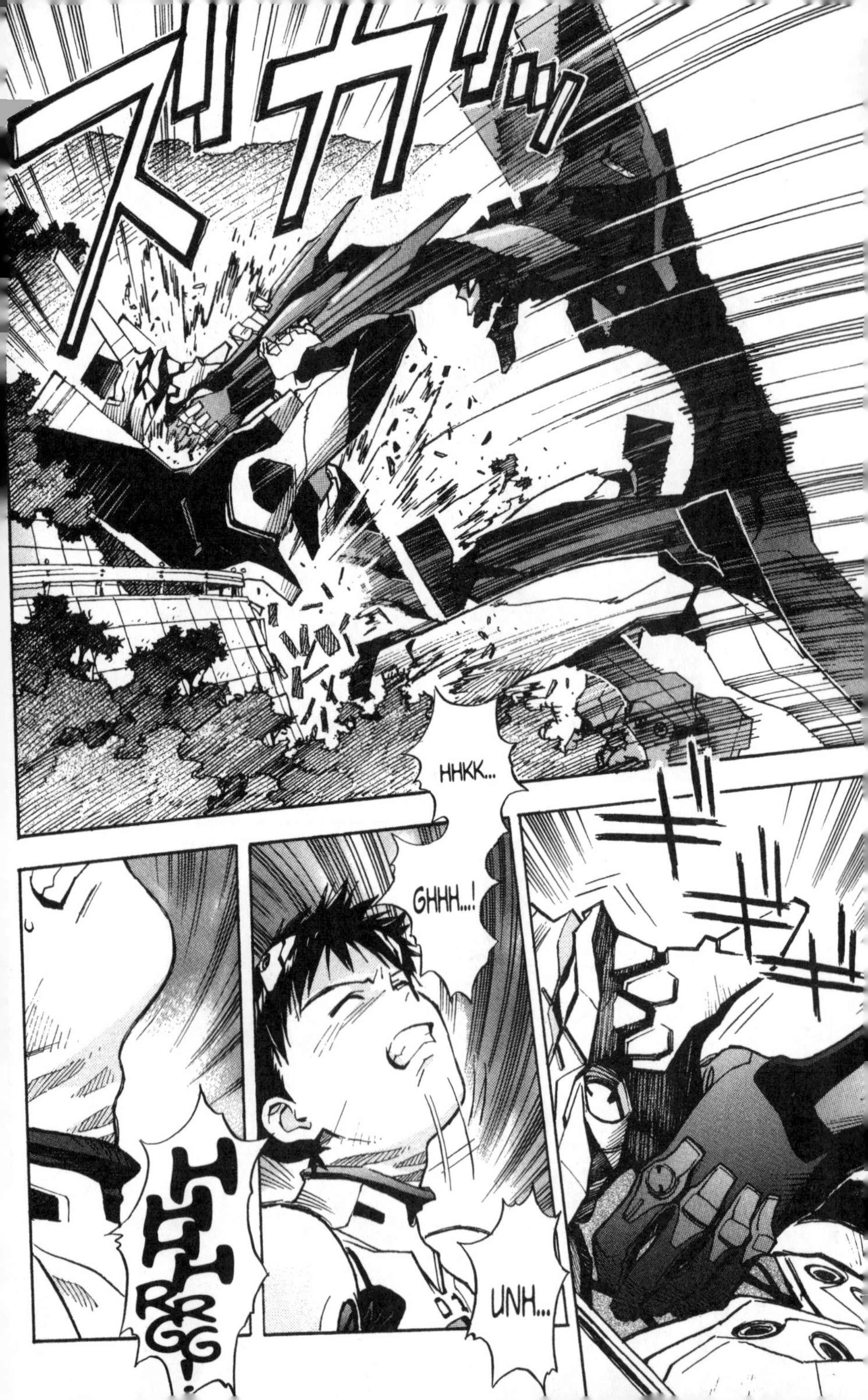
HHKK...
UNH...
GHHH...!
HNGRRGG!

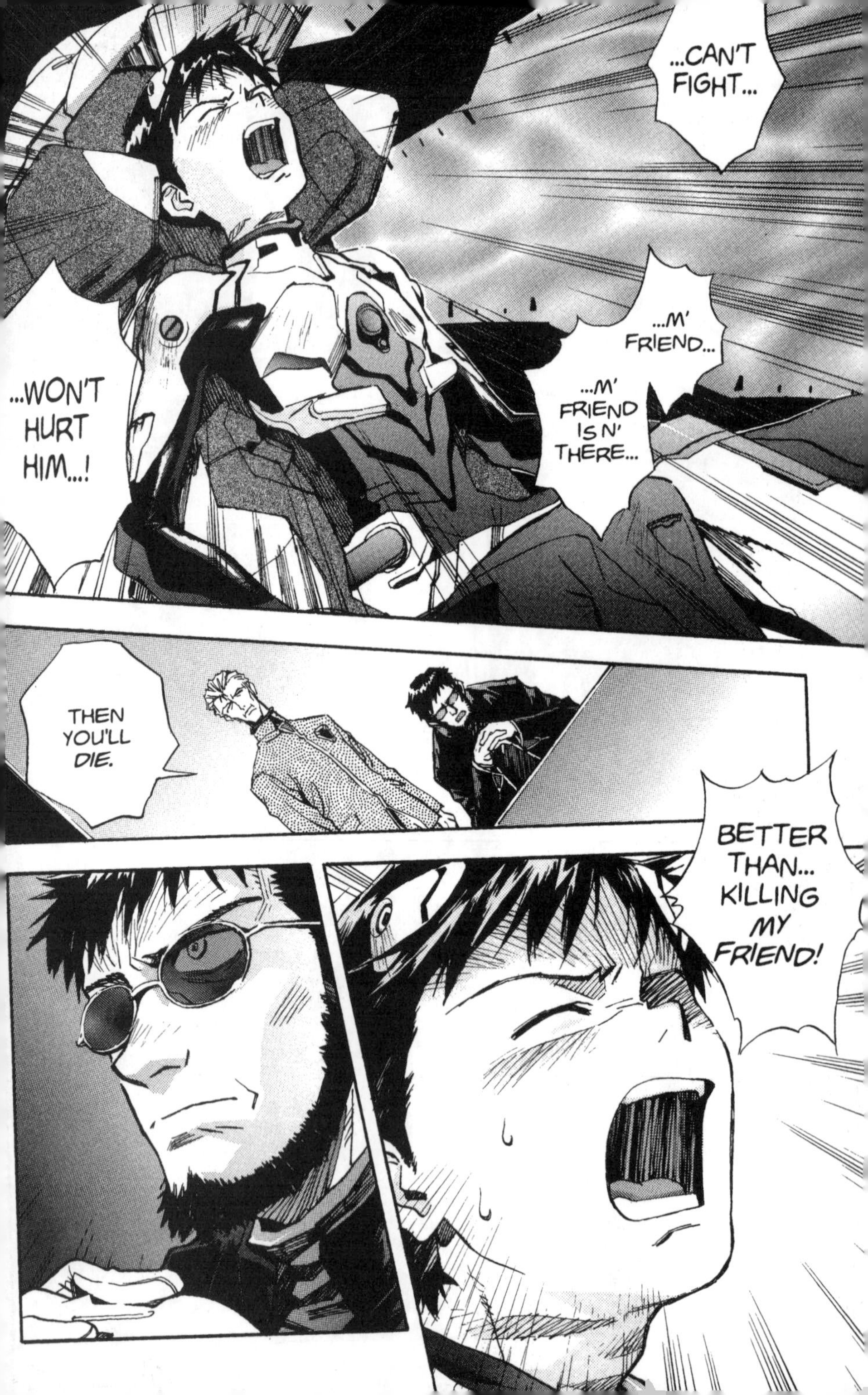
...CAN'T FIGHT...
...M' FRIEND...
...M' FRIEND IS N' THERE...
...WON'T HURT HIM...!
THEN YOU'LL DIE.
BETTER THAN... KILLING MY FRIEND!

CUT THE SYNCH BETWEEN UNIT-01 AND THE PILOT.

?!

SWITCH THE SYNCH CIRCUIT TO THE DUMMY SYSTEM.

...SIR?

"CUT...

DO IT.

CAN'T BE LESS USEFUL THAN OUR CURRENT PILOT.

THE DUMMY SYSTEM HASN'T BEEN DEBUGGED... AND DR. AKAGI IS...ISN'T... HERE RIGHT NOW...

BUT SIR!

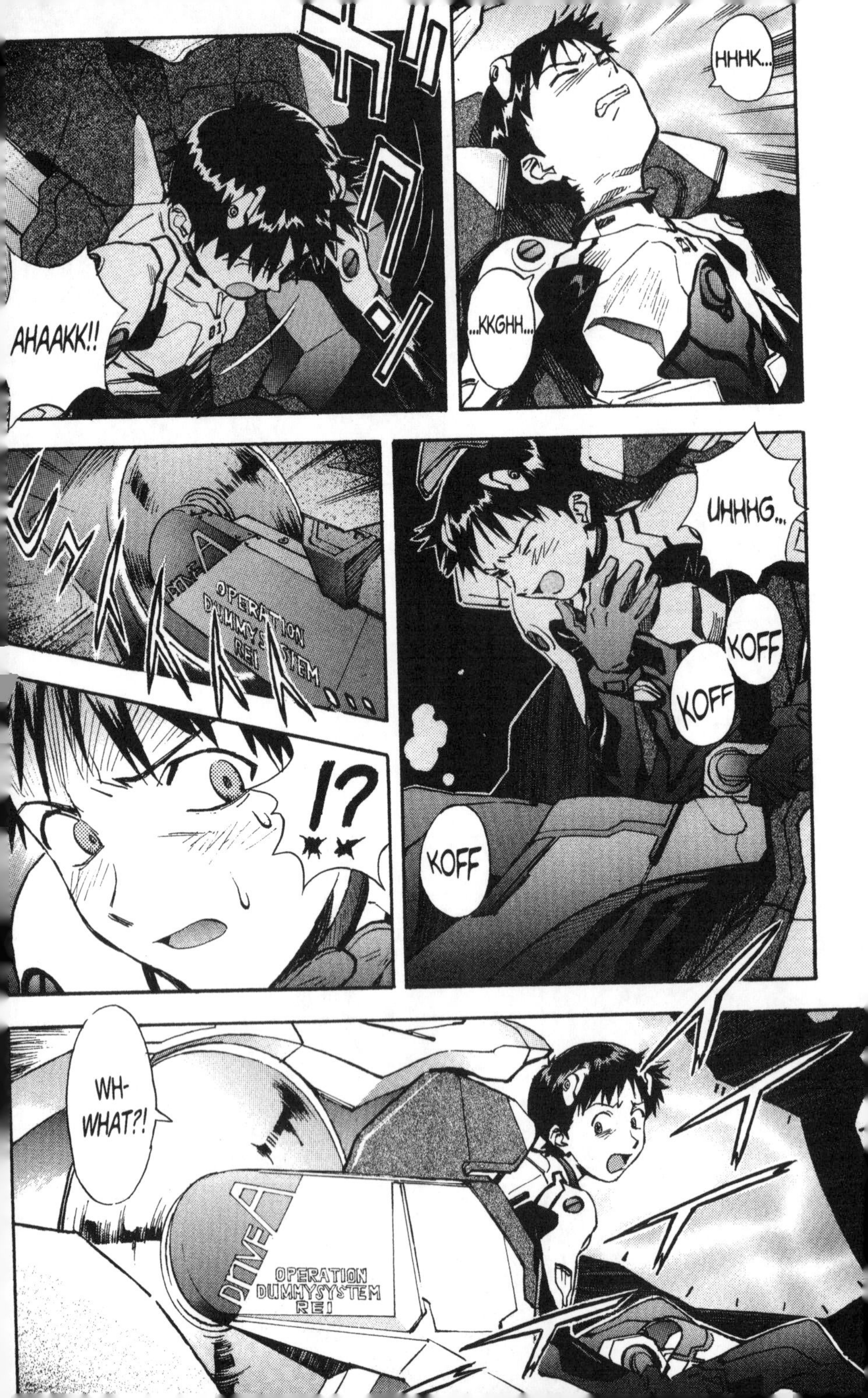
HHHK...
...KKGHH...
AHAAKK!!
UHHHG...
KOFF
KOFF
KOFF
OPERATION DUMMYSYSTEM REI
!?
WH- WHAT?!
OPERATION DUMMYSYSTEM REI

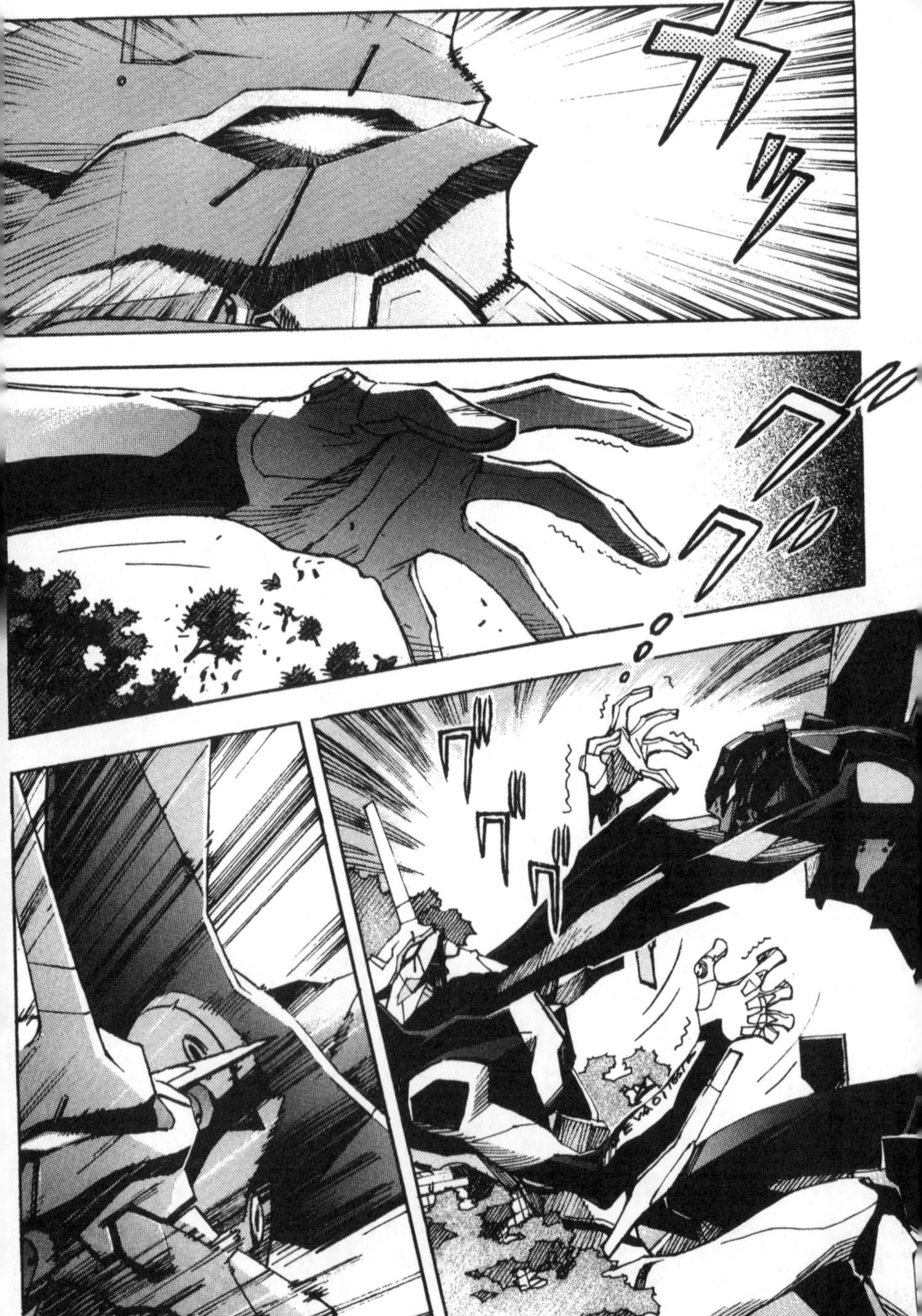
カッ
ググ

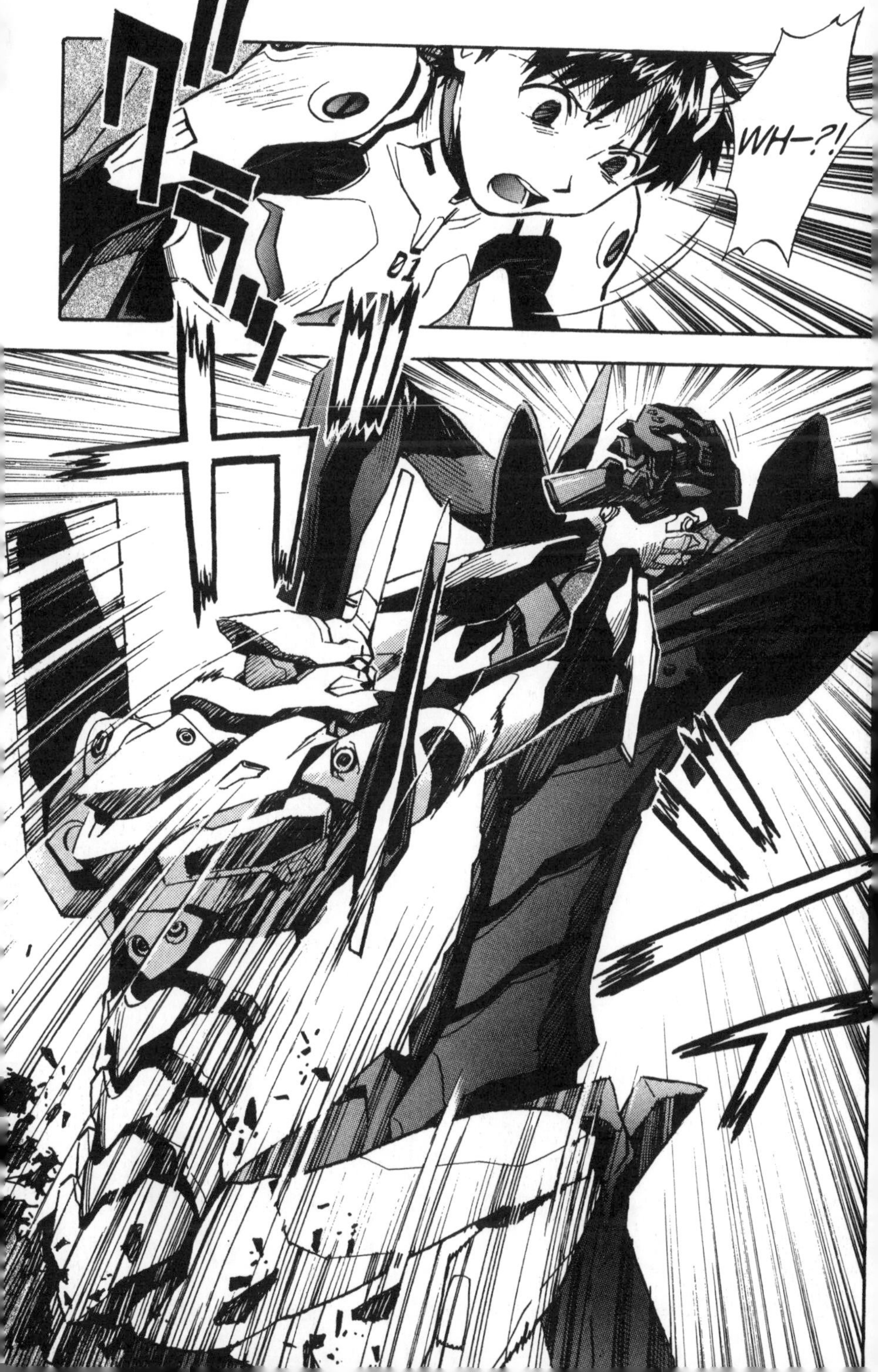
WH–?!

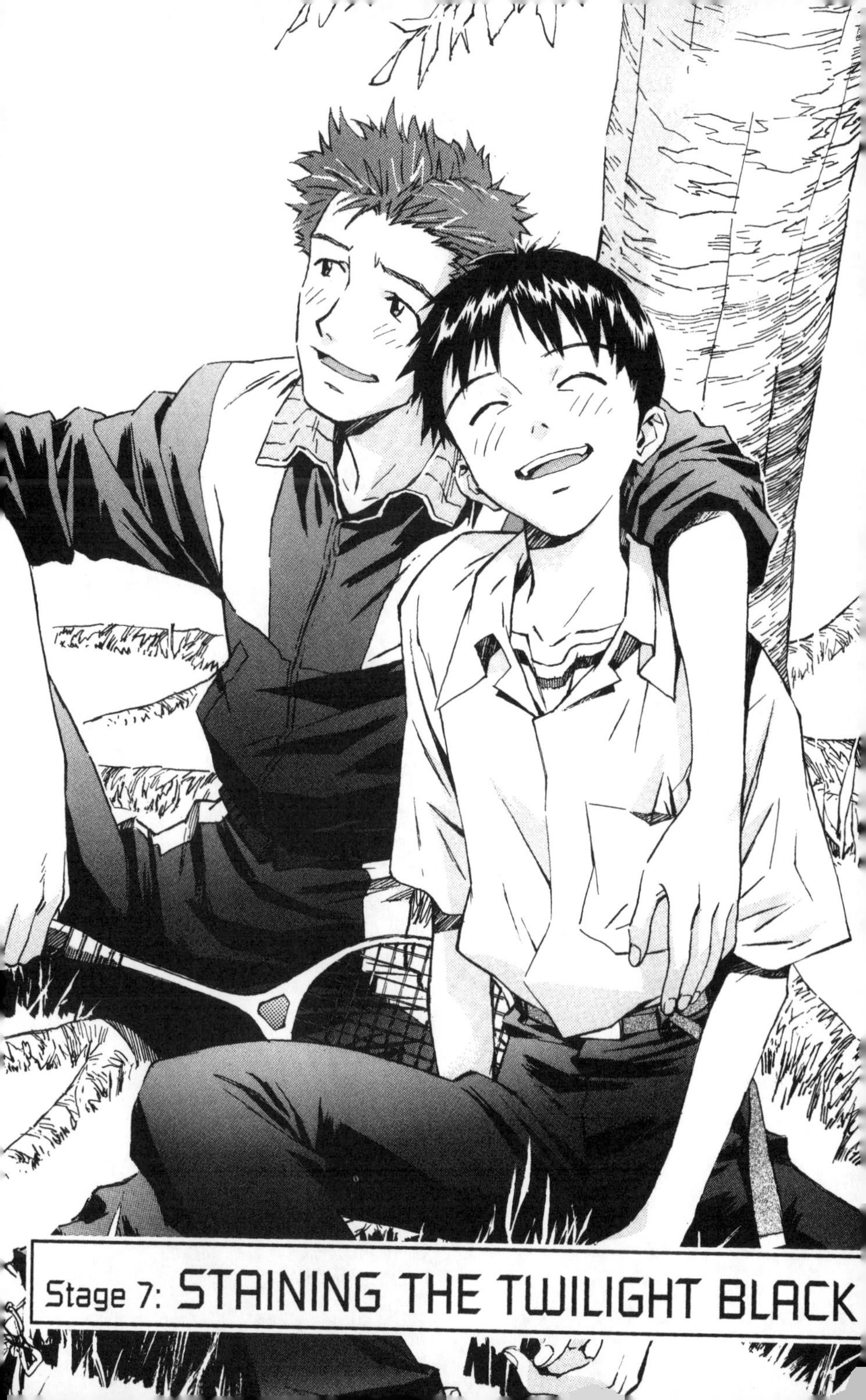
Stage 7: STAINING THE TWILIGHT BLACK

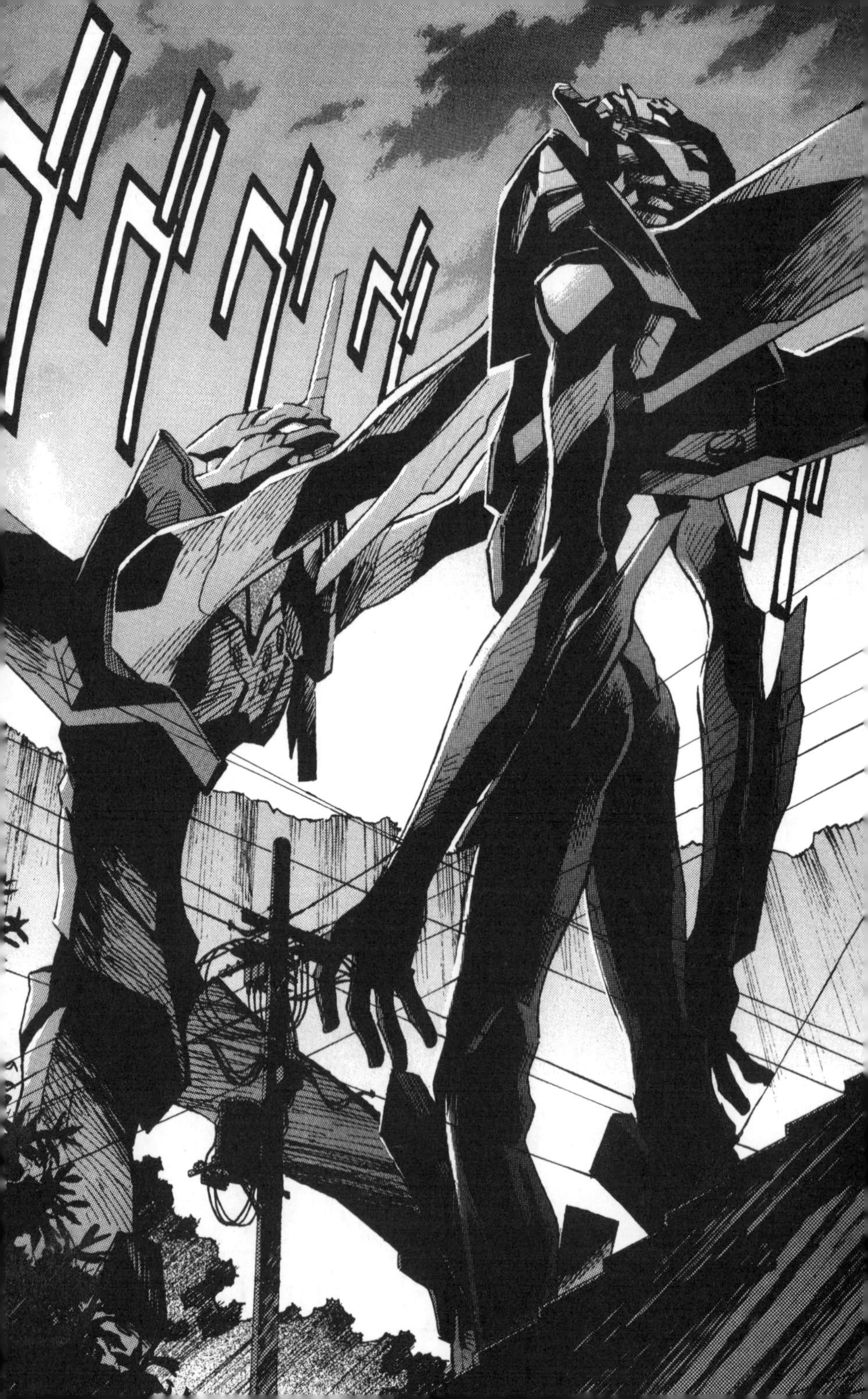

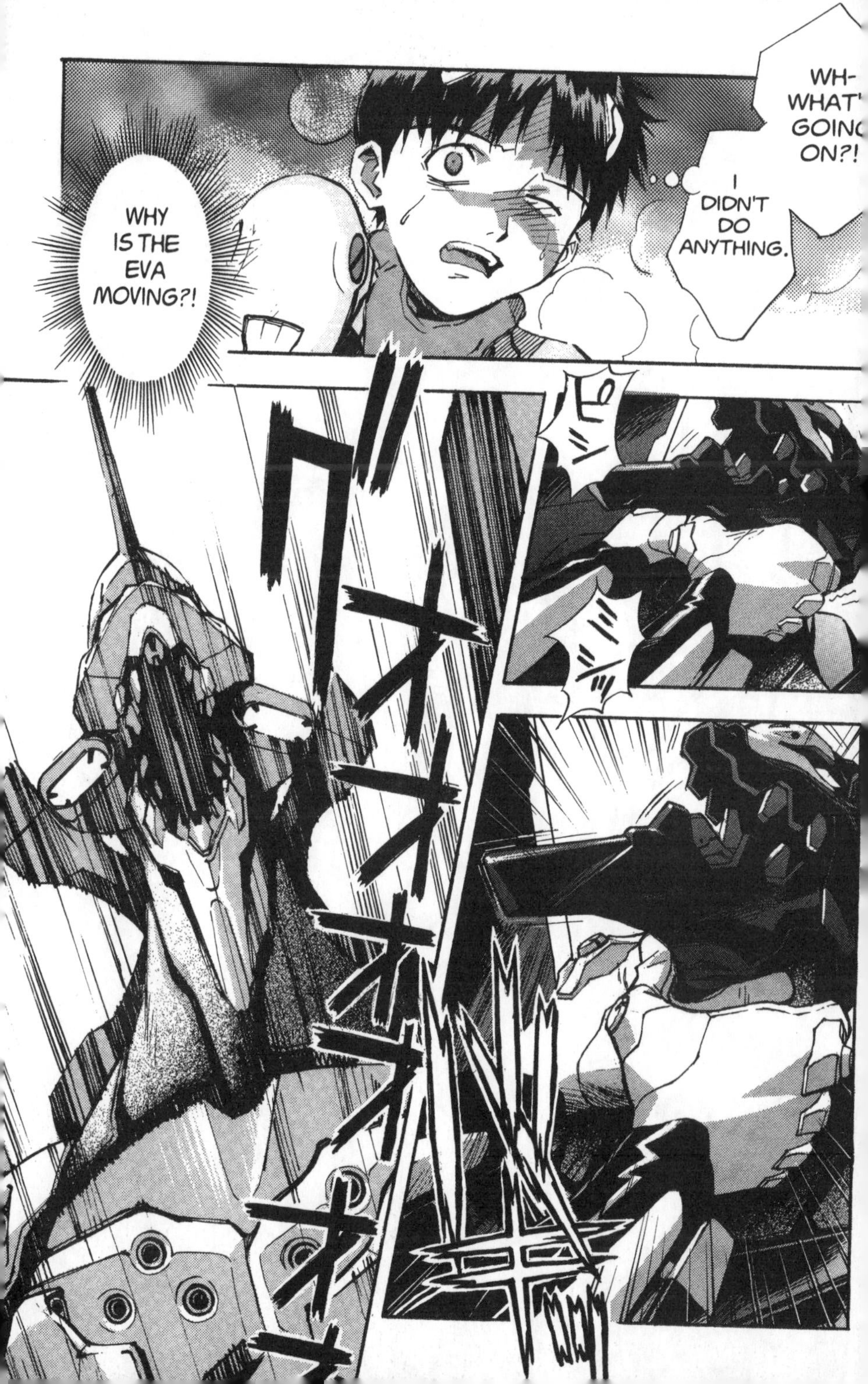
WH- WHAT' GOIN ON?!
I DIDN'T DO ANYTHING.
WHY IS THE EVA MOVING?!

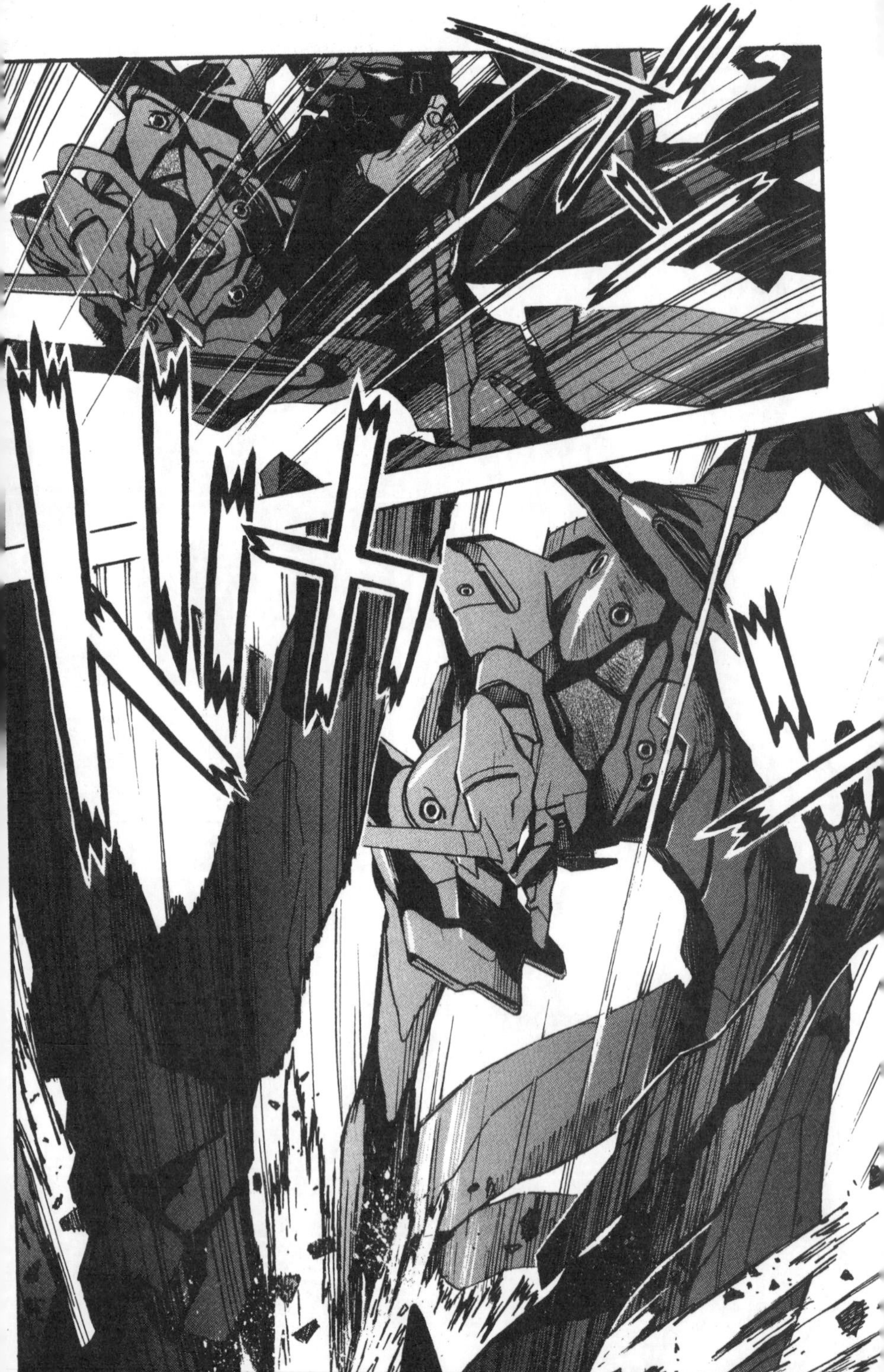

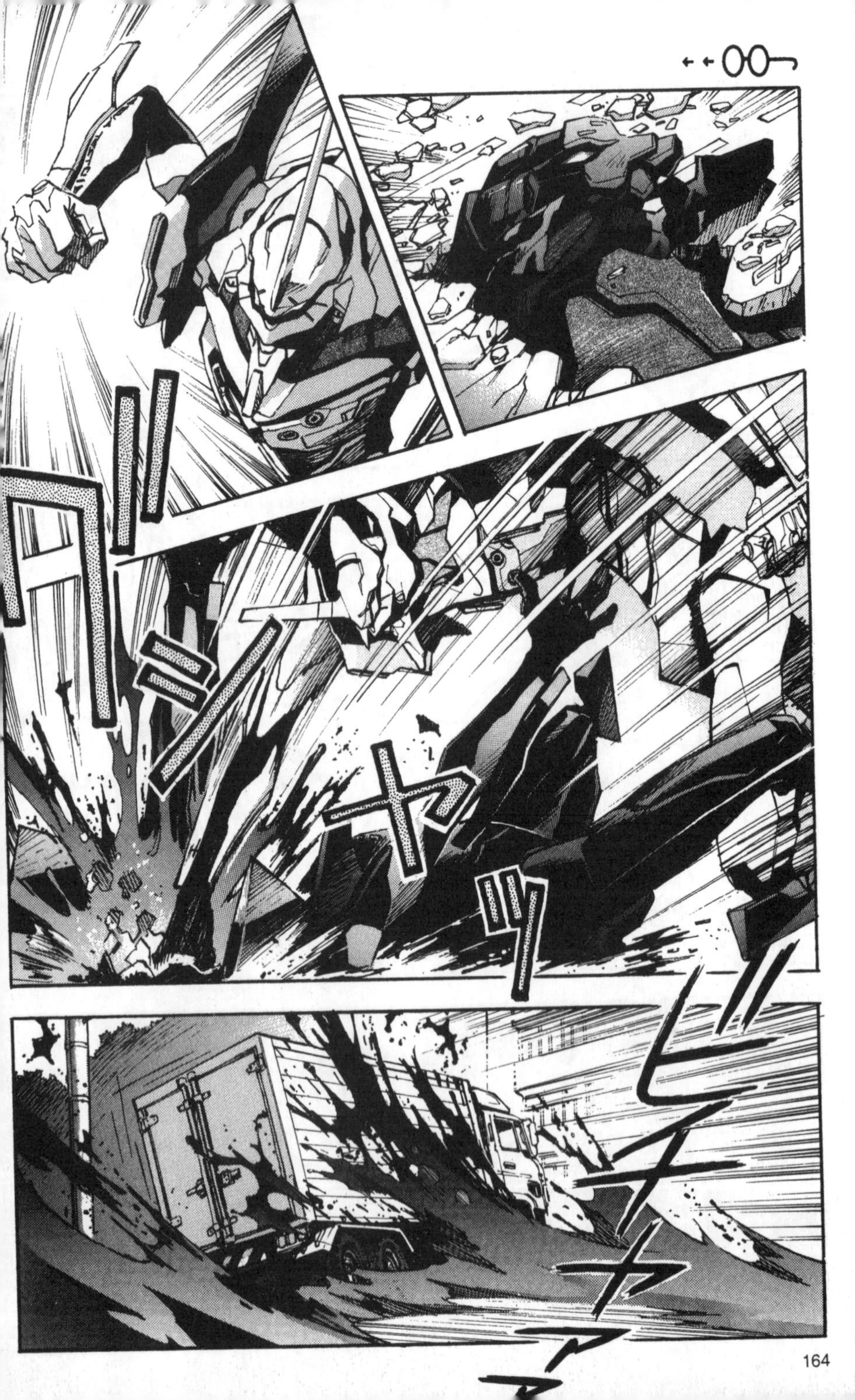

THIS IS THE DUMMY SYSTEM...

IT...

URP.

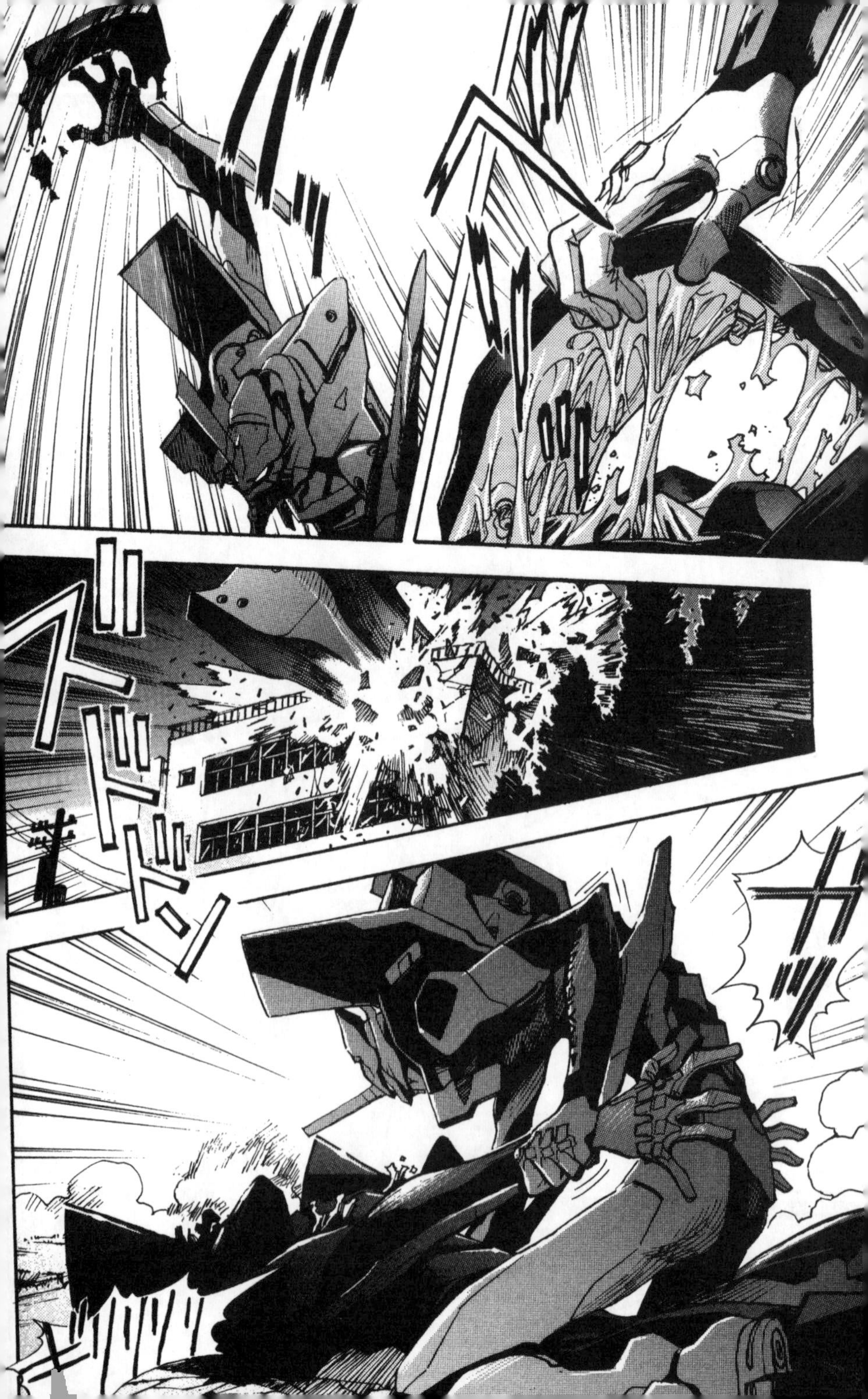
ズドドドッ
ガッ

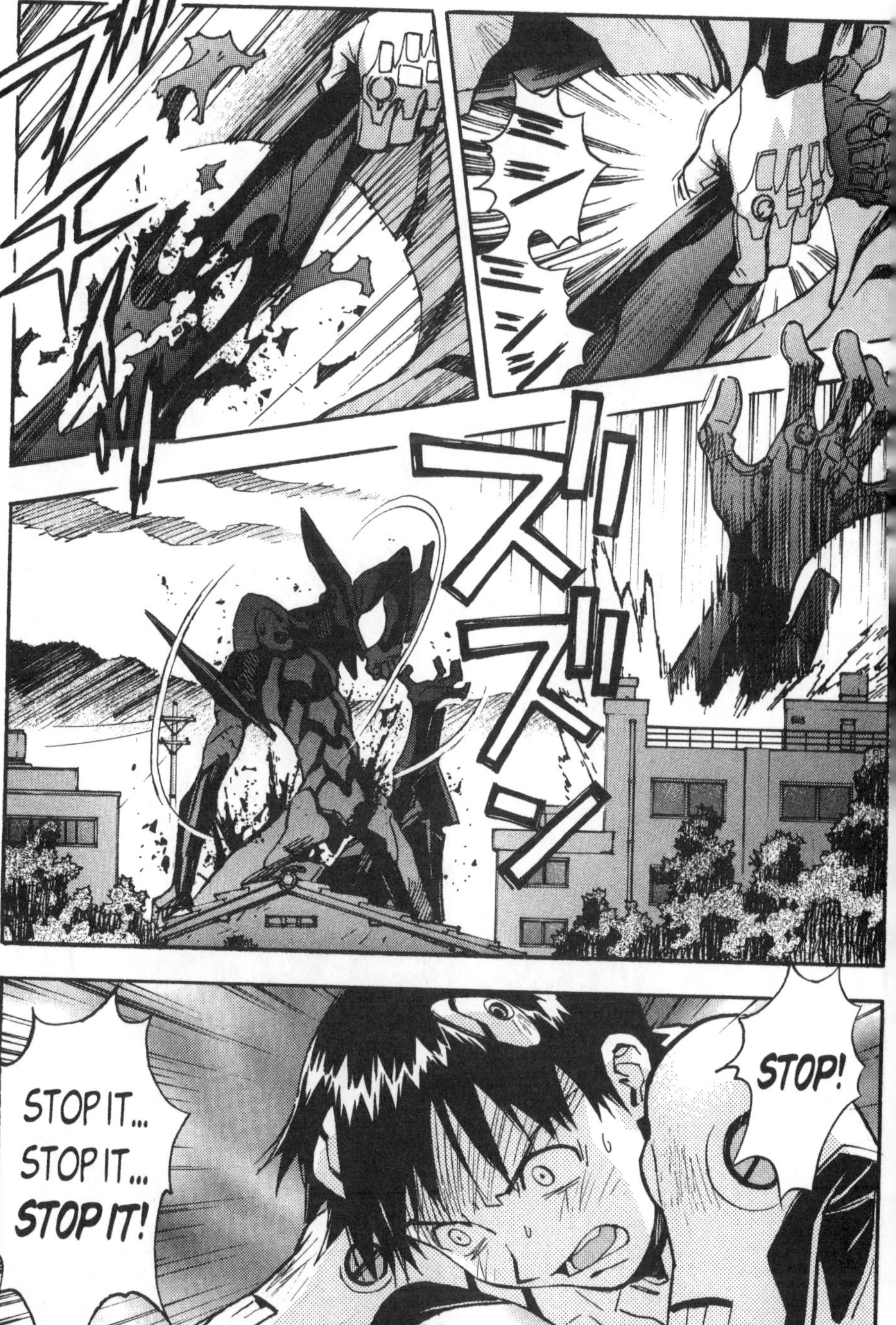
STOP!
STOP IT...
STOP IT...
STOP IT!

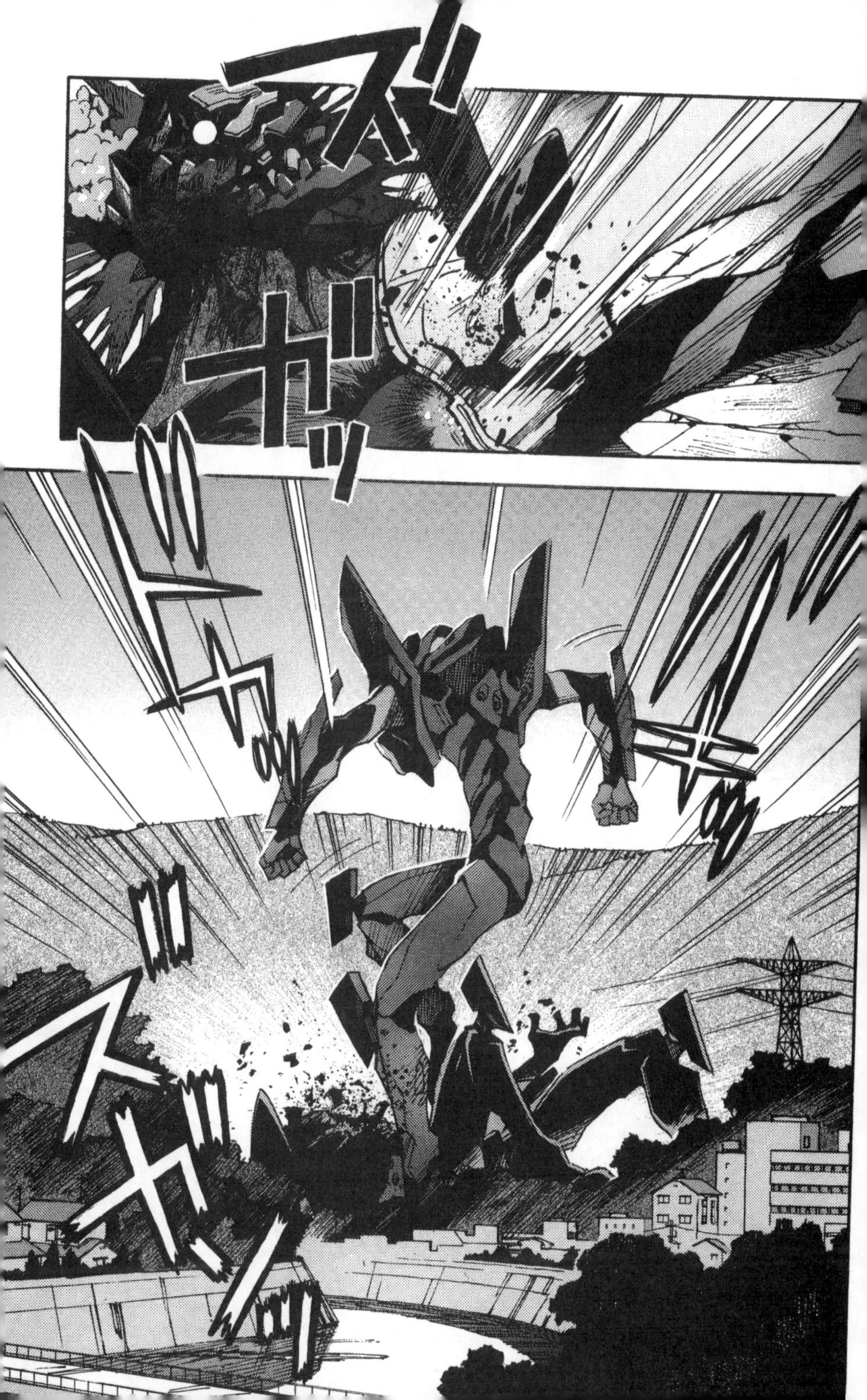
ズガッ
ビュッ
ビュッ
ズザッ

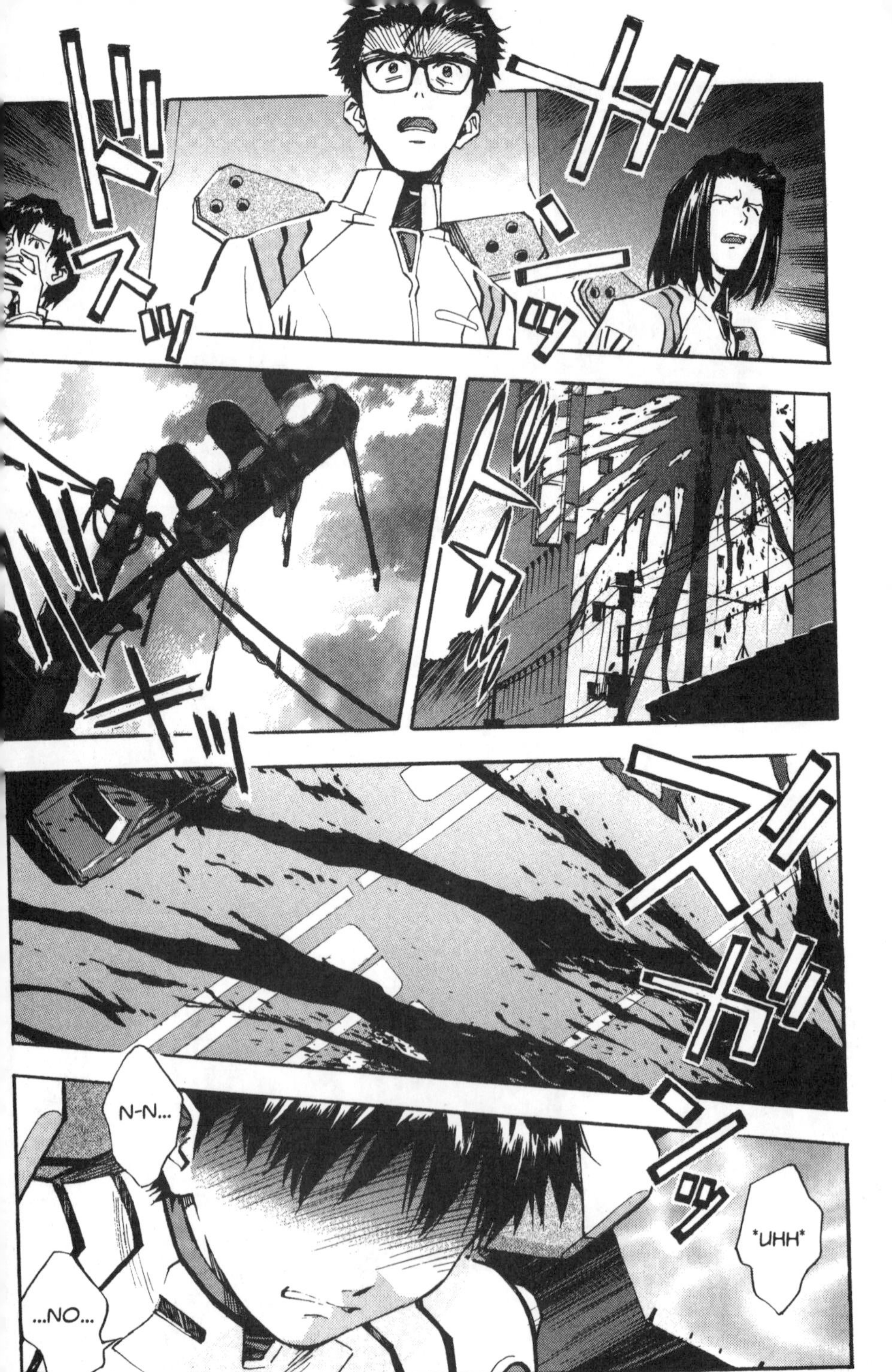
UHH
N-N...
...NO...

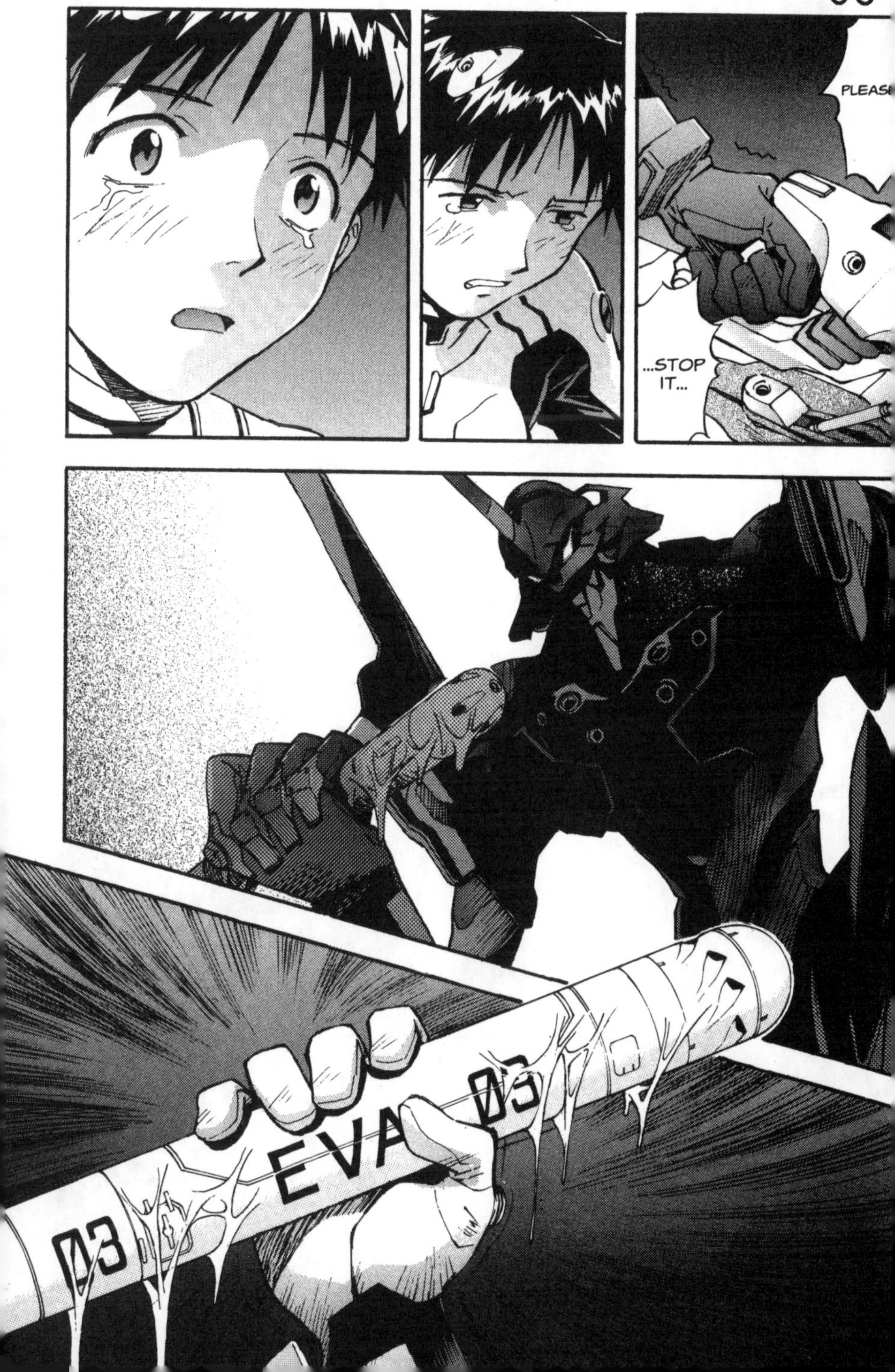
...STOP IT...
EVA 03
03

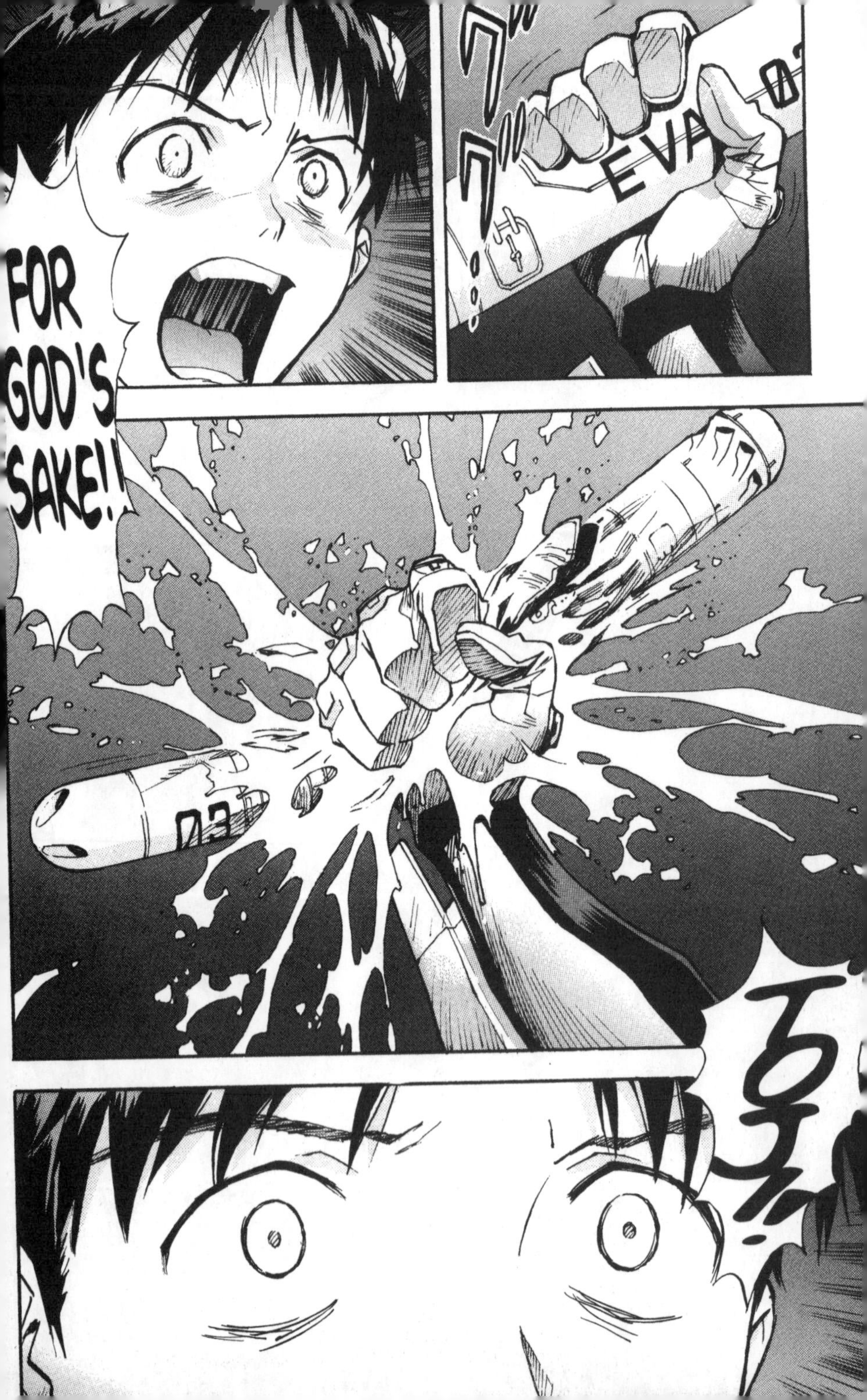
EVA
FOR GOD'S SAKE!!
03

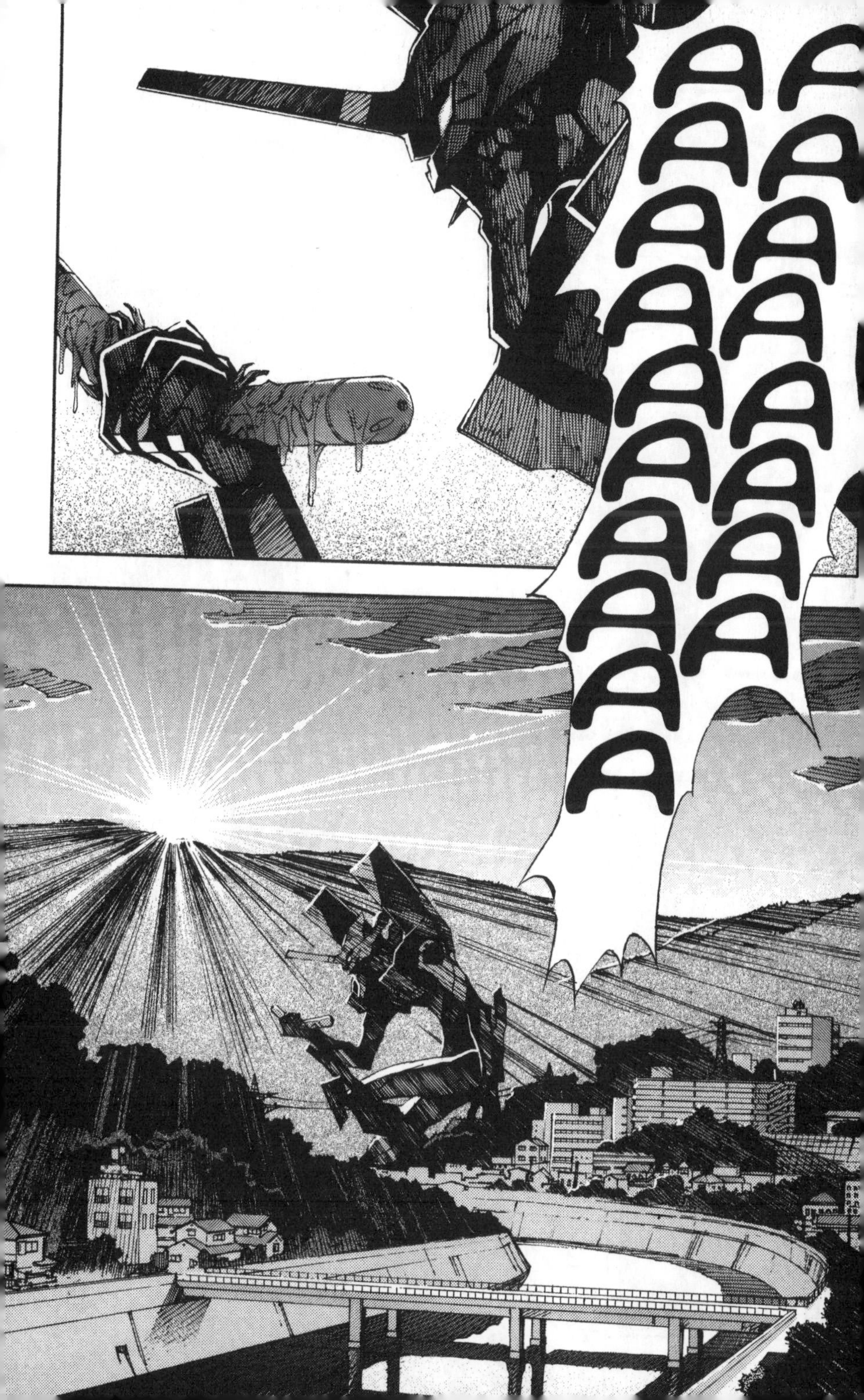
AAAAAAAAAAAAAAAAAAAA

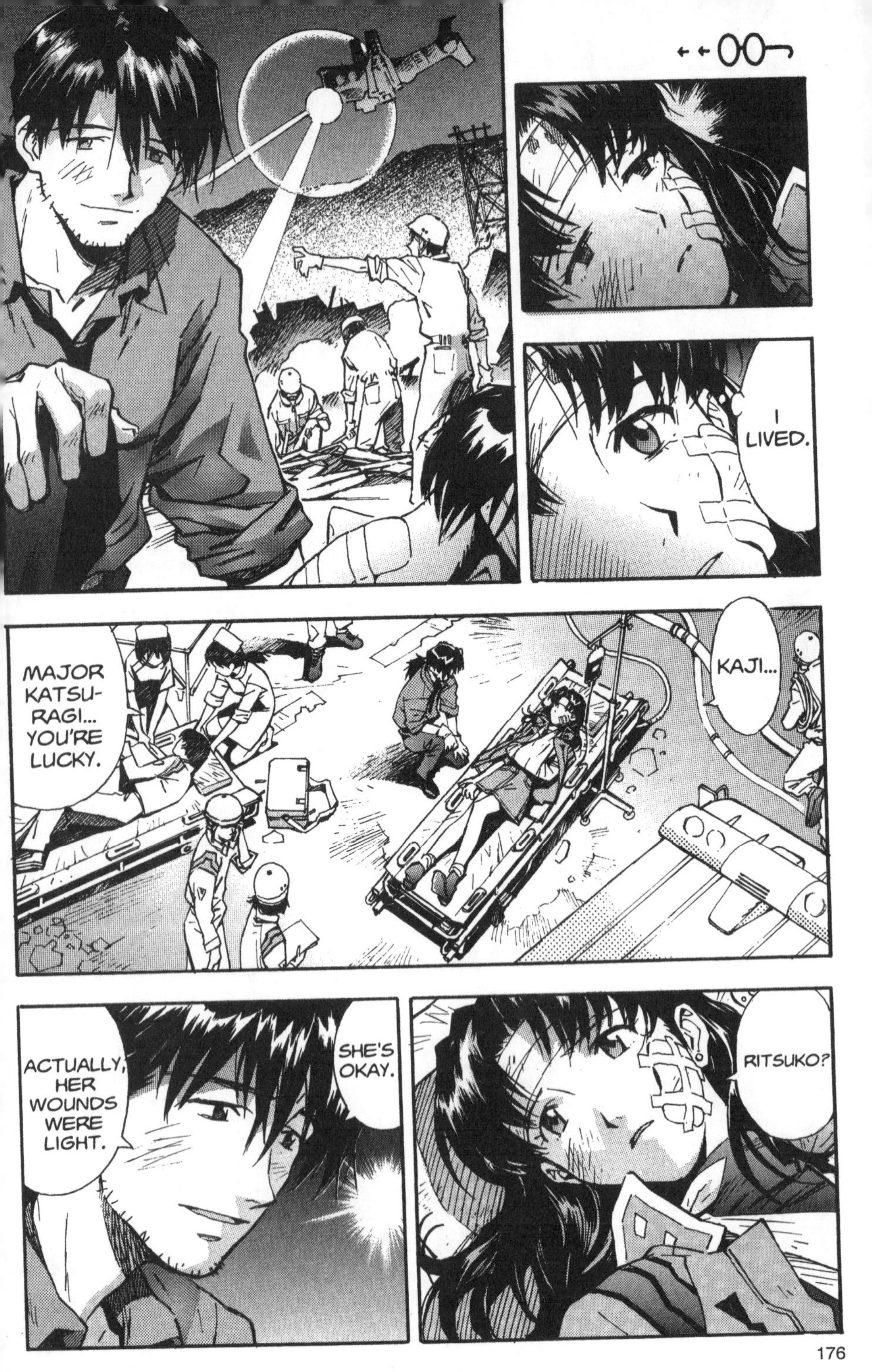
I LIVED.
KAJI...
MAJOR KATSURAGI... YOU'RE LUCKY.
RITSUKO?
SHE'S OKAY.
ACTUALLY, HER WOUNDS WERE LIGHT.

WHAT ABOUT UNIT-03...?

I SEE..

PILOT AND ALL.

IT HAD TO BE DESTROYED... AS AN ANGEL.

WHAT ABOUT SHINJI...?

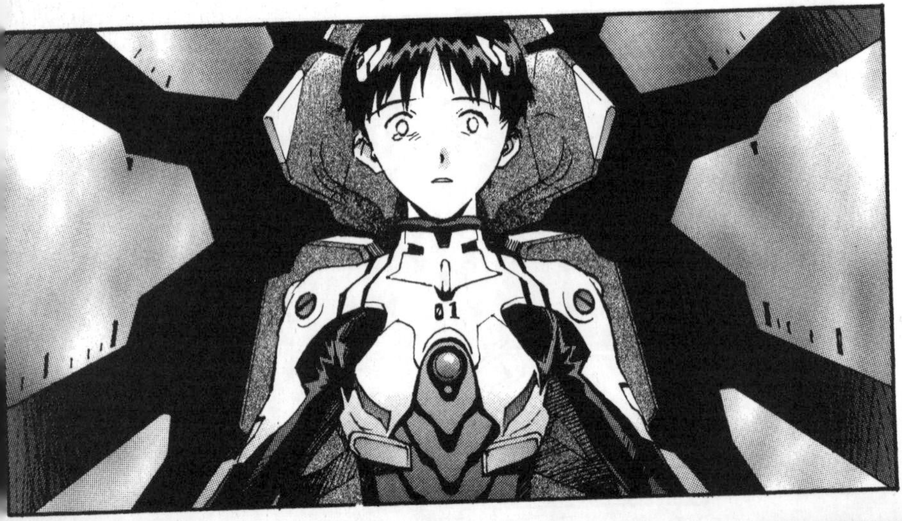
01
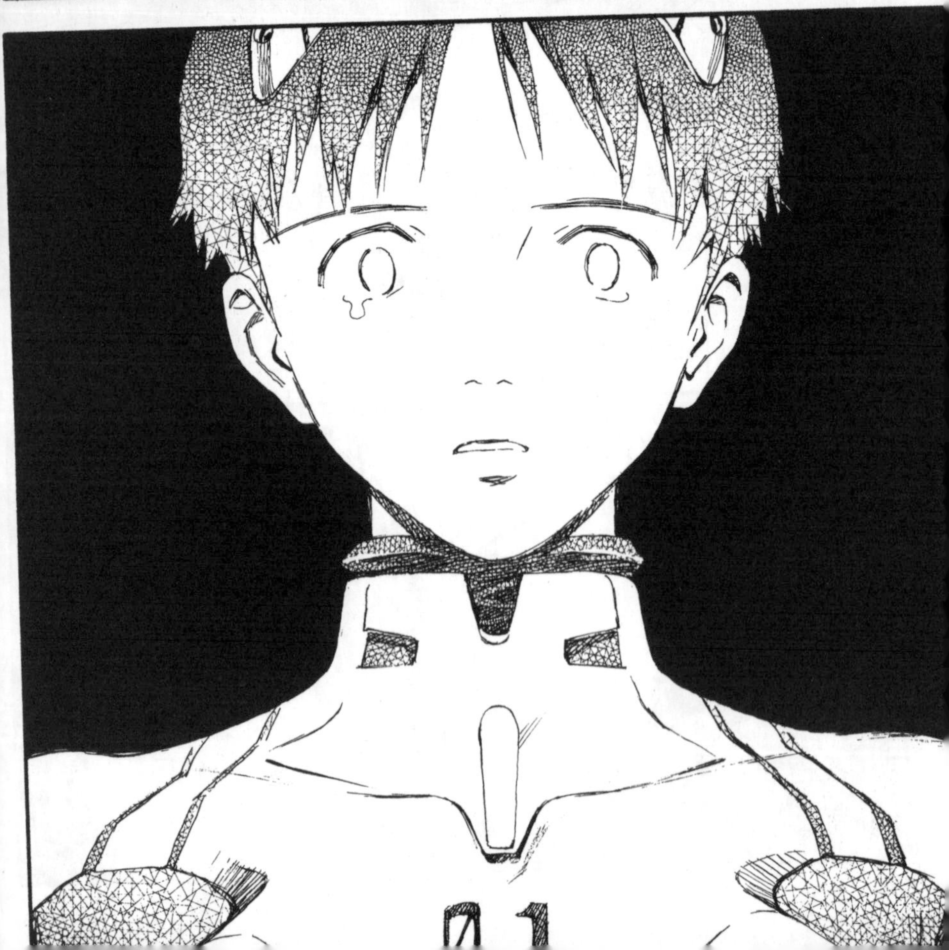
01

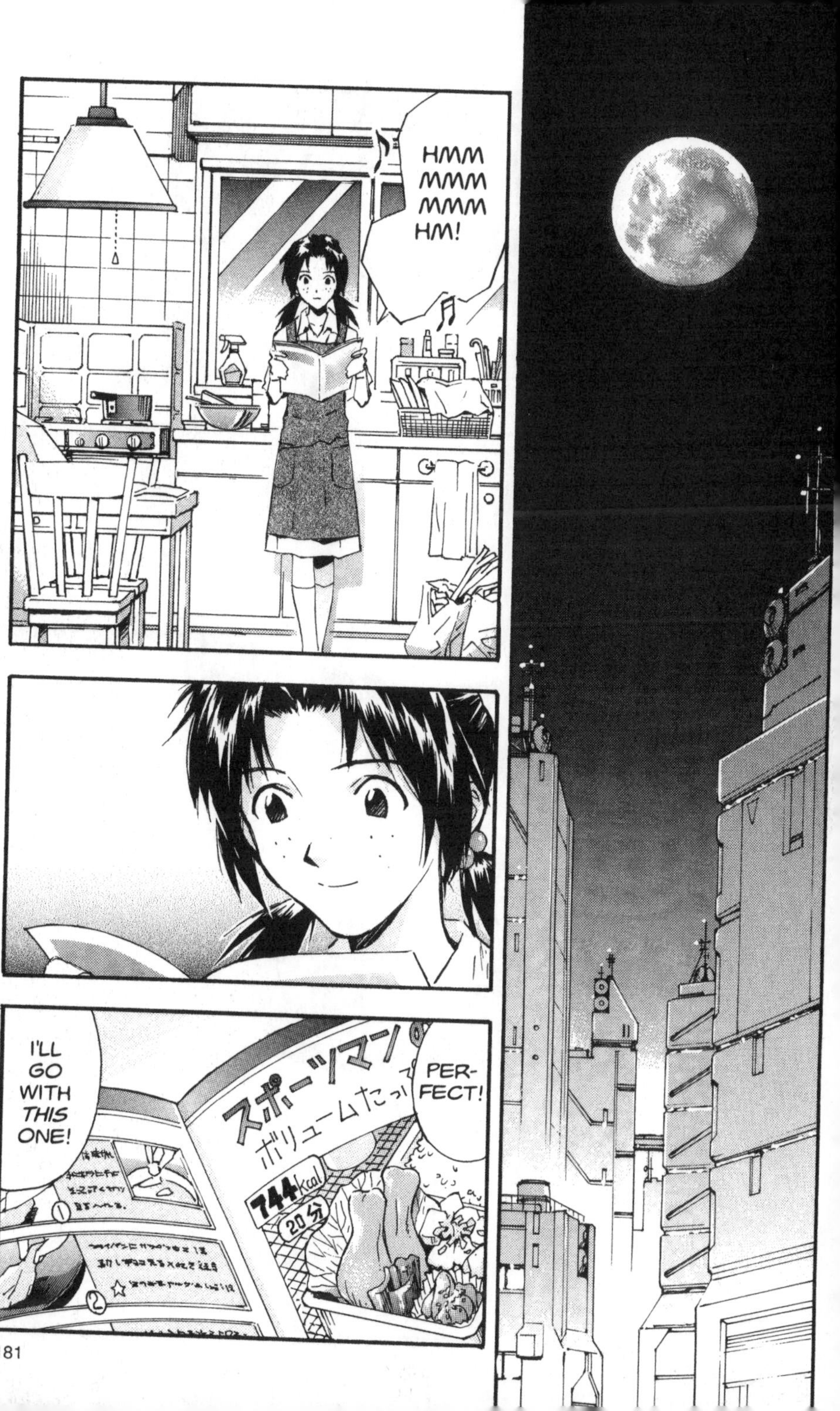
HMM MMM MMM HM!
PER-FECT!
I'LL GO WITH THIS ONE!
スポーツマン
ボリュームたっ
744kcal
20分

Sound Effects Glossary

13.4	FX:	zaa [zzt]
16.4	FX:	miin miin miin miin [cicadas]
20.2	FX:	Uooo! Yappa AK-47 kakkoeee! Chikushyooohosshii! ["Ooh! AK-47s are sooo cool! I want one!" Note the 'eh,' not 'ee' pronunciation of e in Japanese; so what Kensuke is doing is pronouncing kakko ii in the more 'manly' fashion kakkoeee—said kahk'koh-ehhhhh.]
30.1	FX:	pako [wap]
32.3	FX:	den zudedede [slam whamamam]
36.3	FX:	Gatten shite itadake-mashita deshoo ka? ["Do you get it now?"]
37.1	FX:	Gatten! Gatten! Gatten! ["I got it!" "I got it!" "I got it!"]
37.2	FX:	pi [clik]
38.1	FX:	Geee! [gack]
40.3	FX:	kata kata [clacketa]
40.5	FX:	kata kata [clacketa]
41.3	FX:	katata katata [clacketa clacketa]
49.2	FX:	gaa [grr/mreow]
50.3	FX:	pon [pat]
52.4	FX:	biku [urk]
55.3	FX:	kachan [clink]
55.6.1	FX:	pi [eep]
55.6.2	FX:	gaton [clunk]
56.5	FX:	pi [eep]
56.6	FX:	gaton [clunk]
57.2	FX:	kakyo [ckrish- opening can]
59.1	FX:	miin miin miin [cicadas]
60.3	FX:	ba [grab]
61.1	FX:	keho [koff]
61.2	FX:	shuyuun [sniff]
68.2	FX:	suu [breath]
68.4	FX:	gofa [door]
69.1	FX:	kacha kacha [clacketa clacketa]
69.4	FX:	pi [clik]
72.1	FX:	shuru [shwip- ribbon]
76.4.1	FX:	gata [clunk]
76.4.2	FX:	pi [eep]
78.1	FX:	kacha [clink]
79.1	FX:	zaa [fshh- water]
79.3	FX:	kacha kacha [clink clatter- dishes]
87.4	FX:	suu [sliding door]
87.5	FX:	pisha [slam]
88.6	FX:	pon [pat]
89.2	FX:	gachan [clik]
89.4	FX:	goo [roarr]
90.1-2	FX:	goo [roarr]
90.2	FX:	uoo [whoo]
92.2	FX:	gacha [chk- door]
94.4	FX:	guu (grip)
95.1	FX:	bashu (dash)
93.4	FX:	biku [urk]
97.4	FX:	miin miin miin miin [cicadas]
103.3	FX:	tatata [running]
105.1	FX:	gokun [gulp]
105.2.1	FX:	ahahaha
105.2.2	FX:	ban [smack]
105.3	FX:	jii [stare]
106.4	FX:	bashun [fshoom]
109.2	FX:	ka [flash]
109.3	FX:	fii fii fii [alarm]
110.2	FX:	gakon [klang]
110.3	FX:	gugugu [straining]
111.2	FX:	gugugu [straining]
111.2-4	FX:	bago [crack]
111.5	FX:	gigigi [creeak]
112.1-2	FX:	guoo [grrraugh]
113.1.1	FX:	gogogo [rumble]
113.1.2	FX:	zudoon [kaboom]
114.1	FX:	pi pi pi [cell phone]
118.5	FX:	fii fii fii [alarm]
119.1	FX:	bashu [bwoosh]
119.2	FX:	doshu [doosh]
119.3	FX:	gan [klang]
121.3	FX:	von [vmm]
122.5	FX:	bashi [wpsh]
122.6	FX:	bo [bom]
124.1	FX:	kana kana kana [another species of cicada]

Sound Effects Glossary

124.2	FX:	kana kana kana [cicadas]
124.4	FX:	zun [thm]
127.5	FX:	zun zun [thm thm]
128.1	FX:	zun [thm]
128.4	FX:	gan [wham]
128.5	FX:	zaa [sskt- static]
129.1	FX:	zun [thud]
129.2.1	FX:	zun zun [thm thm]
129.2.2	FX:	shuu [fssht]
130.1	FX:	zun zun [thm thm]
131.1	FX:	zun zun zun [dm dm dm]
131.6	FX:	jaki [chk]
132.3	FX:	pipipi [eep eep]
132.5	FX:	zun [thm]
133.1	FX:	gugigigi [creeak]
133.3	FX:	guon [leap]
134.1	FX:	don [slam]
134.2	FX:	zuga [wham]
135.1	FX:	gigigi [creeak]
135.3.1	FX:	dororo [gloop]
135.3.2	FX:	mishi mishi [crackle]
135.4	FX:	biku [!]
136.1	FX:	mishi mishi [crackle]
137.1	FX:	bachi [zzak/snap]
137.2	FX:	bon [boom]
137.4	FX:	zuga [crash]
138.1-2	FX:	goo [whoo]
141.3	FX:	dokun [ba-bump]
143.3	FX:	guooo [graaurr]
143.4	FX:	ban [leap]
144.4	FX:	gan [whack]
145.1	FX:	dodon [slam]
145.2	FX:	zun [thud]
147.1	FX:	zun [thunk]
147.3	FX:	doga [crash]
149.1	FX:	gogogo [crumble]
149.2	FX:	hyun [whoosh]
149.3	FX:	pashi [wpsh]
150.1	FX:	zuga [slam]
150.2	FX:	gigigi [rrk- strangulation]
151.4	FX:	gigigi [rkkk]
154.2	FX:	gakun [oof]
154.4	FX:	hyuii [whirr]
154.6	FX:	iii [whirr]
156.1	FX:	ka [flash]
156.2	FX:	gugu [rrk- raising arm]
156.3	FX:	gugugu [rrk]
157.1	FX:	gura [lurch]
157.2	FX:	gashi [glomp]
160.1	FX:	gugugu [rrkk]
161.2.1	FX:	pishi [crack]
161.2.2	FX:	mishi [creak]
161.3	FX:	baki [snap]
161.4	FX:	guoo [graaugh]
162.1	FX:	bun [fling]
162.2	FX:	dokan [slam]
163.2	FX:	gacha gacha [clacka clacka]
164.2-3	FX:	gusha [smash]
164.4	FX:	bichaa [splorch]
165.3.1	FX:	ga [grip]
165.3.2	FX:	biki [creak]
165.4	FX:	beki beki beki [rip crack]
166.1	FX:	beri [rrip]
166.2	FX:	ba [toss]
166.3-4	FX:	zudodon [crash]
166.4.1	FX:	ga [grip]
166.4.2	FX:	giriri [rrkk]
167.1	FX:	mishi mishishi [creak crack]
167.2	FX:	buchi [rrip]
167.3	FX:	zuzun [crash]
168.1	FX:	gacha gacha [clacka clacka]
169.1	FX:	zuga [stomp]
169.2	FX:	baki doka zugan [smash stomp crunch]
170.1	FX:	gan dosu [wham thud]
170.2	FX:	doka [whack]
170.3	FX:	baki [crack]
170.4-5	FX:	zugan [crunch]
172.1	FX:	gugu [squeeze]
175.1	FX:	piipoo piipoo piipoo [weeoo weeoo- ambulance]
181.4	FX:	[magazine] Sportsman no Volume Tappuri [lit. "A whole lot of volume (i.e., a hearty meal) for the sports man."]

SECRETS OF EVANGELION
Special Bonus Dossier Section

CAUTION: REVISED FOR EVANGELION VOLUM

ADAM: Two different-appearing entities, which may or may not be one and the same, have been referred to by this name at this point in events: a.) an object several cm in length resembling a human embryo, carried by Ryoji Kaji in "suspended animation" within a case and delivered to Gendo Ikari, an object described as "the key to the Instrumentality Project" and "the first human being;" and, b.) several weeks later: a giant, humanoid figure hanging from a cross in NERV's ultimate-level classified facility, the deep subterranean hangar known as Terminal Dogma. Upon first witnessing this figure, Major Katsuragi characterized Adam as "the First Angel;" Kaji added "This is also 'Project-E'."

The appearance of the figure described in b.) is that of a sexually indistinct human, white, hairless, almost blubbery. Its wrists are affixed to the cross by bolts or screws. Where its face would be, is a mask, possibly physically driven into the figure (a dark liquid can be observed oozing from where the mask meets the neck). On the mask is the sigil of SEELE (see below). The "body" is missing its presumed lower half, as if severed at the waist; but close inspection shows many smaller (that is, human-sized) pelvises and legs dangling from the blobby terminus of the figure. A paler, serum-like liquid runs from the figure down to the bottom of the cross.

Kaji told Shinji that his mother, Dr. Yui Ikari, who vanished during the initial creation of the Evangelion series, solved the "primary problem" of "'Eva,' born from 'Adam.'" In an action related to the "Adam Project," Unit-00 pilot Rei Ayanami drove the Spear of Longinus (see below) into the body of Adam, where it currently resides at this point in events.

20th-century rabbi Z'ev ben Shimon Halevi, a student of Kabbalah (an ancient tradition with Judaism that seeks the mystical and esoteric rationale behind Creation) explained the Kabbalistic theory that the Systema Sephiroticum (see below)—a representation of which is on the floor and ceiling of Gendo Ikari's office—represents the model, map, schematic and code for the totality of Creation and, simultaneously, also the diagram for the body of the primal human being, "Adam Kadmon."

In the process of Creation, Adam Kadmon, says Rabbi Halevi, is "the first of four reflections of God to become manifest as existence extends from Divinity to Materiality, before returning to merge again at the end of time." The Adam created in the book of Genesis is *based* on this model of Adam Kadmon; Halevi relates that while mainline Judaism "has it that Adam was created last of all creatures so that he would be humble, the Kabbalistic view is that all other creatures without exception—even the angels and archangels—are based on Adam (Kadmon) but were left incomplete: only the Adam (of Genesis) was a complete image of the Divine. This fact accounts for the myth of jealousy and discord among the angelic hosts..."

ALBINISM: One explanation that has been offered for the unusual appearance of the First Child, Rei Ayanami. Albinism is a genetic defect; the hereditary inability to produce the pigment melanin, which, in different combinations, is what gives human skin, eyes, and hair their different colors. Rei's blue-white hair, pale skin, and red eyes (the red color of the underlying retina) are all highly symptomatic of albinism.

There has been the strong suggestion that the Children are either the product of genetic experimentation or have certain "natural" genetic characteristics. If this is true, then Ayanami's presumed albinism could be either an "acceptable side effect" or "acceptable defect," considering the overall importance of her job. It is interesting to note, however, that while albinism necessarily results in sensitive skin and eyes, Ayanami appears to wear no special protection for either. She has been observed to be taking some sort of medication, however.

...e origins of SEELE and Kiel are unknown, though "Lorenz Kiel" is also a German name, as is both "NERV" and its precursor organization "GEHIRN." Although sometimes communicating only through a hologram, there is certainly evidence to suggest Kiel is an actual person, him having been photographed in a public gathering with Gendo Ikari in 2002. Kiel is a Caucasian and has the appearance of a man in late middle or early old age; he possibly has sensitive eyesight, as he, unlike the other members of SEELE, wears a slitted visor over his eyes, and wore wide dark glasses in the 2002 photo.

It is known for certain that Dr. Yui Ikari, and through her, Gendo, worked for SEELE in the year before the Second Impact. It is possible that SEELE is indeed an organization of ancient lineage and a hidden power in world history (indeed, Ryoji Kaji suggests this is in fact the case, saying they at least are certainly the progenitors of NERV). They may also be of more modern origins, and merely claim an unwarranted, exaggerated, or unproven antiquity to bolster their prestige or sense of mission, as has been the case with other secret societies such as the Masons and Rosicrucians.

In any event, SEELE makes a convincing claim to have access to ancient *knowledge*, including knowledge of both the human past and future based on prophecies and revelations in certain secret "Dead Sea Scrolls" in their possession. A great many of the Dead Sea Scrolls—important early Jewish historical and theological documents dating from circa 250 BC to circa 135 AD—are publicly known to scholars. However, the first of the Scrolls were unearthed under chaotic circumstances in 1947 and were restricted to a small group of scholars for many years thereafter; scholars also assume others remain hidden in private custody, if only for their priceless monetary value. All are factors lending mystery to these documents, and make SEELE's claim to possess secret Scrolls difficult to dismiss on its face.

In fact, even among the publicly-known Scrolls is a fragment of the earliest ever found version of the pseudoepigraphical Book of Enoch, a work not accepted as canonical by mainline Judaism or Christianity but of enduring interest to occultists. This particular fragment, 4Q201, has an odd reso-

...nance with the history of NERV, reading in part, "[They (the leaders) and all...of them took for themselves] wives from all that they chose and [they began to cohabit with them and to defile themselves with them]; and to teach them sorcery and [spells and the cutting of roots; and to acquaint them with herbs.] And they become pregnant by them and bo[re (great) giants three thousand cubits high ...]"

It has been suggested by Taliesin Jaffe that Kiel identifies himself and his committee with the personages described in the Old Testament book of the prophet Zechariah (see also Spear of Longinus, below) chapters 3 and 4, and 8: "For behold the stone that I have laid before Joshua; upon one stone shall be seven eyes: behold, I will engrave the graving thereof, saith the LORD of hosts, and I will remove the iniquity of that land in one day...and he shall bring forth the headstone thereof with shoutings, crying, Grace, grace unto it. Moreover the word of the LORD came unto me, saying, The hands of Zerubbabel have laid the foundation of this house; his hands shall also finish it...they shall rejoice, and shall see the plummet in the hand of Zerubbabel with those seven; they are the eyes of the LORD, which run to and fro through the whole earth....In those days it shall come to pass, that ten men shall take hold out of all languages of the nations, even shall take hold of the skirt of him that is a Jew, saying, We will go with you: for we have heard that God is with you."

Zerubbabel, which means "Seed of Babylon" in Hebrew, was a lineal ancestor of Christ (Michaelangelo depicted him in the Vatican's Sistine Chapel). He was a leader among the Jews who returned to Jerusalem from exile after the "Babylonian Captivity," and it was he who finished the rebuilding of the Temple of Solomon. Solomon's Temple, today a ruin except for its Western, or "Wailing" Wall, was long regarded in esoteric traditions (notably Masonry) to be as close to a physical expression of the majesty, secrets, and perfection of God as human technology ever created. The Branch Davidians, an apocalyptic sect of the 1990s, also believed that the "latter-day Zerubbabel" was among them.

MARDUK AGENCY: Like NERV itself, the even more obscure Marduk Agency is supposedly an organization established by the United Nations' secret Instrumentality of Man Committee, under its chairman, Lorenz Kiel. The founding date of the Marduk Agency is unknown. The purpose of Marduk is to find and identify those 14 year-old "Children" able to "synchronize" with and hence pilot the Evangelion units. At this point in events, four have been found: in order, the First, Rei Ayanami; the Second, Asuka Langley Soryu; the Third, Shinji Ikari, and the Fourth, Toji Suzuhara. Records indicate that the Marduk Agency is a vast concern, with connections to a family of 108 international enterprises. However, NERV's Ryoji Kaji, acting as a double agent for the Japanese Ministry of the Interior, maintains that he has evidence that Marduk is nothing but a vast series of blinds, and the truth about the selection process lies not with Marduk, but with the school all the Children attend.

"Marduk" was the ruler of the gods worshipped by ancient Babylon, the city-state whose armies in 586 B.C. destroyed the original Temple of Solomon in Jerusalem, and then exiled the Jews from their homeland during the forty-eight-year "Babylonian Captivity." This otherwise obscure detail may connect to the Instrumentality of Man Committee. The "Dead Sea Scrolls" consulted by the Committee for their prophecies are believed by many scholars to have been written by the Essene community of Jews—a community which is thought to have had its origins during the Babylonian Captivity (see also SEELE, below).

POSITRONS: One type of antimatter particle; the first variety of antimatter ever created in the laboratory. Although postulated by noted 20th century physicist Paul Dirac as early as the 1930s, their manufacture, even in ultra-minute qualities, was not realized until the 1970s, when the breakthrough occurred at the giant accelerator spanning the Franco-Swiss border of CERN, the *Conseil Europeen pour la Recherche Nucleaire* (European Organization for Nuclear Research). Positrons are the antimatter counterpart to the electrons that surround the nuclei of ordinary matter. Their potential as a weapon is clear when one realizes that while even the most efficient nuclear bombs only manage to release a small percentage of the energy contained in their explosive mass, the intersection of matter and antimatter results in the total conversion to energy of both—a 200% efficient reaction.

The late Joe Bankhead, former USNS Electronics Tech 1st Class/Reactor Operator, commented upon the positron cannon employed by NERV against the Angel Ramiel. Bankhead noted that while a stream of positrons might be a practical weapon in the vacuum of space, where normal matter in the path of the beam would be tenuous, a positron beam used in Earth's atmosphere would be "the equivalent of putting the barrel of your grenade launcher right up against a wall and then pulling the trigger...The matter/antimatter reaction, in other words, would start to occur within nanometers once the positrons leave the (presumed) magnetic containment field within the barrel. Boom." Bankhead added that in theory this could be prevented by surrounding the positron beam with some kind of generated neutrinos, but that in his judgment it remained "a highly dubious prospect."

SEELE: German for "soul" (pronounced "ZAY-leh"), a committee variously shown to be of as few as five or as many as fifteen personages of apparently different ethnic or national origin, to whom Gendo and his sub-commander, Fuyutsuki, have been seen to report. "Seele" is the esoteric name of the (itself secret) Instrumentality of Man Committee of the United Nations. However, neither the existence of the Committee nor the name "Seele" are known to the general public; indeed, it is not known if anyone outside NERV is aware of their existence, and they appear a secret to many inside NERV as well. Also secret is the existence of the Instrumentality Project, the completion of which (and not defeating the Angels *per se*) Chairman Kiel has stated as NERV's primary objective. Adam, the crucified First Angel kept by NERV, bears a mask with marks resembling lunar craters above the sigil of SEELE— an inverted triangle with seven eyes.

...erselves, completes, or corrects an original ...aism that is now irrelevant. Another extreme ...mple of the co-opting of Jewish revelation to jus... a movement or program are the views of present... sects such as the Christian Identity movement, ...o seek to write Jews out of their own history, ...iming that "White, Anglo-Saxon, Germanic and kin...d people" were the actual people of Abraham's ...venant and that modern Jews are somehow impos...s.

...s millennia-old interest in Jewish concepts and ...ought has included conventional religious practice ... well as esoteric ritual, and has included not only ...ures regarded as religious, but philosophers such ... the psychologist C.G. Jung. However, one of the ...rliest non-Jews known to seek occult knowledge ...m the Kabbalah was the mysterious Jesuit schol... Athanasius Kircher (1602-1680). He drew the par...ular diagrammatic interpretation of the Kabbalah ...at appears on the ceiling of Gendo's office, and ...ve it the Latin name "Systema Sephiroticum" ...ystem of the Sephira). Kircher drew controversial, ...yncretic associations between Christian teaching ...nd the Kabbalah, which had by this time already ...xisted separately for centuries as a Jewish disci...ine. It is of course also important to bear in mind ...hat the long history of Judaism has included within ...s own adherents a full range of interpretations of ...abbalah, no less than debate over everyday ques...ons of morals, ethics, practices, and beliefs, with ...ifferences that continue to the present day.

...owever, the pattern does accurately describe funda...mental Jewish Kabbalistic beliefs: to wit, that the ten ..."sephirah," (the word, which is the original Hebrew, ...s an ancestor of the English "cipher") shown in the ...diagrams, are attributes of God, linked together by a ...complex pattern that serves also as a model, map, ...schematic and code for the totality of Creation; there...by, through its study, all knowledge of Creation and ...God can eventually be revealed and understood by ...human beings.

For this to happen, in Kabbalah, is in fact the purpose of existence itself, as Kabbalists believe that Creation—where One made many—occurred because "God wished to behold God," and therefore, "Face must behold Face." Only when our knowledge of Creation—including its experiences and possibilities as brought about by free will—is complete, will all existence be reunited with God.

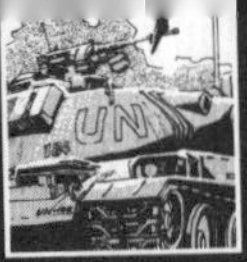
UN

UNITED NATIONS: A... international organization of sover...eign states, established in the immediate aftermath of the Secon... World War in 1945 with its head...quarters in New York City. Originally composed of the victorious Allied Powers, the chartered purpose of the UN was to promote world peace, security and coop...eration in the post-war world, and the organizatio... had come to include nearly all countries by the end o... the century.

The discovery of the Dead Sea Scrolls took plac... against the background of the UN partition of Israe... and Palestine as separate entities, and it was a... member of the United Nations Truce Supervisio... Organization, Captain Philippe Lippens, who brough... in Roland de Vaux, director of the Ecole Biblique, a... French Catholic theological school in Arab Eas... Jerusalem, to oversee research on the Scrolls; he remained director of the project until his death in 1971... It was de Vaux who discovered the fragments of the Book of Enoch in 1952.

The Antarctic Treaty of 1959, which suspended the claims of any individual nation to that continent... opening it up to extensive research, was written to "further the purposes and principles embodied in the Charter of the United Nations." It was the Unite... Nations that investigated and published the officia... explanation of the Second Impact in 2002, claiming i... resulted from a meteor strike. The UN gained in the aftermath of that catastrophe a heretofore unsee... level of power and influence that made it, for the firs... time, an agency capable—if it deemed so neces...sary—of action independent of the major survivin... world governments. Of those governments, that o... Japan appears the most susceptible to UN influenc... (although the mistrust and rivalry between the tw... organizations is also evident). The headquarters o... the 21st century United Nations is in fact now i... Japan's own capital of Tokyo-2, formerly calle... Matsumoto City.

NERV
GOD'S IN HIS HEAVEN. ALL'S RIGHT WITH THE WORLD.

SPEAR OF LONGINUS:

In the account of the Crucifixion given in John 19:34, we are told that after Christ died, "one of the soldiers with a spear pierced his side, and forthwith there came out blood and water," an act interpreted by John to be a fulfillment of a description of the Messiah as given by the prophet Zechariah (Zechariah 12:10). In the apocryphal Gospel of Nicodemus, it is said that this Roman soldier's name was Longinus and—perhaps significantly—that Longinus pierced the living, not the dead Christ. Longinus is regarded as a saint and martyr by both the Catholic and Orthodox churches; he is said to have been converted to Christianity by the experience. His supposed name ("Longinus" may simply be taken from the Latin word for "lance," as this relic is also known), his biographical origins, and the true location, if extant, of his Spear are shrouded in uncertainty.

In previous centuries the Spear has been variously claimed to reside in Rome, Vienna, and Cracow. However, according to a discussion (recorded by classified UN documentary footage, and recovered by Brendan Jamieson) amongst scientists of the Katsuragi Expedition that first discovered Adam beneath their base at Mt. Markham on the Shackleton Coast of Antarctica, the Spear was found in the Dead Sea itself. It was subsequently delivered to the base's dock the week of August 7, 2000. The Second Impact occurred on September 13 during the experimental insertion of the Spear into Adam; the UN scientists attempted to pull it back after "the planned limit values" were exceeded. The Spear, however, continued to sink into Adam, whose A.T. Field released itself in an explosion causing massive tsunami, climactic change, and subsequent civil strife that led to the death of 50% of humanity within the next year. The Spear was recovered and brought to Tokyo-3 in 2015 by an expedition to Antarctica led personally by Gendo Ikari and his second-in-command, Kozo Fuyutsuki.

The lore surrounding the Spear has extended into modern times, as it is maintained by some that Hitler's interest in the occult included this relic. From the gigantic dimensions (the length of an aircraft carrier) of the "Spear" recovered by NERV, it is evident that it cannot literally have been a weapon wielded by any human being. Neither does the "Spear"'s design, that of a military fork whose tines emerge from the unwinding of a progressively tightened double helix, resemble any Roman weapon known to have been in use during the 1st century A.D. NERV, however, and its putative seer SEELE, are organizations steeped in symbo and seeking an esoteric meaning behind the plain of scripture and prophecy. The association of the S with the structure of DNA may have been quite li one of the very last remarks recorded in the UN foot mere seconds before the Second Impact, is "The ge implanted into Adam have already achieved phys merging."

Taking that into account, as well as the uncerta regarding the relic itself, speculation suggests on more of the following: a.) the Spear is an authentic whose suprahuman origins, like those of the Ang were revealed only through secret revelations to wh SEELE and NERV have access, b.) "Spear of Longir is a code name, chosen for its mythological asso tions in the manner of the names given to many m ern military weapons, or even c.) the Spear conta encased *within it* the actual artifact; interestingly, of the massive pillars over the high altar of the Vati is said to contain the Spear.

SYSTEM SEPHIROTICUM: Inscrit

on the ceiling (and floor, in a differ form) of Commander Ikari's office, a diagrams of Creation as conceiv within the ancient Judaic mystical tradition known Kabbalah. It is important to note that because of t antiquity and basic primacy of Judaism and Jewi writings within the Western (and also Islamic) theolo ical tradition, historically, many non-Jews ha attempted to adapt, or co-opt, such to their own sy tems of belief or practice. While this has often be done without malign intent, it has also often taken an expression that could be characterized as an Semitic.

This occurred notoriously with the chief editor of th Dead Sea Scrolls research project himself, Harva Divinity School's Dr. John Strugnell, who was dis missed from his position after voicing supersessionis views about Judaism in a November 9, 1990 intervie with the Israeli newspaper *HaAretz*. Supersessionisr is the practice of believers in newer religions based o Judaism (for example, faiths such as Christianity founded c. 27 A.D. and Islam, founded 610 A.D., both c which regard the God with whom the Jewish patriarc Abraham made a covenant in c. 1850 B.C. as also bein their God) expressing the idea that their new religion

AGAINST A MACHIN
THAT EATS PLANE1
DOES THE THREE-N
STAND A CHANCE?

VIZ GRAPHIC NOVEL

galaxy express 999

vol. 5

232 pag
$18.95 U
$30.95 Ca

松本零士

STORY and ART by
L. MATSUMOTO

LEIJI MATSUMOTO'S EPIC QUEST THROUGH SPAE
TIME CONTINUES THIS APRIL ONLY FROM VIZ CO

VIZ
www.viz.com

ANIMERICA.
www.animerica-mag.com

j-p⊛p.com
www.j-pop.com

©1998 Leiji Matsumoto/Shogakukan. First published by Shogakukan, Inc. in Japan as "Ginga Tetsudo 999"

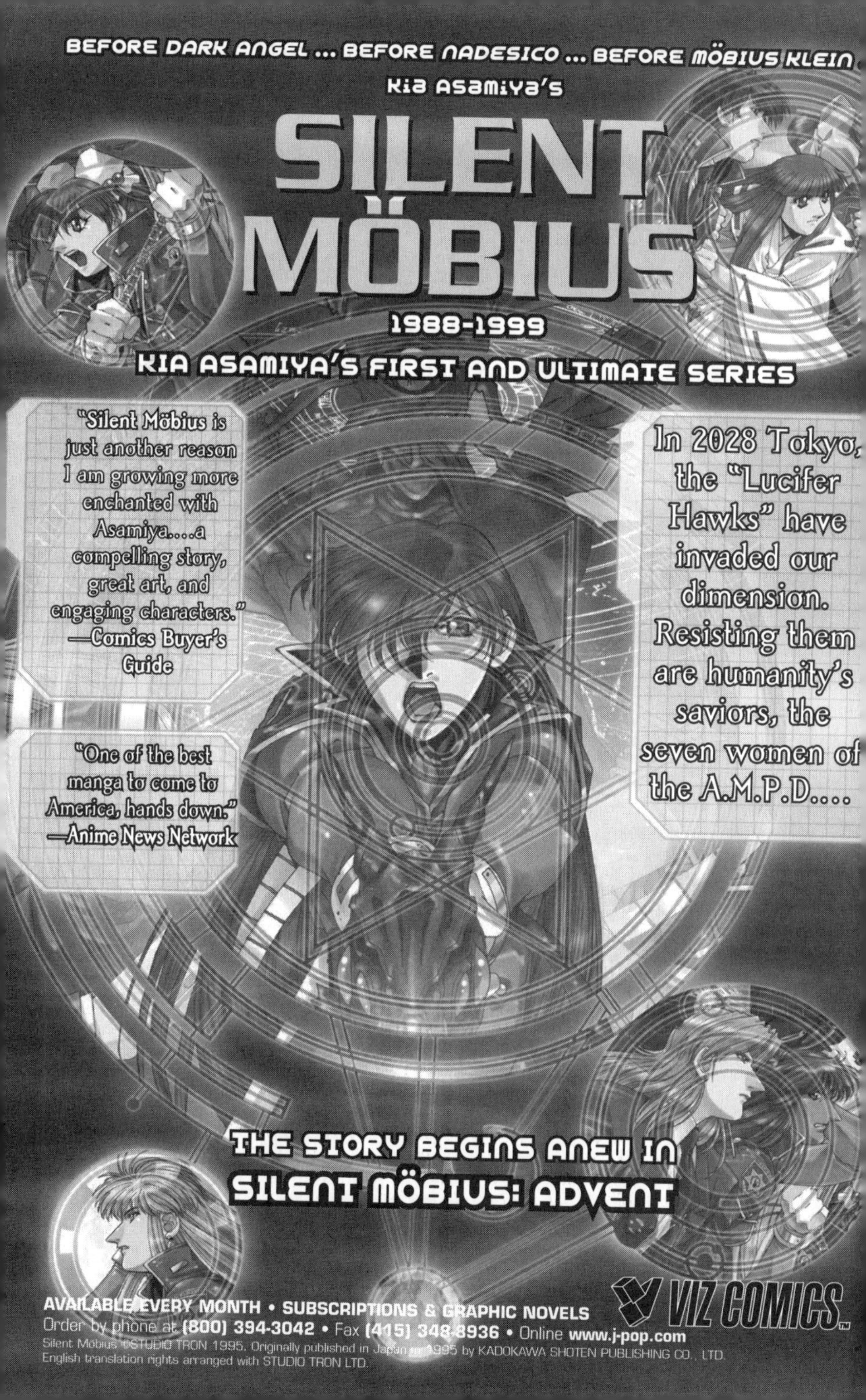
BEFORE DARK ANGEL ... BEFORE NADESICO ... BEFORE MÖBIUS KLEIN
KIA ASAMIYA'S
SILENT MÖBIUS
1988-1999
KIA ASAMIYA'S FIRST AND ULTIMATE SERIES
"Silent Möbius is just another reason I am growing more enchanted with Asamiya....a compelling story, great art, and engaging characters." —Comics Buyer's Guide
"One of the best manga to come to America, hands down." —Anime News Network
In 2028 Tokyo, the "Lucifer Hawks" have invaded our dimension. Resisting them are humanity's saviors, the seven women of the A.M.P.D....
THE STORY BEGINS ANEW IN
SILENT MÖBIUS: ADVENT
VIZ COMICS
AVAILABLE EVERY MONTH • SUBSCRIPTIONS & GRAPHIC NOVELS
Order by phone at (800) 394-3042 • Fax (415) 348-8936 • Online www.j-pop.com
Silent Möbius ©STUDIO TRON 1995. Originally published in Japan in 1995 by KADOKAWA SHOTEN PUBLISHING CO., LTD.
English translation rights arranged with STUDIO TRON LTD.

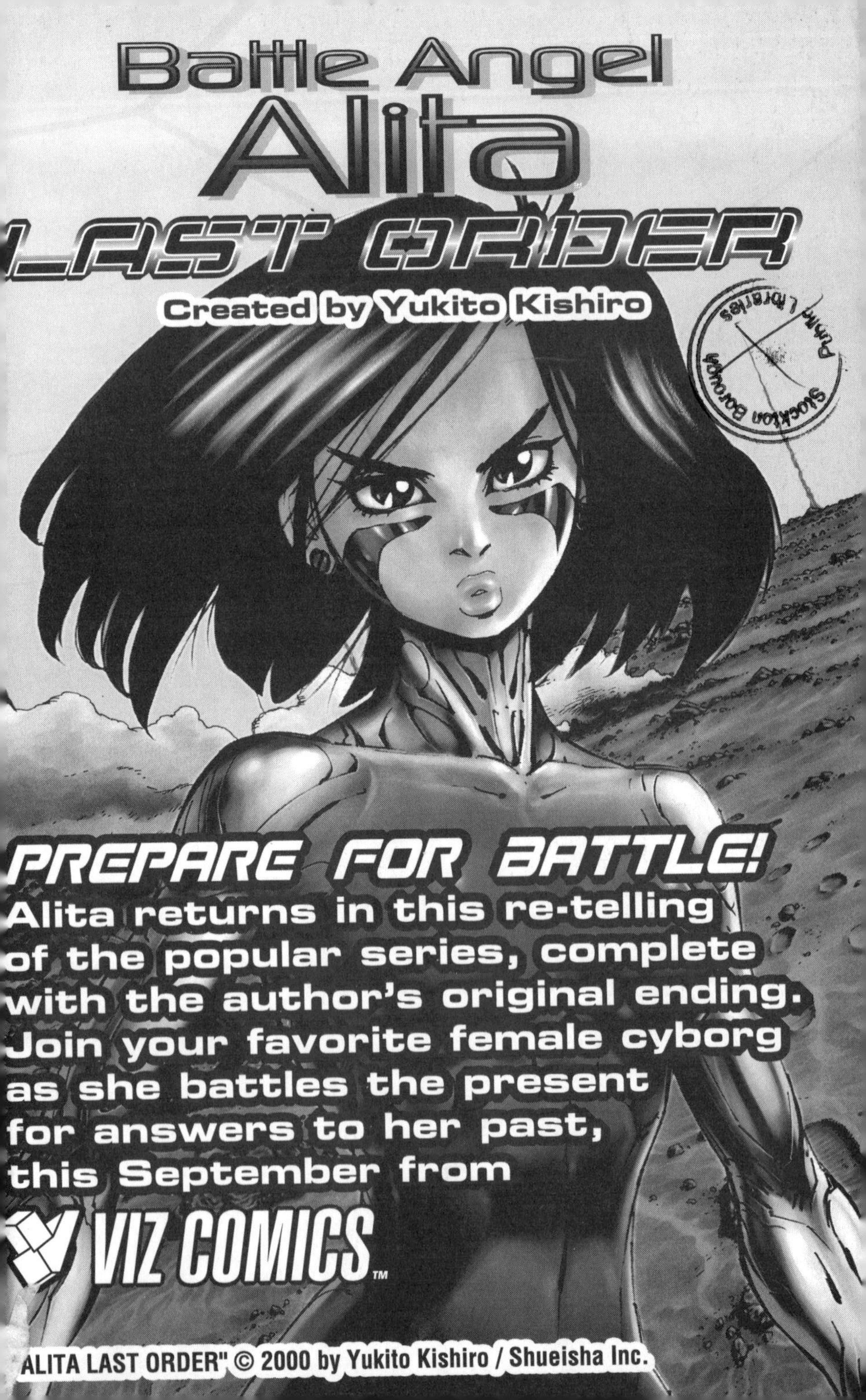
Battle Angel
Alita
LAST ORDER
Created by Yukito Kishiro
Stockton Borough Public Libraries
PREPARE FOR BATTLE!
Alita returns in this re-telling of the popular series, complete with the author's original ending. Join your favorite female cyborg as she battles the present for answers to her past, this September from
VIZ COMICS™
"ALITA LAST ORDER" © 2000 by Yukito Kishiro / Shueisha Inc.